PLANTED:

120 DEVOTIONS FOR DEEPENING YOUR ROOTS IN CHRIST

BOBBIE PERKINS

3 TREES
PUBLISHING

3Trees Publishing

18024 Dedeaux Clan Road

Gulfport, MS 39574

3TreesPublishing@gmail.com

FOREWORD

Just over 20 years ago, we met the most amazing family at our church. Our young daughters had the opportunity to play basketball together in the church league.

It was during this season that I had the chance to meet Bobbie—a wife, a mom of three girls, a nurse, and a friendly little lady with lots of energy. For several years, we enjoyed fellowship, friendship, and community at that wonderful church.

Then, our family moved to a new city and a new church. And I lost touch with Bobbie for a while.

However, through the magic of social media, we were able to reconnect online and keep in touch through Facebook and messaging.

What an encouragement Bobbie has been to me over the years—always leaving a good word, a heart, or a kind remark. She has cheered me on from afar.

Then, a couple of years ago, I got an online message from Bobbie telling me she was interested in writing a book. She wanted to put her words on paper and share them with others. Without hesitation, I encouraged her to do so!

This lovely volume that you hold in your hands is that book!

"Way to go, Bobbie! Thank you for sharing your heart, your story, your poetry, your struggles, your faith, your family, your pictures, and your passion to encourage the hearts of women. Truly, I believe every single reader will be incredibly blessed!"

So, dear reader, take your time with this beautiful project.

Read every page—the introduction, the daily devotions, the prayers, the reflections, the appendices, and the poems. Savor each word. Enjoy every photo. Be encouraged by each verse.

Breathe in the hope unsparingly sprinkled over each page.

My prayer is that your journey alongside my friend Bobbie will plant you deeply in the love of Christ and ground your faith firmly for whatever lies ahead.

Blessings on your journey,

— MELANIE REDD, BEST-SELLING AUTHOR OF LIVE IN
LIGHT: 5-MINUTE DEVOTIONS FOR TEEN GIRLS

CONTENTS

MY GREAT LEAP OF FAITH	xv
Prologue	1
January	17
1. WHAT IS YOUR SOMEDAY?	19
2. THE MASKS WE WEAR	23
3. A NEW YOU	27
4. SWEET LITTLE BABY ON THE SCREEN	31
5. HOPE FOR THE NEW YEAR	37
6. NEW BEGINNINGS	41
7. AND GOD REMEMBERED	47
8. BLOOMS FOR THE NEW YEAR	51
9. RECKLESS	55
10. HOT OR COLD	59
FEBRUARY	63
11. REVIVAL	65
12. WHAT IS GOD ASKING YOU TO GIVE?	69
13. WHO IS IN THE MIRROR?	73
14. 5 WAYS IT AFFECTS OUR LIVES THAT GOD KNOWS US	77
15. ARE YOU A BIBLE STUDY GIRL?	81
16. I DIDN'T ACT LIKE A CHRISTIAN	85
17. IS GOD WITHHOLDING FROM YOU THE DESIRES OF YOUR HEART?	89
18. WASHING THE WOUNDS OF WORDS	93
19. HOW IS YOUR PROGRESS?	97
20. SET FREE FROM THE STICKY TRAP BUT SO MUCH MORE	101
MARCH	105
21. RESTING IN THE RHYTHM OF GOD'S FAITHFULNESS	107
22. GOD IS YEARNING FOR YOUR RETURNING	111

23. TO KNOW HIM   115

24. FAITHFULNESS FOR ALL OUR FEARS   119

25. YOU ARE NOT INVISIBLE   123

26. WHEN YOU DON'T FEEL GOD'S FORGIVENESS   127

27. HOW TO FIND THE HIDDEN TREASURE   131

28. THAT ALL MAY COME TO REPENTANCE   135

29. ARE YOU LIVING AN EASTER LIFE?   139

30. LET OTHERS BLESS YOU   143

APRIL   147

31. ARE YOU CONVINCED AND COMPELLED?   149

32. COME TO THE CROSS   153

33. HOW TO HAVE MORE PATIENCE   157

34. THE ME ON THAT HILL   161

35. ARE YOU LEAVING RIPPLES?   165

36. THERE IS NO GREATER LOVE   169

37. THE TRUTH ABOUT REPENTANCE   173

38. ARE YOU EMAILING GOD?   177

39. HOW TO LIVE A GODLY LIFE   181

40. KEEP LOVING   185

MAY   189

41. DO YOU NEED TO FEEL SPURRED ON?   191

42. FORGIVE YOURSELF THIS MOTHER'S DAY   195

43. 10 WAYS THE HOLY SPIRIT HELPS US REBUILD OUR LIVES   199

44. HOW TO BRING LIGHT TO A DARK SITUATION   205

45. MAMA PRAYERS   209

46. TRUSTING GOD WHEN IT DOESN'T MAKE SENSE   213

47. WHERE ARE YOU PARKED?   219

48. MY REVIVAL FAUX PAS, GOD'S SENSE OF HUMOR, AND TRUTH   225

49. FREEDOM FOR THE CAPTIVES   229

50. HOW TO LEARN TO LOVE YOURSELF   233

JUNE   237

51. ARE YOU A FOLLOWER OR A DISCIPLE?   239

52. HOW TO KNOW YOUR FAITH IS REAL   245

53. SPIDERMAN WISDOM   249

54. WHAT IS THE ARMOR OF GOD?   253

55. YOUR LAST NIGHT ON EARTH   257

56. ONE VOICE   261

57. POTHOLE BLESSINGS AND FLAT TIRE RICHES   265

58. LIFEJACKET LESSONS   269

59. REDEEMING YOUR EGYPT: HOW TO GET OVER YOUR PAST   275

60. HOW TO PROTECT YOUR MENTAL HEALTH   279

JULY   285

61. AMAZED BY YOU   287

62. I SALUTE LAURA INGALLS WILDER   291

63. THE MARKS LEFT ON YOU   295

64. VULTURE PRAYERS: 10 QUESTIONS TO IMPROVE YOUR PRAYER LIFE   299

65. 10 REASONS WE SHOULD PRAY (PART 1 OF 3)   303

66. 10 REASONS WE SHOULD PRAY (PART 2 OF 3)   307

67. 10 REASONS WE SHOULD PRAY (PART 3 OF 3)   311

68. GOD ISN'T DONE YET   317

69. MORE SPIDERMAN WISDOM   321

70. DRIVING, DIRECTION, AND DECISIONS   325

AUGUST   329

71. CRACKER CHICKEN TEARS   331

72. BACK TO SCHOOL WISDOM   337

73. PRO-LIFE ARGUMENTS AND PRO-CHOICE FRIENDS   343

74. ONCE AND FOR ALL   349

75. HOW CAN WE HAVE HOPE IN SUFFERING?   355

76. HEINIE HAZARDS   361

77. 15 THINGS JESUS ACCOMPLISHED ON EARTH   365

78. UNREACHED BUT NOT UNREACHABLE   371

79. MY REFUGE   375

80. LESS THAN   379

SEPTEMBER   383

81. WHAT IS THE LIE?   385

82. DO YOU MAKE GOD SMILE?   389

83. THE MIRACLE OF JUSTICE AND MERCY   393

84. HOW TO BE HAPPY   397

85. STARTING OVER   401

86. THE FRAGRANCE OF CHRIST   405
87. ACTING LIKE A TWO-YEAR-OLD   409
88. WILDERNESS   413
89. SUCCESS   417
90. PLAYGROUND PRISONERS   421

OCTOBER   425

91. ARE YOU ASKING THE RIGHT QUESTION?   427
92. STRENGTH TRAINING   431
93. MARRIAGE GOALS: LEARNING TO LOVE   437
94. MARRIAGE GOALS: LEARNING TO FORGIVE   441
95. MARRIAGE GOALS: LEARNING TO COMMUNICATE   445
96. MARRIAGE GOALS: LEARNING HOW TO LIVE   449
97. TASTE AND SEE   453
98. HE ISN'T SAFE, BUT HE'S GOOD   457
99. DADA   461
100. SOJOURNERS   465

NOVEMBER   469

101. WHAT BRINGS US GRATITUDE?   471
102. TURNING THANKSGIVING INTO THANKSLIVING PART 1   475
103. TURNING THANKSGIVING INTO THANKSLIVING PART 2   479
104. TURNING THANKSGIVING INTO THANKSLIVING PART 3   481
105. CONVERT YOUR GRATEFUL THOUGHTS TO ACTIONS   487
106. SPIRITUAL BLESSINGS   491
107. GOD'S GIFTS   495
108. LOOKING BACK   499
109. THE THINGS WE AREN'T THANKFUL FOR   503
110. THANKSGIVING AND LYME DISEASE LESSONS   507

DECEMBER   513

111. CAN WE SEE GOD?   515
112. ALL ABOUT JESUS   519
113. WHAT I LEARNED FROM THE YEAR OF COVID CHRISTMAS   523
114. HAPPY BIRTHDAY JESUS!   527

115. HOW TO GET READY FOR CHRISTMAS   531
116. GETTING PAST THE CHRISTMAS CHAOS   535
117. GOD'S MERCY MANGER   539
118. GOD WITH US   543
119. A LEGACY OF FAITH   547

APPENDIX A   555
APPENDIX B   559
Acknowledgments   563
About the Author   565

To my faithful husband Denny, who taught me how to step out in faith. We are total opposites, yet you are God's perfect match for me. To my daughters Hannah, Regan, and Emery...One of my greatest joys in life has been watching you grow into women who make a difference in the lives of those around you, especially mine. To my sons-in- law, Ross, Weston, and Kevin...for being men worthy of entrusting my daughters to and being the sons I never had. To my precious grandchildren....for bringing me unspeakable joy...may you all grow to know and love God and follow His path for your lives. But most of all...To the One who sought me out and planted His Spirit within me. May my roots continue to deepen and bring Him glory.

> *Blessed is the one who does not walk in step with the wicked or stand in the way that sinners take or sit in the company of mockers, but whose delight is in the law of the Lord, and who meditates on his law day and night. That person is like a tree planted by streams of water, which yields its fruit in season and whose leaf does not wither— whatever they do prospers.*

> — PSALM 1:1-3 (NIV)

www.bobbieperkins.com

MY GREAT LEAP OF FAITH

My first book! I'm not sure if there are more to come, but at least saying "first" leaves that option open! This venture has been a long, refining process of following the Lord's call on my life. The words have been in me for many years, but my technology handicaps have limited me to pages of words scattered in stacks of notebooks. Armed with the knowledge that God is big enough to make it happen, I took the leap of faith.

Why do I write? First of all, I love the beauty of carefully crafted poetry, books, and written words, especially THE WORD. I had been a Christian for quite some time before I began seriously studying Scripture. It changed my life and brought power to my walk with God! I want others to discover the treasures in God's Word, so I write to share some of the nuggets I find.

The second reason I write is because writing is therapy. When I was seven years old, I discovered a book of poetry at our school library. I was entranced by the beauty of the words and painstakingly re-wrote every poem in the book on notebook paper so I could keep my own copy of the words! I was a weird little kid. (Not a lot has changed!) Soon I was writing my own poems, and I found that writing helped me sort through the emotions of growing up and discovering a relationship with God. My poems became my letters to God, and quite honestly, His letters to me as He taught me through the process.

The third reason I write is to minister to others. Since words are my love language, they are also the way I show love to others. Hand-written notes are a dying art, but I still enjoy sending hand-written notes to encourage the people in my life who have impacted me.

I have had the privilege of knowing and being involved in Bible studies with many precious women through the years. Their friend-ships have encouraged me to put down deeper roots and have kindled the desire in me to leave a godly legacy of faith. It was through my love of writing, of studying God's Word, and of connecting with other women that the idea of my blog Deeper Roots was born. My talented daughter Emery designed the perfect logo for me, highlighting my desire for deeper roots in Christ but also my love of the outdoors and trees. This book grew from my friends asking for my blog devotions in book form.

It is my prayer that this devotional book will help you grow deeper roots of faith.

—

BOBBIE

PROLOGUE

BEGINNINGS CAN BE COMPLICATED. I DIDN'T PLAN TO INCLUDE MY testimony at the beginning of this book. But God has a way of leading us into obedience in His own gentle way.

My faith journey has also been complicated. It would take a REALLY thick book to include all the twists and turns of my life that led me to where I am with Jesus today. God continues to turn over the tapestry every now and then to show me some more of the back story with tangled up threads that He weaved with purpose. And those threads continue to amaze me.

In many ways, I had a great childhood. My mom had the gift of hospitality and loved to feed people, so our friends often stayed for dinner. We had fun as a family with camping trips, card games, and visits with cousins and other relatives. As I was growing up, I knew my parents loved me. I have some great memories of my parents, and everyone who knew them loved them. They were kind, fun, generous people, but they were typical unbelievers. The choices they made were worldly choices, and that's the lifestyle they taught me and my older sister. God's name wasn't mentioned in our home except as a swear word. We had a full professional bar at our house, and my parents would let me and my sister take sips of alcohol, even as small children, laughing and saying, "They gotta learn to hold their liquor at an early age!" So we did learn to do that, and by the time I was twelve years old, my mom was buying my cigarettes for me, and I could drink a grown man under the table.

But we had wonderful godly neighbors who told me about Jesus. Their daughter Rita was my best friend. Rita's mom had a beautiful voice, and she was always singing hymns. I had never heard a hymn before and didn't understand all this talk about the blood of Jesus. But I felt something special at their house, and I recognize now that it was the stirring of the Holy Spirit as He put a desire in my heart to know God and prepare my heart for the gospel. I went home to excitedly tell my parents all the things our neighbors were telling me about God. But my dad made fun of me and asked if I thought I was going to float off to heaven with the good Baptists across the street. I was crushed! I had really hoped that the things Rita's family had said about God loving me were true. I decided then that God must be for families like Rita's, but not families like ours.

Another thing happened when I was young that distorted my view of God. I was sexually abused by a family friend over a period of about a year…it's a convoluted web that abusers weave in order to lure their victims, especially children who don't have the judgment of an adult. It greatly impacted my self-esteem and reinforced the view that I wasn't good enough for God and that God didn't love me the way He loved girls like Rita. The most tragic thing about abuse isn't just the abuse itself—it's the way the enemy uses it to distort the victim's perception of God. I wrote this poem in junior high school, when I decided that if God did exist, He must be distant and uncaring.

Hearts of Stone

You don't have to cry
When you let your soul die.
It's really not that sad a thing.
The dead can't be hurt,
Buried deep in the dirt.

They escape what tomorrow may bring.
You might feel alone
When your heart turns to stone,
But it's the way that is safer and best.
Stone can't be broken
By pain that's unspoken
Like a heart that is made out of flesh.
They don't have to know
Everywhere that you go
That you've killed your soul deep down inside.
Put it all on the shelf.
Never show your true self.
For there's no other place you can hide.
If someday you start longing
For a sense of belonging,
Your soul might try to resurrect.
Quickly cast it away,
Or it soon becomes prey,
And God will not care or protect.

— ©1977 BOBBIE PERKINS

Later as the Lord began to heal me, I learned the name Hagar used for God, El Roi, the God who sees me, and I wrote this poem.

The Pen

Writing has become to me
My kind of private therapy—
My only way to let things out,
From things too hard to talk about.
Remembering a little girl
And how back then she saw her world...
It's the only way I can express
The shame and hurt and worthlessness.

And something happens as I write.
Though it doesn't make the past all right,
It changes something inside me
So I can see truths God can see.
How each and every time I cried,
God was there right by my side.
And when He saw what I went through,
My God cried out in sorrow, too.
And I wondered why He didn't stop
The pain like some great heavenly cop,
But that would mean we'd also lose
Man's free will to think and choose.
And so, I hope that with this pen,
God keeps healing me within.
Though I've come far, it's not complete
Until one day when I'm at His feet.

— ©1998 BOBBIE PERKINS

I want to push the pause button right here. Have you ever felt as if God didn't see you or care about you? Maybe you've prayed and prayed about something, but it seems like God is just ignoring your cries. I want you to know that is a lie straight from Satan himself. Satan WANTS you to believe God doesn't care about you. He wants you not to trust God. Psalm 10:14 says, "But you, God, see the trouble of the afflicted; you consider their grief and take it in hand." God sees your grief. When we take something in our hands, we are doing something with it. God takes your grief in hand, because HE IS DOING SOMETHING WITH IT! The thing is... we don't always see what He's doing. And sometimes the grief you're experiencing today is God's way of working something beautiful into your life ten years down the road. I PROMISE you...God is trustworthy. Any time we are tempted to doubt God's love for us, we just need to go back to the cross. If God loved me enough to give His Son to die for me when I was His enemy, how can I think He doesn't love me now that I'm His child? The problem is we're trying to look within ourselves to find a reason God should love us, and if you're like me, I find plenty of reasons why He shouldn't. But if you're a believer, when He looks at you, He sees you united to his beloved Son, clothed in His righteousness. He loves us not because we are loveable, but because of His character. And He loves us because we are in Christ. Colossians 3:3, one of my favorite verses, says "For you died, and your life is now hidden with Christ in God." Hallelujah! I love the idea of my life with its mistakes being hidden and God seeing the righteousness of Christ instead of my mess when He looks at me! No matter what you are going through, God loves you. As I began to understand God's love better, I later wrote this poem with a new perspective.

Innocence

She skips down the street, her pigtails flying,
But did you hear her last night in her bed softly crying?
The secrets are kept. It's her way to survive.
Her childhood is gone. Is she really just five?
She longs for the innocent play days of youth.
They were stolen from her. Now she must hide the truth.
"Don't touch me..." yet longing for someone to hold.
It's strange to be so young and yet feel so old.
The pain is well hidden as she grows through the years.
There are honors accomplished. She's admired by her peers,
Yet she cries on the inside and feels so defiled.
Can you be an adult without ever being a child?
And now she's still searching—An unreachable goal—
To retrieve what was lost, to be pure, to be whole.
White lace gown—she yearns so much to be a pure bride.
Dressed in white, she still feels like she's tarnished inside.
But there is One who brings healing and removes her heart's
    shame.
There is purity found only in One Righteous Name.
His Spirit within her, her spirit joins in.

Now she's one with a Spirit NEVER tainted by sin.
A remnant of childhood in her heart has grown...
A purity found in Him, not her own.
God's Spirit within her has never been touched.
It is holy and pure—what she longed for so much.
Now grown, she has found what her heart had been after.
She's at last learned to play. She has found childish laughter.
Only Christ could make her feel more young and alive
Than she did in those days when she was just only five.

— ©1999 BOBBIE PERKINS

To backtrack back to my story ... during junior high and the first half of high school, I began hanging with a wild crowd and doing drugs. God mercifully shielded me from addiction. I sometimes took drugs from friends and didn't even know what I was taking, and I had some scary experiences, but God protected me. I was in a weird battle of wanting to know God but also being angry at Him. But when I was sixteen years old, one of my friends invited me to Young Life, where I heard the same things about God that Rita's family had told me years before. (By this time, Rita and I had drifted apart). I was so hungry to learn about God that I began to go to Young Life every week after that. I had heard before that Jesus "died for our sins," but I had never understood what it meant. I thought it meant He was so upset over our sins that He died (like died of a broken heart). I had never grasped the concept that it meant that He died in our place as our substitute.

One night the leader said, "Jesus took the rap for you." (Don't you know they had to put it in hoodlum terms for me to understand it?) The light bulb went off in my head, and I felt like I'd been slapped with the truth! I suddenly understood! I deserved to die for my sin and be separated from God. But Jesus took MY punishment on that cross...He took the rap for me...so I could be declared innocent before God and have a relationship with Him. Not just ANY relationship...I could be a daughter of the King!

I was so overcome with conviction and sorrow for my sin, and for the first time, I realized that God did love me, even if I wasn't like Rita. So it was then, at the age of sixteen, that Jesus became my Savior. I gave all that I knew of myself to all that I knew of Him. Now...I would like to say it was smooth sailing after that, but it wasn't! I hold the title of the slowest growing Christian ever! I STRUGGLED as a new believer. I had no clue how to live the Christian life and didn't even own a Bible. My Young Life leader gave me a Bible, and I began reading it but didn't understand a lot of what I was reading. I needed to be in church but had no idea where to go because I was so confused by all the different denominations. I actually looked up churches in the yellow pages (if you're too young to know what yellow pages are...go ask someone over fifty). I ended up going to some pretty strange churches.

It was a lonely time in my life because I lost my best friend who didn't want to hang around me anymore now that I was a "Jesus Freak." That's hard when you're a teenager. I knew I needed to get away from my old friends, but I also didn't think the Christians I knew could relate to my struggles. I wrote the following poem/song about it:

Changing

My friends still walk in darkness.
They think I've lost my mind.
And the Christians that I know don't have
The same struggles I find.
So I'm stuck in the middle.
There's nowhere to fit in.
Where do the new believers go?
I'm struggling with my sin.

Chorus
It's all changing. God's rearranging my heart.
The more I see just what's inside, I give Him one more part.
And He peels off the layers and shines His light within.
And I find another part of me that I must give to Him.

It hurts to be made fun of
By those who once were near.
I try to tell them how I've changed,
But they don't want to hear.
So, wrap me in Your presence, Lord,
Contempt and scorn will fade.
You know the hurt I feel inside—
You were once betrayed.
©1981 Bobbie Perkins

My freshman year of college I met a wonderful Christian friend named Linda Dale. She helped me find a good church, and I began to learn, but I had a LOT to learn. I once told someone I was going to seminary because I thought seminary was another word for church! LD began praying with me, and I can honestly say she is the one who taught me how to pray. I gradually dealt with the sin in my life as God revealed it to me. Thankfully, He didn't reveal everything at once or I would have been overwhelmed! But I started trying to follow the rules instead of the Rule Maker. I was trying to be a carbon copy of my new Christian friends because I wanted to be like them. I met a nice Christian guy at church, (I'll call him Craig) and we began dating. Back when Jesus saved me at the age of 16, I had previously been promiscuous sporadically for a few years, but I had made the commitment at the age of sixteen when I gave my life to Christ that I would go forward from that point on with staying pure until marriage. And I had kept that promise...for five years. So here I was at twenty-one years old, and my boyfriend "Craig" and I were alone at the apartment I shared with LD. We were watching a movie, and "Craig" picked me up off the couch and carried me into the bedroom. I listened to the voice of the enemy telling me that it didn't matter because I wasn't a virgin anyway. I was so disappointed with myself afterward that I had broken my promise to God but even more horrified to later learn I was pregnant.

I couldn't tell anyone. I couldn't tell my Christian friends because surely they wouldn't understand. I already felt I didn't measure up to them, and I was sure they'd judge me. I couldn't tell my parents because I wanted SO DESPERATELY for them to come to know Christ. They knew about my faith. If they knew I was pregnant, I reasoned it would just confirm to them what they already believed to be true...that Christianity was a joke. LD, my sister, and one other friend were the only ones I told. Like David, I was desperate to hide my sin and hurry up and have an abortion before "it" became a baby. All of my emotions bubbled up in anger at God. I was angry that He allowed me to get pregnant after I had been trying to live in obedience. Angry about the abuse in my childhood. Angry that God didn't give me a home like Rita's. ANGRY enough to want to HURT God the way He had allowed me to be hurt. Angry enough to have an abortion because maybe that would be a way I could lash out at God. (How God didn't just strike me down I'll never know...that I actually had the mentality of thinking I could take vengeance against God???)

I was miserable after my abortion. The conviction and depression were so heavy upon me, but I couldn't talk about it because I was determined to keep it a secret. I broke up with "Craig." My dad died suddenly, and even though now I know it isn't true, back then I was convinced that his death was God's way of punishing me. I bought a gun with the intention of ending my life but had no idea how to shoot a gun and was afraid to handle it. I then decided an easier plan would be to swipe a vial of insulin from the hospital where I worked and inject the whole vial. Before I could carry out that plan, LD convinced me to go to a huge crusade with her. (She knew about the gun I had bought for "protection" and was worried about me). I went to that crusade almost as a last-ditch effort with God, and I don't even remember anything specific that was said at the crusade. But I do remember leaving that night with hope. I'd like to say it was the beginning of me running back to God, but really...it was the beginning of me seeing that God was running after me. I felt overwhelmed when I realized that while I had been shaking my fist in His face, He still loved me. Amazed by His grace and mercy all over again, I realized that there truly is nothing that can separate me from His love! It wouldn't be until decades later that I would find out that my current beloved pastor was the one who had organized that crusade. God is so deliberate with those tangled threads of tapestry He weaves into our lives. As far as my abortion, I did what most women who've had abortions do. I mentally stuffed the memory of my abortion in a neat little box and hid it in the closet of my mind to pretend it never happened.

And that worked for a while. I left my church to get away from "Craig" and ended up at a wonderful church where I really began to blossom and grow as a Christian. I learned to study the Bible and spent hours in the Word, falling deeper and deeper in love with Jesus. I discovered how Scripture memory renewed my mind and helped with flashbacks of bad memories that haunted me. My relationship with God no longer consisted of trying to copy the Christians I knew or legalistically trying to follow a bunch of rules or abstain from sin. It was just about learning to know God more and love Him more. And a funny thing happened...loving Him more made me love sin less! Obedience became easier because Jesus was the most important relationship in my life. I married my sweetheart Denny and we had three beautiful children. Our lives became busy with children and church activities, and I was growing deeper roots of faith. But I still had that little box hidden in my closet.

One day I was at work (I'm a nurse), and I had a patient who miscarried her baby at ten weeks. I held that tiny baby in my hand and was shocked to see the development even down to the little fingers, and I realized that this was not a blob of tissue... It was a baby! The lid started to slip off that box in my closet. Soon after, I was at church on Sanctity of Life Sunday and heard a speaker from Life Choices of Memphis share her story of abortion. She talked about freedom from guilt and shame and told about a Bible study that helps women who have had abortions. I remember my heart was beating so fast and feeling like my face was all flushed....surely everyone could just look at me and KNOW! By this time I was very active in church, so I didn't want anyone to know about my past abortion. But I knew I needed that Bible study.

I ended up doing both their post-abortion Bible study and their sexual abuse Bible study along with individual counseling that year. It was a brutal but necessary time of tearing down lies and putting up truth. God used those studies to change my life! God also gave me a new precious friend who walked with me during that year, and she is still my best friend today. She had wrestled with deep sorrow herself. Despite losing her two- year-old daughter in a tragic accident, she had clung to the truth that God is always good, even when we don't understand. I learned about trusting God from my dear friend Lilly.

It makes me sad to know that so many Christians don't read their Bibles. Jesus prayed before his crucifixion, "Sanctify them by the truth; your word is truth." I see the evidence of that in my life. God used His Word through those studies and personal study time to continue the sanctification process (that growth process) in me, bringing me freedom, joy, and peace that I never dreamed possible. I gained a boldness in my faith that I didn't have before. I no longer felt like a second-class Christian or that I had a secret to keep. I had a story to tell! A story of freedom and grace!

One of my favorite passages is Psalm 40 because it so clearly describes what God has done in my life. I encourage you to open your Bible and read it for yourself. It reminds me of this picture that I have hanging in my office as a reminder of the great love my Savior has for me.

It takes a reckless kind of love to leave all the other obedient sheep in order to go after that one rebellious lamb who is knee deep in mud. Jesus came after me when I was running from him and stuck deep in the mud pits of sin.

Psalm 40:

> *"I waited patiently for the Lord; He turned to me and heard my cry."*

Jesus heard my cry and saw my pain. He hears yours, too!!! He not only hears your audible cries, but He hears the SECRET cries of your heart that you can't share with anyone else.

*"He lifted me out of the slimy pit, out of the mud and the
     mire."*

I don't know what kind of pit you've been in. Maybe a pit of grief from losing someone or something, and you can't get past why God would allow that in your life. Some of you have been in the pit of a failed marriage, depression, or health problems. Or maybe like me, you're carrying a load of guilt and shame from the past that makes you feel less than other Christians. I know what it's like to feel less than. But I want you to STOP listening to the lies of the enemy...you are not less than! Like this little lamb, Jesus is running after you with all His might, longing for you to understand how much He loves you.

"He set my feet on a rock and gave me a firm place to stand."

HE is my Rock. Nothing can separate me from His love. Not even my own stupid choices.

"He put a new song in my mouth, a hymn of praise to our God."

My soul is so satisfied in Him, I can't help but praise Him! Singing is NOT my gift. But I praise Him through my writing and the opportunities He gives me to share Him with others. And even though I often fail miserably, my deepest desire is to praise Him in how I live.

"Many will see and fear the Lord and put their trust in him."

I knew God was calling me to help other women find the freedom I'd found.

So I began volunteering at Life Choices of Memphis and eventually was hired as their Director of Nursing. I would have never dreamed that the place that ministered to me so greatly would eventually become the place where I now get to minister. Way back when I thought God was uncaring, He was actually TAKING MY GRIEF IN

HAND AND DOING SOMETHING WITH IT. He knew I would one day be counseling women who had experienced abuse, abortion, family issues, and other problems.

Oh, and that best friend I lost way back when I first became a Christian? I ran into her about ten years after high school. She came running up to me and hugged me and apologized, telling me she had given her life to Christ. And even more exciting...I eventually got to help lead my mom to the Lord. I know my Mama is in heaven now. In 2024 I completed my certification as a Biblical Counselor. God is GOOD! He loved me in my brokenness and relentlessly pursued me, even when I was shaking my fist in His face. He's pursuing every one of you, too. If you don't know Him, I want you to have that opportunity by reading this book. Please turn to appendix B to learn more about how to know the One who is pursuing you!

I know there are a lot of women like me. In fact, in the United States alone, One out of every four women has had an abortion and one out of every five has experienced sexual abuse. These are staggering statistics...Women who are silently keeping their secrets, crippled by feelings of shame and unworthiness. Maybe it isn't abuse or abortion for you. Maybe it's some other issue that makes you feel less than. Isn't that what the enemy wants? If he can't have us, then he'll do everything he can to make us live as a crippled believer. God is abundant in grace and mercy and longs to show compassion. The sacrifice that Jesus made on that cross was enough to cover ALL sin—abortion, or anything else.

I wrote the following poem for one of the women I counseled. She was wrestling so hard with God and struggling to accept His grace. I wanted so badly to just drag her down that path of healing...I wanted to do it for her...but I couldn't. The Holy Spirit had to take her there. But it was so beautiful when it finally happened. It is so amazing to see the changes even in the countenances of these women when they finally embrace God's grace. God's grace is also there for you. And maybe this poem is for you, too.

The Journey

I want you to be there. I want you to see.
It's just over that hill, and you'll finally be free.
Through your tears and regret, you still don't understand-
That it's for YOU that He holds out that grace in His hand.
It's hard work digging up pain from the past.
You can stuff it or numb it or keep wearing a mask,
But the sorrow's still there, and you still carry that load.
I know. I have walked down that long, lonely road.
Please- just keep trudging a little further with me.
I want to see when it happens-- when God sets your soul free!
I long to reach down in that pit where you are,
But I can't pull you out—for my hand has no scar.
HIS hand reaches and rescues. It's been there all along
To set your feet on a rock and give your mouth a new song.
Repentance and sorrow with obedience renewing
Bring the mystery of grace and God's relentless pursuing.
Beloved, He's redeemed you in powerful glory.
Accept now His peace. And then go tell your story.

— ©2020 BOBBIE PERKINS

***PLEASE READ APPENDIX B TO SEE HOW YOU CAN HAVE THIS SAME KIND OF RELATIONSHIP WITH GOD!

***PLEASE READ APPENDIX A FOR HELP WITH EMOTIONS FOLLOWING AN ABORTION OR SEXUAL ABUSE

JANUARY

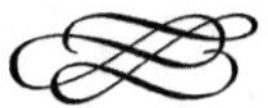

WHAT IS YOUR SOMEDAY?

> *"Now devote your heart and soul to seeking the Lord your God."*
>
> — 1 Chronicles 22:19

HAS GOD EVER TOLD YOU TO DO something, and you promised Him you would do it "someday?" But someday still isn't here? Maybe life just got busy. Maybe you wonder if it's too late to obey. Or maybe you are afraid because His directions take you out of your comfort zone. I had all three of those reasons for not acting. I had known God was calling me to write since I was a little girl. I had been telling God "someday" for years. Oh, I had continued to write, but I had only shared my writing with a small number of people. I had never tried to take steps to share my writing with the big, scary world. My "maybe someday" turned into a lot of days and a lot of years. But I found out something about God. When He tells us to do something, our lack of obedience doesn't cancel His orders. He is so patient to work that obedience into our lives.

God first had to get my undivided attention. I was training for a marathon. I was so excited about it and committed large blocks of time to the training program. Then it happened. I injured my knee and had surgery that would require eight weeks of rest and rehabilitation. I not only couldn't run, but I couldn't even work and had to do a lot of sitting! Suddenly I had a lot of free time on my hands. I listened to God's nudge to dive deeply into His Word. My morning Bible reading routine grew into hours spent studying the Word and having longer conversations with God. In I Chronicles 22:18, David admonished the Israelites for not seeking God during their time of rest. He challenged them, "Is not the Lord your God with you? And has he not granted you rest on every side?" Whoa! I could relate to that! My busy life was suddenly at a standstill. I kept reading, and verse 19 was God speaking directly to me. "Now devote your heart and soul to seeking the Lord your God." I knew that my season of rest was not to be idle. It was to seek the Lord more deeply so that I could obey Him more completely.

It was also no coincidence that a close friend had been hounding (ok- gently encouraging) me to pursue writing in a more serious way. She had no idea that God was using her to reveal to me that my procrastination was actually disobedience. I just wasn't trusting God. I wrestled with my fears. I might fail. People might not like what I write. I'm not a Bible scholar. How can I tell others how to grow in their faith when I am so imperfect? Sharing my personal struggles makes me feel too vulnerable. I'm technologically challenged. On and on…the excuses came. And I knew I was not trusting God. It was time to obey. My pastor's latest sermon included this quote from Hudson Taylor, "Unless there is an element of risk in our exploits for God, there is no need for faith." So, Lord, here is my obedience, lifted up to You with trembling hands of faith. Please take it and do with it things that I cannot do!

REFLECT:

Have you planned to get back in church someday, but someday still hasn't happened?

. . .

Have you planned to someday become more faithful with prayer or reading your Bible but still haven't started?

Is God nudging you toward a particular ministry, but you are wrestling with your fears?

What is your own "someday"?

—✝—

Dear God, Please forgive me for the times I hesitate to trust You because of my fears. Help me to step out in faith, knowing You are trustworthy. Thank you that I can be confident You equip me to do things that I cannot do on my own. Amen.

THE MASKS WE WEAR

WHEN A NEW YEAR BEGINS, I LIKE TO reflect back on the previous year to think about what I should do differently in the upcoming year. There are often lots of things I wish had been different, but I also have to remind myself that some things are out of my control.

2020 was definitely one of those years that was out of everyone's control! None of us will forget the Covid outbreak that caused people to lose loved ones and live in fear and isolation. The masks!!! When the pandemic began to subside, oh, how glad I was to finally shed my mask! But after wearing it for so long, it felt weird not having it. I felt naked!

We wear other kinds of masks, too. Removing them can also make us feel exposed. Masks of humor. Control. Conformity. Perfectionism. Indifference. We don't like to be vulnerable, even to our friends. Removing those kinds of masks can make us feel naked, too.

The truth is, we don't feel so vulnerable when others are also vulnerable. When one person is brave enough to take that first step, it gives the next person the courage to do the same. Is there someone in your life who needs to confide in you but may be waiting for you to be the first one to remove your mask?

The Mask

I walk by your side; I call you my friend.
Can I trust you enough to let you peek in?
My life is a blur of mistakes and wrong turns.
Your world seems so perfect with no real concerns.
So, though you're my friend, I'll live out my charade,
And keep my tight mask on. I'm much too afraid.
Your opinion of me would change if I told
All the dark, ugly secrets that are burned in my soul.
Then it happened! My mask slipped! I turned quickly away
Before you could see all my scars on display.
But you caught a quick glimpse before I could adjust,
And I braced myself for your recoil of disgust.
When it never came, I stared back in surprise,
As you lifted your own mask, and I saw your eyes.
I saw the deep pain that you had been through,
As you nervously showed me that you have scars, too.
How foolish I was to not see that God uses
The comfort of others to help heal all our bruises.
Then, our masks laid aside, we can look face to face
As our ashes are traded for beauty and grace.
For it's when we're transparent by bravely revealing
Our true selves to others.... Those scars begin healing.

— © 2020 BOBBIE PERKINS

REFLECT:

What kind of masks do you tend to wear and why?

. . .

Who in your life may be waiting for you to remove your mask so they can also remove theirs?

Are you willing to go first?

What has God taught you through your scars that enables you to help others?

—✝—

Dear God, When I think of the vulnerability of Jesus hanging naked on a cross for me, it convicts me to give of myself instead of living in self-protection. Help me to have a healthy balance of being transparent without oversharing. Help me to walk with others through their hurts. Amen.

A NEW YOU

I GREW UP IN MY SISTER'S SHADOW. She was older than me, pretty, and popular. I was the tag-along little sister. Her friends didn't even call me by my name. They called me "Little Rich" because our last name was Rich, and I was the little version of my sister. But I really wasn't like my sister. I liked music, books, and daydreaming. I wasn't as good about doing my chores as she was. Oh, the fights that we had! I can't imagine fighting with my sister today. But we are different people now. I am no longer "Little Rich." I have a new name, carved by my own mark in the world.

Think back to the person you were many years ago. What were you like? Did you have a nickname formed from your own life foibles? How have you changed? It would be discouraging to be the same every year, with no progress or growth. I'm so glad God is faithful to continually transform me into the image of Christ. He promises to do that for all believers, but we have to cooperate with the process! "Being confident of this, that he who began a good work in you will carry it on to completion until the day of Christ Jesus," (Philippians 1:6). Sometimes my progress toward that goal seems dismally slow. In fact, I often claim that I hold the world title of the slowest growing Christian ever! When I look at yesterday, I seem the same, but when I look further back, I see growth. Every day I am a new me, continuously shaped by new experiences, struggles, triumphs, and fashioning by the hand of God Himself.

You are, too! God is working in your life. I don't know where you are in the growth process, but He is transforming you. You may not see it yet. Growth is hard to see. We look at our children and see they've grown, but do we actually see it happening before our eyes? The earth is continuously moving, but do we feel it move? Slow growth is still growth. So be as patient with yourself as God is with you, but in your patience keep your focus on Him. Strive with all you have to know Him more. And He will give you a new name and make you a new you!

Jacob had a name, too. His name meant "deceiver," and he lived up to that name by cheating his brother. It wasn't until Jacob was the victim of deception, instead of the perpetrator, that his heart began to change. God was working to slowly change Jacob's character and to ultimately change his name and reputation. In Genesis 32:28, God gives Jacob a new name, Israel, which means "to prevail." Jacob prevailed in his quest to know God better. I hope all of us will do the same.

You are not bound by yesterday, so keep growing! God is in the process of making a new you. Like Jacob, keep wrestling to know Him. "You will seek me and find me when you seek me with all your heart," (Jeremiah 29:11).

REFLECT:

What name would you give to the "old you"?

. . .

What new name has God given you or would you like Him to give you?

What do you need to do in order to grow?

—✝—

Dear God, Thank you that you have a good plan for my life and are continually working to carry it out. I commit now to seek you with all my heart, so that I can know you in a deeper way and walk differently as a believer. Amen.

SWEET LITTLE BABY
ON THE SCREEN

*"The Spirit of
God has made me;
the breath of
the Almighty
gives me life."*

– Job 33:4

I wasn't getting anywhere. She had emphatically rejected the gospel. She was a brick wall, and I could find no breach to penetrate. I silently prayed for the Holy Spirit to be my voice.

I explained that her pregnancy was so far advanced her baby could already survive outside the womb, even if born that day. I discussed the option of adoption. I explained fetal development—that her baby could feel pain. She seemed to have no connection to her baby, saying she just had to think about herself.

So I appealed to her god of self. I explained abortion procedures and the risks involved. I even talked about the emotional risks. Oh, the emotional risks….

I remembered the stoicism and self-focus of my own abortion many years ago and how the emotions came later. I silently pondered that surely her suffering would be even greater with a pregnancy so much more advanced than mine had been. Not that one life is more valuable than another. These babies all have value. But there is something about seeing that fully developed baby on the ultrasound screen that often helps women bond with their babies. I prayed it would happen as we walked into the ultrasound room together.

Little Baby on the Screen

Little baby on the screen, I saw you dance today.
Only weeks till you're ready for birth,
I pray your Mama sees your worth,
And that God uses this ultrasound machine,
Sweet little baby on the screen.
Little baby on the screen, your heart was beating and strong.
Safely snuggled in your Mama's womb,
She looked away from her belly's tomb.
Your eyes were open, your face serene,
Sweet little baby on the screen.
Little baby on the screen, you are formed by God.
When you raised up your tiny hand,
I was praying your mom would understand.
Were you saying, "Mommy, please just try"?
Were you asking why you had to die?
Little baby on the screen, I entrust you to a faithful God.
She looked away at your heartbeat,
Said you'd keep her from goals to meet.
She didn't even shed a tear that day,
Just picked up her purse and walked away.
Little baby on the screen, your life has purpose.
Now I keep your picture in a drawer
To remind me there are many more.
All beautiful, though unplanned,
Precious, perfect when I scanned.
Little baby on the screen, your brief life still counts for good.
I will shed the tears for you,
Even if it's something your mom can't do.
You are known, honored, loved, and seen,
Sweet little baby on the screen.

— ©2023 BOBBIE PERKINS

I don't know why that particular baby impacted me more than the others. Perhaps because the pregnancy was so far advanced, and the baby was so animated on the ultrasound. Maybe because the mom seemed so cold-hearted. Probably because God had a lesson to teach me....

You see, I went home that day mad at that mom. Good grief! Her pregnancy was almost over! What's a couple more months to let her baby live? It may have been righteous anger, but I realized something else that brought conviction to my heart... If that mom were to later return for post-abortion counseling, I would have to work through my own anger at her in order to be able to counsel her. And God revealed the sin in my own heart....that there was a corner of my heart that believed she didn't deserve to experience the freedom from guilt that I had experienced.

I'm so ashamed to admit it, now that the Lord revealed my pride. I was like Jonah with the Ninevites, when he was mad at God because he believed he deserved God's forgiveness more than they did. Pride is so ugly. I am no more deserving of God's grace and mercy than that lost woman who killed her baby in the third trimester. Sin is sin. We are all hopelessly lost without means to save ourselves. We ALL need the blood of Jesus applied to our iniquity. I began praying harder....not just for that woman's baby, but for her soul. I also prayed that she would go into early labor, delivering her baby before she would have a chance to get an abortion.

God gave me a deeper glimpse of His grace and mercy that day. He had to reveal the ugly darkness of prejudice in my heart, but He's good like that...gradually leading us down that path of sanctification, finding corners of our hearts that need to be made more like Christ. "Create in me a pure heart, O God, and renew a steadfast spirit within me," (Psalm 51:10). He's going to have to pour a lot of bleach on this old heart of mine. The bleaching blood of my Savior, making me more like Him. I'm so grateful that He does.

***In the United States, the third Sunday in January is desig-nated as National Sanctity of Human Life Day. Please see*

Appendix A for more information on how you can support life and for resources to help those hurting from a past abortion. ***

REFLECT:

Why is it important to honor the sanctity of human life? (see Genesis 1:27; Psalm 139:13-16; Galatians 1:15)

What emotions do you think a woman typically struggles with after an abortion? Do you think men also struggle with these emotions?

Can a woman who has aborted her baby be forgiven by God? (See I John 1:9; Isaiah 43:25; Isaiah 30:18; Romans 8:1; Lamentations 3:22,23)

How can the body of Christ help these women and men?

—✝—

Dear God, Thank you for the forgiveness we have through Christ that covers even the sin of abortion. Help me to take a stand for life while still supporting the women and men who have been hurt by abortion. Please reveal my pride and the corners of my heart that need to be cleansed by You. Amen.

HOPE FOR THE NEW YEAR

"But if we hope for what we do not yet have, we wait for it patiently."

— Romans 8:25

IT WAS THE TYPICAL DAY-AFTER Christmas scenario. We had a fridge full of leftovers. Good stuff. Taco fixings. Chicken Enchiladas. Chicken poppyseed casserole. Cheesy potatoes. Quiche. The little smokie sausage roll ups. Cookies were scattered in various containers, taking over the counters.

And we didn't want any of it. We ordered soup and salad from Chick-Fil-A delivery. After several days of rich food, we just wanted something lighter.

The old quote that you can have too much of a good thing is true.

Have you ever loved a particular song until the radio overplayed it, and you got tired of it? Sometimes it is the wait for something that increases its value. There is even a country song with lyrics that say, "the longer the waiting, the sweeter the kiss."[1]

---

1. Turner, Josh. "The Longer the Waiting." Lovin' You On My Mind, MCA Nashville, 2007.

So why are we so impatient about what we want? Why do we take away joy from our kids by buying them too much? And why do we pursue material things so much when Luke 12:15 tells us "life does not consist in an abundance of possessions"?

Having too much can take away the joy of the little.

My husband and I have plenty. More than enough and more than many people. But we still wouldn't be considered wealthy. And I'm really happy about that. I wonder if great wealth would take away some of the joy I have in simple things, like a nice vacation that took us two years to save for. Planning it and anticipating it was so much part of the fun!

Proverbs 30:8 says, "Give me neither poverty nor riches." I am grateful that is where I am. I get excited anticipating things that are probably humdrum to the wealthy, but I don't have to worry about day-to-day needs like those who live in poverty. What a blessing!

So, as I look forward to the New Year, instead of longing for things I think I want, I am grateful for what I don't yet have. Like that upcoming vacation. When we don't have something, we hope for it. And hope is even a more beautiful thing in the spiritual realm.

Hope is part of the redemptive process.

"We ourselves, who have the firstfruits of the Spirit, groan inwardly as we wait eagerly for our adoption to sonship, the redemption of our bodies. For in this hope we were saved. But hope that is seen is no hope at all. Who hopes for what they already have? But if we hope for what we do not yet have, we wait for it patiently," (Romans 8:23-25)

The next time I am frustrated at myself for my sinful responses to life, I will remember that I am not there yet, but I am hoping for the day when my redemption from this decaying, sinful body is complete. I have to remember that the redemptive process has three parts, and I'm just partially through the second one! I have been justified. It is finished. I am being sanctified, the gradual process of being made like Christ. And I have the eager, expectant hope for the day I will experience the last part of that redemptive process—the glorification of being made perfectly sinless! Paul felt the same way when he said, "We wait for it patiently."

It is not a "wishing for something" hope. It is an excited anticipation of a "for sure thing" kind of hope. We will behold Him and will be made perfect because of the glorious gift of salvation.

Just as Denny and I paid that vacation deposit, guaranteeing us what was to come, God "put his Spirit in our hearts as a deposit, guaranteeing what is to come."

It's a for-sure thing! As I look forward to this year with hope, I am grateful for what I do not yet have—but will someday!

REFLECT:

Are you absolutely confident in the redemption God has given you through Christ? (If not, please read Appendix B).

Do you think we can be totally sure we are going to heaven? (See 1 John 5:13; Romans 8:16).

What is something that you waited for that seemed to increase its value to you?

—✝—

Dear God, Thank you that You had a plan even before the creation of the world to redeem not only mankind, but the entirety of creation. Please help me to live with an eternal perspective, remembering that my life on earth is so short in comparison to eternity. Thank you for the hope we have in You. Amen.

NEW BEGINNINGS

THIS PICTURE IS FROM MY RUN THIS morning. The trees that just a couple months ago held leaves of various colors now all have empty branches. It's as if the trees themselves are celebrating the New Year with the shedding of the old in order to welcome in the new. A fresh start!

I love the thought of a new year with new beginnings. The thought brings hope for growth and change. What new things will you embrace this year in your walk with Jesus?

I don't do New Year's Resolutions in the traditional way, but I incorporate my "resolutions" into our Christmas celebration. I think of my goals for the new year as a gift of obedience that I bring to the Lord, and that is my birthday gift to Jesus. Some years I do better at fulfilling my commitment than others. What gift of obedience is God asking of you this year?

Lately God has been leading me into some new ventures—things to stretch my faith and help me learn to trust Him more. As I look back at other faith-stretching experiences in the past, I see the journey He has had me on—a journey that reflects His goodness and mercy in my life.

His goodness and mercy stand out as an antithesis to some heavy baggage that I carried for years. I had so many leaves I didn't want to shed. Ugly leaves, fertilized by the enemy's lies, stuck to my life like glue, preventing new growth from occurring. I don't know what baggage you are carrying from the past, but the new year is a perfect time to let go of it. Like the trees have shown us, new growth can't come until you let go of the old.

The enemy doesn't want you to let go of it. He wants to keep you chained to regret, sorrow, or shame from the past. His plan is to "steal and kill and destroy," (John 10:10). He wants to steal your joy, to kill the fulfillment of God's purpose in your life, and to destroy your peace. But Jesus came to stop Him! "The reason the Son of God appeared was to destroy the devil's work," (I John 3:8).

Jesus came to stop the destruction from the enemy in your life. I have to ask you...Are you still letting it happen? Are you still listening to his lies?

"I have come that they may have life, and have it to the full," (John 10:10b). Jesus speaks truth over us and wants us to experience the fullness of walking with Him in a new way by letting go of the old.

I used to beat myself up because I thought that as a Christian I was supposed to forget the past, and I had some painful memories that I just couldn't seem to forget. I mean...Isn't that what Paul was saying in Philippians 3:13? When I read, "Forgetting what is behind and straining toward what is ahead," I would chastise myself for not being able to forget the past as Paul seemed to be doing. The leaves of regret stayed on my tree, keeping me from moving forward with God.

God eventually showed me the real meaning of that passage. God doesn't expect us to just forget our pain. But He doesn't want us to stay there. He doesn't want us to focus on it so much that we lose sight of Him. He wants to have such preeminence in our lives that anything that held our focus in the past seems insignificant in comparison to Him. Paul says in the following verse, "I press on toward the goal to win the prize for which God has called me heavenward in Christ Jesus," (Philippians 3:14).

He is our goal. And when we are moving toward that goal, everything else fades in comparison. In that growing process, He gently removes those ugly leaves off our trees. He replaces them with new leaves of healing and restoration, bringing ministry and purpose.

"See, I am doing a new thing! Now it springs up; do you not perceive it?" (Isaiah 43:19)

The Goal

Lord, I read it in the scriptures—
"Forget what is behind."
So I smother painful memories
In locked closets in my mind.
Sometimes those memories creep out,
But every time they come,
I detach myself from feeling,
So emotions can grow numb.
I press on to walk with Jesus,
But as I'm straining toward the goal,
It's hard to ignore the gaping wound
In the middle of my soul!
But, Lord, I thought I'd been made new!
Why does this pain still last?
I must be a weak-kneed Christian
To still struggle with my past.
But You see me with compassion,
As I pretend that all is fine,
And you whisper the true meaning of
"Forget what is behind."
...To forget my former trophies,
Things once held in high esteem...

I'm to count them loss for the sake of Christ
For a glory yet unseen.
For in placing higher value
On the goal to know my Christ,
Pursuing You with passion,
I find You, Lord, as my prize.
I see now how misled I've been
To trust in my own denial.
As you walk the valleys with me, Lord,
Your love can reconcile.
I've only made things worse
Each time I heap on self-contempt
Because I've tried to "forget the past"
But failed at each attempt.
I've learned Your plan is not for me
To bury what I'm feeling.
You've a greater journey planned—
It's called the path to hope and healing.
Anything that hangs me up,
Keeping me from liberation,
Should be brought to You and not denied—
You're a God of restoration.
Oh, Lord, open all the closets
That stayed locked within my soul,
So that nothing else can hinder me
From You, Lord...You, my goal.

— ©1999 BOBBIE PERKINS

REFLECT:

What kind of leaves in your life need to be removed?

What leaves bring you an opportunity for ministry?

. . .

Which of the following trees best describes you? (A) Full of brown lifeless leaves I need to shed (B) I have shed leaves, but now my branches seem bare and I'd like to grow new beautiful leaves (C) I have new sprigs of green growth sprouting forth (D) I have lush green branches of growth (but always room for more).

—✝—

Dear God, Thank you that You can make even the ugly leaves in our lives look beautiful as You teach us to shed them in preparation for growth. Thank you for Your Holy Spirit to teach us and guide us in that growth. Help me to not necessarily forget my pain, but find You as the Healer for all of it. Help me to pursue You as the only prize worth focusing on. Amen.

AND GOD REMEMBERED

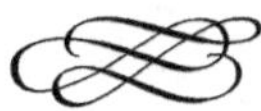

THE SCRIPTURES THAT STATE "AND God remembered" used to baffle me. Wait a minute. Isn't God omniscient? If He remembered something, does that mean that prior to that He forgot? Then how could He be all-knowing? When I began looking at the examples in Scripture where it states that God remembered, I learned that in those passages, the word "remembered" doesn't mean to recall something that had been forgotten. It carries more of the idea of looking upon someone with regard or seeing someone as worthy of attention, especially after a period of struggle (See Hannah, Rachel, Abraham, Noah, David). Scripture repeatedly tells us that God remembers His people, and sometimes He even causes us to remember them! That is exactly what God did at the St. Jude virtual marathon. Let me tell you about my friend Ashley.

Ashley was running her first full marathon after months of training. She had made the sacrifices. Running at dark-thirty. Running in the fog, rain, heat and cold. She had suffered through hills and cramps, blisters and chafing, and all those things that marathoners go through to discover capabilities and strengths they didn't know they had. And she had done it. She had completed the training that meant that she was ready to conquer that 26.2 miles.

What was hard in training, however, became even harder on the day of the race. Ashley struggled through the last several miles, suffering painful muscle cramps. She fell further behind her anticipated finish time and began to fight that little voice inside her head that tried to tear her down. She began to criticize herself for struggling, for trying to do something that was so hard. But Ashley had another voice inside her head. It was the voice of her sister, Lori, who had passed away eight years prior. It just so happened that the race was on the anniversary of Lori's death, and it was Lori who had encouraged Ashley to make healthier choices, lose weight, exercise, and stop drinking sodas. Ashley couldn't help but to think how fitting it was that the race fell on this particular date, giving her a way to honor her sister for encouraging her to live a healthier life.

photography by Jay Snow, used with permission

Those last few miles were ruthless as Ashley struggled to continue putting one foot in front of the other. Her friends and family began cheering as they saw her approaching the finish line, and they witnessed the determination on her face. The exact moment she crossed the finish line, the civil defense test siren sounded the loud noon whistle. We began laughing and saying, "Look, Ashley, even the siren is cheering for you." She immediately burst into tears. I thought she was just overcome by the momentous achievement she had just accomplished, but the blood drained from my face when she sobbed, "Lori passed away at exactly twelve noon."

It was at that moment that we realized why it was meant for Ashley to struggle toward the end and finish at a slower pace than she expected. It was meant for her to reflect upon the words of her sister. And to finish at that exact moment in time.

Ashley honored the memory of her sister that day and celebrated her life. And God did, too. "Remember me, Lord, when you show favor to your people," (Psalm 106:4). Oh, how God remembers...in the most impressive ways.

photography by Jay Snow, used with permission

REFLECT:

Think about a time God has "remembered" you or shown unusual favor to you. Have you ever thanked Him for it?

What would you like to be remembered for?

What can you begin to do today to make that happen?

Dear God, Thank you that You are in the details. Your sovereignty over even the little things in life is a comfort and encouragement for me when I am struggling. Help me to remember that You care about every detail of my life, and You are in control. Amen.

BLOOMS FOR THE NEW YEAR

MOST PEOPLE WHO KNOW ME ARE VERY aware that I am a plant murderer. Seriously! Plants hate me, and my plants always die without Denny's intervention.

But something interesting happened recently. I received an amaryllis bulb while attending a women's retreat. I heard an especially impactful message at this retreat—one that gave me a deeper glimpse into God's love for me. I saw His hand through different seasons of my life, and to be honest, some of those seasons were ugly.

But God was working even in those ugly seasons, creating something of beauty. And that little amaryllis bulb taught me that sometimes beauty is born through the winter seasons of our lives.

I didn't hold out a lot of hope that this plant would survive, given my track record. But I so wanted it to. As silly as it may seem, that little plant signified something to me. It reminded me that God had been doing a lot of new things in my life over the last decade. And He promised it would be beautiful.

I carefully planted the bulb, watered it, and turned it in the window so it could receive some indirect sunlight. It was slow, and I waited patiently for growth, without seeing any for several weeks. It reminded me of my own growth as a Christian, as I have often claimed the title of "the slowest growing Christian ever." But God's timing is always perfect. Just as growth had occurred in my own life ever so slowly, my little amaryllis also began to grow. It took over a month for the first bloom, but soon after, it was bursting with beautiful blooms!

I love the way God's creation points us to His goodness. I see Him in the way trees go through seasons of life much like we do, shedding leaves that need to go so that new growth can occur. I've had to shed a lot of ugly leaves in my life. But God has brought new leaves of beauty. And that is what I love about this amaryllis! It has the courage to bloom in the winter! What a visual reminder of God's work in the winter seasons of our lives!

It takes great courage to bloom in the dark seasons of our life, when we can't see the light. It involves trusting God and believing that He is good even in our sorrows and that He brings good from them. And in His perfect timing, He brings those blooms of growth.

"But grow in the grace and knowledge of our Lord and Savior Jesus Christ," (2 Peter 3:18).

REFLECT:

What beauty does God want to display through the amaryllis blooms of your own soul's winters?

Will you be patient with His timetable?

Will you consider sharing your blooms with others?

—✝—

Dear God, Thank you for the Holy Spirit who brings growth and new knowledge of You to my life. Help me to be patient with the growth process, recognizing that I may not always understand what You are doing. Help me to trust the refining You are doing in my life through the dark seasons of my soul. Amen.

RECKLESS

I ONCE HAD THE HORRIBLE EXPERIENCE of seeing a dog get hit by a car. Blinded by pain, the poor animal recklessly ran even deeper into traffic, bolting one direction and then another, trying to escape the pain but only getting deeper into trouble.

I pulled over to try to help but then saw a man stopping traffic while another man cautiously approached the dog. Knowing an injured dog may become defensive due to pain, I hoped the dog would allow the man to help. A few people got out of their cars to form a barricade to force the dog to safety. Speaking in a calm, soothing voice, the man, whom I then realized was the one who had hit the dog, gently eased the dog into his car to take him to a veterinarian. The injury appeared to only be on his leg, so I hoped that all would turn out okay for the dog and was grateful that the man had cared enough to stop to help him.

There was a time in my life when I was a lot like that dog. Running recklessly into deeper dangers, trying to escape pain. Defensive against the very One who was trying to help me. I didn't understand that God was my help instead of my enemy, and I honestly have to admit that the injured dog was more cooperative than I was.

I'm so grateful that other people got out of their cars….well,….off of their pews….to help me. I can think of several specific mentors who invested time into teaching me Biblical truths so that I could find my way to the Healer. The tapestry of threads God weaves into our lives looks like a tangled mess that makes no sense, but as I look back and see the people God placed into my life at specific points in time, I am amazed. God is so good, and sometimes it takes years before we can look back and see it in perspective.

He brought people into my life at exactly the right time to lead me to Him, the One who could bind up my wounds. He came after me. He healed all the broken places.

I was recklessly running, but His love was even more reckless. And it still is. He is still healing the brokenhearted and binding up their wounds. What wounds do you need to bring to Him today?

Reckless

Reckless in my heart and soul,
Rebellious in my choices...
Angry at an unknown God,
Haunted by past voices.
Reckless to destroy my world,
Impetuous behavior...
I fought the One who loved me most.
I didn't know there was a Savior.
Reckless love that sought me out,
While my fist shook in Your face...
Relentless love that took my sin
So my heart could find Your grace.
Reckless love! My soul sings out.
You drew me from the pit
And silenced the accuser's voice—

Those lies that counterfeit.
Reckless love I have for You.
You are my God who knew...
This hungry soul could still be healed
And live to worship You.
Reckless love! I love to tell
Of chains that were released...
And how you drew me to Yourself
To bring my soul a lasting peace.

— ©2000 BOBBIE PERKINS

REFLECT:

Have you ever been uncooperative with God as He was working in your life?

If so, what did you learn about God through the process?

How has God's love been reckless in your life?

Name some people God placed in your life to draw you closer to Him.

✝

Dear God, Thank you for Your incredible love that I don't deserve, yet You give because of Your grace and mercy. Thank you for the people You have used in my life to point me to You. Help me to do the same for those You place in my path. Help me to have a reckless love for You! Amen.

HOT OR COLD

WHEN I WAS A LITTLE GIRL, MY friends and I used to play a game called "hot" and "cold." One person would hide an object, and the others would hunt for it. The person who hid the object would give hints to the people searching, saying, "cold" when they were way off base and "hot" when they were getting close. It's definitely different from the games now being played by children in today's age of technology!

Sometimes I think it would be nice for God to give us the same kind of appraisal as we go through life—yelling, "hot" when we are walking in proximity to Him and "cold" when we are wandering away from Him!

I think of the Israelites wandering in the desert for forty years, so far from the promised land but not turning totally away from God and going back to Egypt. Just kind of stuck in the middle of the luke-warm life. The promised land could have been theirs so much sooner, but they refused to embrace the life of holiness and faithfulness that

God desired for them. But God in His goodness used even those wilderness years to teach them.

I believe that a large number of Christians are like those Israelites. Oh, they assent to the foundational beliefs of Christianity. They have received the free gift of salvation with gladness but now have wandered away from the cross, letting the world capture their gaze instead of their Savior. Every now and then they feel a spark of the flame after a church service or a song on the radio, but they don't come closer to the flame to be warmed to the soul.

I've been in that wilderness, too. Times of a chill overtaking my heart, the flame of faith sputtering and drowning in the liquid wax of the world. Escaping hell but not growing toward abundant life. Planted, but not blooming.

Thankfully, our gracious God will not cast wilderness wanderers away, for salvation is based on faith in Christ, not works. But what a tragedy to prefer wandering in the desert over living in the abundance of the promised land! The Holy Spirit will not audibly yell, "hot" or "cold," but sometimes He will whisper it to our soul.

And sometimes God uses the body of Christ as that gentle whisper. Through different stages of my Christian growth, I remember being around other Christians who were just different somehow. I couldn't identify what it was at first, but eventually the Holy Spirit began to whisper to me that I was missing the warmth of something they had. And He was inviting me to draw closer to the flame instead of living the lukewarm life. He was whispering, "cold" and asking me to adjust the thermostat of my heart.

I found that changing the temperature of my heart doesn't just happen once. It is a daily choice that I must still choose today and every day.

I want to choose every day to have it blazing like a woman in menopause!

Where is your heart's thermostat set? Is God whispering, "hot" or "cold"?

REFLECT:

With 0 being frozen and 10 being boiling, what number would you give the temperature of your own heart right now? If less than 7, what can you do to increase that number?

What has God taught you in the wilderness seasons?

How has God used the body of Christ to reveal the temperature of your heart?

—✝—

Dear God, Oh, how I want to be on fire for You! Please help me to continue to grow in my love for You, and please reveal to me when my heart is growing cold. I commit to establish spiritual habits of discipline to keep me connected to You and ask You to help me be faithful. Amen.

FEBRUARY

REVIVAL

<table>
<tr>
<td>

</td>
<td>

I LOVE READING ABOUT THE GREAT revivals in history, such as the Great Awakening that began in the 18th century or the Jesus Movement of the late 1960s and early 1970s. There have been pockets of revivals since then, but I wonder what it would be like today to see a widespread revival of people turning to God in abandon.

</td>
</tr>
</table>

But it doesn't have to look like that. There can be revival on a church pew in just one person. There can be revival in a hospital room when a heart reaches for the God of all hope. Sometimes there is a bigger revival in one heart than there is at a whole tent crusade.

Maybe instead of looking outward for revival, I need to be looking inward for it. Maybe revival starts with me.

Grow My Heart

Holy Spirit, grow my heart...
That I might grow flowers, not weeds...

To look past my own selfish needs,
And see those straining and trying,
Yet have souls lost and dying.
Holy Spirit, grow my heart...
That while I lament this sick world,
I will see Your kingdom unfurled.
Greed, crime, drugs, and gender
Will all bow in surrender.
Holy Spirit, grow my heart...
To cast off pride, seek Your face,
To know I'm no more deserving of grace
Than the most murderous, lewd, men.
The cross includes even them.
Holy Spirit, grow my heart...
Quench my complacent indulgence
To move past my reluctance
To carry Living Water in glasses
To the lost, thirsty masses.
Holy Spirit, grow my heart...
Move my gaze toward what You see,
To follow Your path for me,
To repent of my dwindling fire,
To live holy as You require.
Holy Spirit, grow my heart...
To not give up in defeat
At the worldwide needs I can't meet...
For You'll show me what to do,
Because I can reach the nearby few.
Holy Spirit grow my heart...
So that I no longer care
If people think I'm "way out there,"
To know the task that You've given me
Is one blind eyes will never see.
Holy Spirit, grow my heart...
And help my own eyes to see

That this world's not all that's meant for me.
Help me to point redemption's way
To those who cross my path each day.
Holy Spirit, grow my heart...
To tell when I'm the only one.
To tell when I'm scared, made-fun.
To tell of this heart made new...
To tell all those I meet of You.

— ©2022 BOBBIE PERKINS

REFLECT:

What needs to happen in your heart for revival to happen?

When we reflect back on what God has done in our life, it can often kindle a revival of our love for Him. On a separate paper, write out a short testimony of how you came to know God and what He has done in your life since then. Consider sharing it with someone if God brings you the opportunity.

—✝—

Dear God, I give my heart anew to You today to be revived in love and commitment. Help me to grow more excited about You with each passing day because the more I know of You, the more I have to be excited about. Help me to become more comfortable sharing the gospel with others, so that revival can spread! Amen.

WHAT IS GOD ASKING
YOU TO GIVE?

> *"They gave themselves first of all to the Lord."*
> — 2 Corinthians 8:5

When it comes to ministry, have you ever felt God was asking you to do something that was over your head? I don't know about you, but I kind of like to stay in my comfort zone. There are some things that I feel fairly confident doing— leading a small women's bible study, participating in a committee, writing a devotion. Other ministry opportunities (things that you may consider easy) I consider more difficult, like teaching a large group of children, decorating for an event, or singing a solo. We definitely all have different talents!

Even within those areas of strength, however, God sometimes likes to stretch us. He doesn't want us to get so comfortable that we are serving in our own strength. Because when we start serving without seeking Him, our ministry is devoid of the thrill of seeing God at work.

I have a friend who sings in the choir. He has a decent voice and occasionally sings some solos. I should preface this with the fact that our church has TREMENDOUS musical talent with some very gifted musicians and soloists. This friend knows he is not in that category. But he can sing pretty well. He just gives God what talent he has and enjoys serving.

Our choir director recently asked my friend to sing a solo in a very difficult song. He didn't want to do it. He felt the song was over his musical ability. He could have said no. He could have let someone else do it. Surely someone else had more talent suitable for that song.

In John 6:1-14, there was another person who felt he didn't have enough. But instead of saying no, the small boy gave Jesus everything he had. And Jesus took the boy's five loaves and two fish and blessed the boy's trusting willingness with the tremendous miracle of feeding five thousand people. The twelve baskets of leftovers confirmed that God loves for us to trust Him instead of trusting in our own resources.

In the same way, my friend decided to trust God and sing the solo. He was nervous, but he decided to step out in faith and practice plentifully. He also asked for prayer. I remember praying for him and feeling nervous for him because I knew he did not feel confident.

That lack of confidence in his own ability forced him to trust God. The song stretched his vocal range, but his obedience stretched his faith. And God showed up. His voice was strong and on pitch with no hint of nervousness. It was definitely the best solo I have ever heard him sing. The part that made it so incredible was that it taught me something about trusting God and allowing Him to stretch us.

God blessed his obedience, and my friend had a moment. He even got a standing ovation. It is a blessed memory in our church because we knew we had witnessed something special. We felt the presence of God, and when he finished the song, it was as if we were reveling in the twelve baskets of leftovers.

We all saw God work that day because my friend gave not out of his ability, but out of his lack. And God took care of the rest. Where is God asking you to step out of your comfort zone? Are you serving in your own strength or trusting in the unlimited resources of God? You might just see a miracle.

REFLECT:

What is God asking you to give in order to trust Him more?

Describe a time when you saw something happen that you know was the result of God's intervention.

Name someone who has taught you something about trusting God

—✝—

Lord, Please forgive me for my lack of trust in You and help me to step out in faith. Help me to rely on You rather than my own strength. Remind me that whatever you call me to do, You will equip me to do. Amen.

WHO IS IN THE MIRROR?

I'M GOOFY. I KNOW IT, EMBRACE IT, and much to my family's chagrin, have no shame over it! I love to laugh, even if I'm laughing about something silly I have done. Sometimes God gives me little glimmers of truth from my goofy antics. Like my elevator incident.

I was staying at a hotel with my husband while we attended a wedding. I was alone in the elevator and began looking around, observing my surroundings. I looked up toward the ceiling and felt a rush of adrenaline! Someone was staring back at me! I immediately screamed, then began laughing hysterically (mind you, still alone in the elevator) when I realized that the person staring back at me was my own reflection. The elevator happened to have a mirror on the ceiling. How had I not recognized myself?!

After I recovered from laughing, the Holy Spirit immediately brought to my mind the sobering passage in James 1:22-25, which says "Do not merely listen to the word, and so deceive yourselves. Do what it says. Anyone who listens to the word but does not do what it says is like someone who looks at his face in a mirror and, after looking at himself, goes away and immediately forgets what he looks like. But whoever looks intently into the perfect law that gives freedom and continues in it—not forgetting what they have heard, but doing it—they will be blessed in what they do."

I began to think about the times I have listened to a sermon or read a particular scripture with a feeling of conviction to respond in a certain way but then walked away and lost my focus. Forgotten to reach out to that person who is hurting. Forgotten to confess that sin. Forgotten to release my tight grip on something Jesus should be carrying for me. James says I will be blessed if I look "intently." The enemy loves to keep me busy and distracted so that I don't take the time to look intently. He wants me to have an emotional reaction to the truths in God's Word but not take the time to incorporate those truths into my life. Focusing intently takes conscious effort. God wants more than my emotions. He wants my will and my focus. It is my prayer that we will all mull over God's Word intently, so that our lives will reflect His truths.

Mirror

Brought face to face with the mirror, I wonder if people can see
Not just my outward reflection, but the Jesus who lives
    inside me.
And You, Lord, what do You see there? Do You have the throne
    in my heart?
Or do I take charge of my own life? And leave Jesus just one
    little part?
It's a question of total commitment. Like a sculptor, You give
    my life form
Only if it is yielded in fullness, not a half-hearted faith that's
    lukewarm.
You have called me to share it with others. So many are
    searching for You.

How sad if I fail to take notice and sit complacently on the
*   church pew.*
Lord, give me the boldness to step out and share the love in my
*   heart that keeps growing*
to millions of people who are longing to hear of a Christ that
*   they die without knowing.*

— © 1988 BOBBIE PERKINS

REFLECT:

Do you read the Bible or go to church expecting that God has a message for you?

Do you take notes during the sermon to help you focus on the message?

How can you narrow your focus to continue "intently" in your faith?

Is there a part of your life that you still need to yield to God?

─✝─

Dear God, Please forgive me for not following through with the truths You communicate to me. Help me to respond to You in obedience, not losing my focus or forgetting what You teach me. Thank You for Your Word to reveal what is in my heart and to direct my path. Amen.

5 WAYS IT AFFECTS OUR LIVES THAT GOD KNOWS US

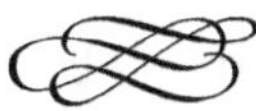

"I love you," is one of the most often said phrases around the world, especially on Valentine's Day. But there sure are lots of different kinds of love, aren't there?! I love coffee, books, and my next-door-neighbor, but not in the same way I love my husband! There is a special kind of love that comes with deeper intimacy.

> "I will give them a heart to know me, that I am the Lord."
> — *Jeremiah 24:7*

My husband knows me intimately. He can finish my sentences. He could order my food at a restaurant because he knows what I like. I will pick up the phone to call him, only to find that he is calling me at that moment, as if our hearts and thoughts are connected. Being loved by him is a lot like being loved by God because I can be vulnerable and know that I am fully known, yet fully loved.

When describing our relationship with God, Scripture uses an interesting word in Hebrew. It's the word "yada." We find it first in Genesis 4:1. "Now Adam knew (yada) Eve his wife, and she conceived." The type of knowing that results in children is more than just a casual knowing! It means to know intimately. It encompasses a cherished relationship, a special type of communion with total transparency.

5 WAYS IT AFFECTS OUR LIVES THAT GOD KNOWS (YADA) US:

1. WE CAN BE SECURE IN GOD'S LOVE BECAUSE HE FULLY KNOWS US AND FULLY LOVES US.

"He knows (yada) the secrets of the heart," (Psalm 44:21). Yet you know (yada) me, Lord; you see me and test my thoughts," (Jeremiah 12:3). God already knows every little thing about us, including the worst things, and He still loves us.

2. GOD DOESN'T JUST KNOW US INTIMATELY. WE CAN KNOW HIM INTIMATELY, TOO.

"I will give you hidden treasures, riches stored in secret places, so that you may know (yada) that I am the Lord..." (Isaiah 45:3). "I will give them a heart to know (yada) me, that I am the Lord. They will be my people, and I will be their God, for they will return to me with all their heart," (Jeremiah 24:7). God knows (yada) us and CHOOSES us so that we can know (yada) Him! I think of those sports teams back in middle school where the captains chose the team members, and that last person was chosen by default because they weren't really wanted on the team. Friend, God CHOSE you because He wanted you on His team! He gave you a heart to know (yada) Him, and to direct your heart and affections toward Him!

3. BECAUSE GOD KNOWS US FULLY, HE FULLY UNDERSTANDS OUR SORROWS.

"For you saw my affliction and knew (yada) the anguish of my soul," (Psalm 31:7). Sometimes even our closest friends and family can't understand how we feel. God understands us because He sees what is in our heart.

4. BECAUSE OF OUR INTIMATE RELATIONSHIP WITH GOD, WE CAN KNOW HIS WILL AND HIS PATH FOR US.

"Trust in the Lord with all your heart and lean not on your own understanding; in all your ways acknowledge (yada) him, and he will make your paths straight," (Proverbs 3:5,6). The closer we get to God, the easier it is for us to discern His will. Letting Him be an intimate part of our life helps us to live the way He wants us to.

5. BECAUSE OF OUR INTIMATE RELATIONSHIP WITH GOD, IT CHANGES HOW WE LIVE SO THAT OTHERS CAN SEE HIM IN OUR LIVES.

"I want to know Christ..." (Philippians 3:10). The Greek word in that passage used for "know" is "ginosko," which is similar to the Hebrew "yada" in that it means to know deeply. It means to know from personal experience, not just secondhand. I love that! Like Paul, I want to know Christ deeply through personal experience. Faith can never be secondhand. I don't know Him because I read about Him. I know Him because I experience Him in my life daily. I want to be like Paul, to "press on toward the goal to win the prize..." (Philippians 3:14). The prize is to know Him even more deeply!

REFLECT:

Would you say you have a deep desire to to know God better?

Does knowing God change the way you live?

. . .

Are you relying on a secondhand faith?

⁻✝⁻

Dear God, Thank you for the great love You have for me. I want to know You better and press on with passion like Paul to have a deeper relationship with You. Help me to seek You and experience You daily in my life. Amen.

ARE YOU A BIBLE STUDY GIRL?

<table>
<tr><td>

"For as he thinks in his heart, so is he."

— Proverbs 23:7

</td><td>

IT'S FUNNY HOW OUR THOUGHTS affect our actions. Proverbs 23:7 says, "For as he thinks in his heart, so is he." I have seen this evidence first-hand in my running journey and in my spiritual journey. When I first started running, I never called myself a "runner." I would always say that I was "someone who runs sometimes."

</td></tr>
</table>

There was something about designating myself with that title of runner that brought higher expectations of my performance.

Gradually my running improved in pace and distance. I honestly don't remember when the transition happened in my mind, but somewhere along the course of time, I began to think of myself as a runner and call myself a runner. The thoughts and actions were intertwined. As I improved, my thoughts about my ability improved, which brought more confidence, which further enhanced my performance, which brought more confidence. Follow me? Thoughts feed actions. Actions feed thoughts. They can't be separated. I became a runner.

Not long ago, someone called me a "Bible study girl." This

resonated with me because as much as I love and study the Bible now, I so very clearly remember the days when I didn't know one single verse. I remember when I was in high school and beginning to seek God after the death of a friend. I visited a church and was caught off guard when the small group went around in a circle, sharing their favorite verses. I was embarrassed when they got to me. I didn't know any verses by heart. This did intrigue me to study the Bible, however, because the verses the others shared spoke to my heart. It was that same year that I began my own thrilling journey of knowing Jesus as my Savior.

Knowing Jesus, however, didn't instantly make me a "Bible study girl." In my early years as a Christian, I struggled with low "spiritual self-esteem." I was constantly comparing myself to other Christians and feeling I would never measure up to them. I didn't know the Bible the way that they did. I wasn't raised in a Christian home, so I didn't understand all the doctrines and terminology that they did. I didn't know how to pray beautiful prayers like they did. I had things in my past that they didn't. The enemy used this mind game with me for YEARS. I never considered myself a Bible study girl. I considered myself based on my past, grateful for salvation, but resigning myself to sitting on the sidelines, admiring the other "runners." But gradually, my walk grew stronger, and my faith grew deeper. As I spent time in God's Word, I began to see myself as God saw me. I wasn't inferior to all of my Christian friends. I was chosen! For a purpose! I began to understand the glorious riches of the inheritance I had been given. And I found my purpose—to learn all I could about how to walk closer to Jesus and help others to do the same. I became a Bible study girl.

I want other women to see themselves as God sees them, so that they can stop listening to the lies of the enemy and listen to the truths of their identity in Christ. Hebrews 12:1,2 says, "Let us throw off everything that hinders and the sin that so easily entangles [lies from the enemy, negative thoughts, insert your own struggles]. And let us run with perseverance the race marked out for us, fixing our eyes on

Jesus, the pioneer and perfecter of faith." A runner always begins with that first step. Go for the prize. Be a runner. Be a Bible study girl!

REFLECT:

Do you struggle with feeling "less than" or unworthy?

If so, where do you think those thoughts come from?

Meditate on the cross for a moment. Is there anything more God could have done to demonstrate your worth to Him?

—✝—

Dear God, thank you for the cross. There is no greater demonstration of love than that sacrifice made for me. Remind me when I feel "less than" that I am more than "a conqueror in Christ Jesus." Remind me that You have promised to finish the work you started in me and help me to cooperate with that sanctification process through obedience. Amen.

I DIDN'T ACT LIKE A CHRISTIAN

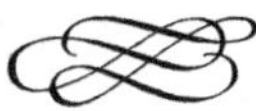

I DIDN'T ACT LIKE A CHRISTIAN THAT day. It was one of THOSE days, the kind where I was hit from every side, and my stress level was at breaking point. My condescending words spewed out like a sixth grade volcano science experiment. What I had said was true, but the manner in which I said it was not how I want to be known. I went home that day vacillating between remorse over my response and justification that I had been right. After all, SHE had spoken wrongly to me first. SHE wasn't doing her job. SHE was just being lazy. SHE wasn't dealing with the same stress that I was. All the while, I knew that even though my coworkers who saw what happened might have agreed with me, in God's eyes I still wasn't justified in reacting the way I did.

But how could I apologize when she had been rude to me first? Shouldn't she be apologizing to me? My pride continued to rationalize that I should just forget the interaction and move on. But I couldn't. The words of Philippians 2:14,15 convicted me. "Do everything without grumbling or arguing...then you will shine among them like stars in the sky." I hadn't shined very brightly that day. I felt the Holy Spirit whisper to me, "If you apologize, you are humbling yourself in a way that is unlike how the world lives. The grace that has been given to you should overflow to others. Go shine... and tell her why you are different. Don't react the way everyone else does. Responding in a way that is different is what makes you shine as a Christian."

It was hard to make myself obey, but I was glad that I did. And because I don't want to go through that again, I will choose my words and demeanor more carefully in the future! My apology seemed to surprise her, but she was receptive and forgiving. My explanation of how God had convicted me seemed to intrigue her as I explained that I felt I had been a bad example of the joy that lives in my heart. She assured me that all was well, and I noticed our next few interactions were more friendly than they previously had been. I detected a hint of respect that had not been there before.

Will I make this same mistake again in the future? Probably. But most likely to a different person, in a different situation. But maybe to this one person, I am shining a little brighter now...like stars in the sky, standing out as a little different, making her wonder about that difference...A difference I told her was because I have the light of the world inside of me. May He shine more brightly as I learn from my mistakes.

Shining

I'm just a little candle, shining in the night
To a lost and dying world that needs to know God's light.
I set my light upon the stand for all the world to see
The source that makes my candle burn is Jesus inside me.
Sometimes troubles come along, and the dark hours seem to
*   stay,*
But I just let my little candle burn, and its light shows me
*   the way.*

My little flame may not be much, but God says there is a need
For candles like me to lend out their light, to make a way
through the darkness and lead.
Sometimes I wander from my kindling source, or I let my wick
get too low.
My flame dies down to a flicker and has only a smoldering
glow.
In the darkness I struggle and stumble, but as soon as I call on
His name,
He's always right there to build up my fire back to a bright
shining flame.
Yes, I'm just a little candle, burning bright in the dark,
Hoping to start a huge fire from the warmth of my tiny spark.

— ©1983 BOBBIE PERKINS

REFLECT:

Is there someone you've had cross words with you should offer an apology to?

If a stranger were to follow you for a week, would they know that you are a believer by observing your interactions with others?

How does Jesus make a difference in the way you live?

—✝—

Lord, I confess there are times I don't act in ways that bring You glory. Please help me to walk in the Spirit rather than the flesh in my daily interactions with others. Thank you that the Holy Spirit enables me to do things that I cannot do on my own. Help me to shine for You. Amen.

IS GOD WITHHOLDING FROM YOU THE DESIRES OF YOUR HEART?

> *"Take delight in the Lord, and He will give you the desires of your heart."*
>
> — Psalm 37:4

"Take delight in the Lord, and He will give you the desires of your heart." It's a beautiful verse that seems to hold a promise for happiness if we perform the required prerequisite of "taking delight in the Lord." But what if God isn't giving you that intense desire of your heart? What if you are seeking Him the best you know how, begging Him for something specific, and He hasn't fulfilled that deep yearning within? When our unmet longing is for something good and honorable, we can feel as if God has let us down when He doesn't grant it. It makes us question our faith. It makes us question God Himself.

Perhaps you are feeling the pain of this unmet longing. You may be thinking to yourself, "It's not like I'm asking to be rich or famous. I just want this person I love to come back to God….Or I just want my husband to stop drinking….I just want God to heal my child from cancer….I just want the pregnancy test to be positive this time…." whatever your prayers are, they are whispered in desperation from a grieving heart. I think we all have been at a place where we have wondered why God wasn't answering our prayers.

The truth is, God is so much bigger than that. We can't put Him in a box with a cookie-cutter formula that if we do A, then God will do B. Sometimes God has choice C in mind, a path we may never have envisioned. And we must be careful when we handle Scripture, that we don't turn principles into promises to suit our own desires. God is not a transitive property math equation. He sees what we don't see and knows what we don't know. He desires what we don't always desire, but He longs to make our desires the same as His.

And that is where we are on the struggle bus —in making our desires like His. It's hard to imagine that He is doing something good in the things that we see as painful. We usually don't see it until we are on the other side of the pain. Is it possible that your intense desire for that THING you are praying for has taken preeminence over God Himself in your life? God's gift of children, a husband, relationships, health...are we lifting these desperate pleas up so high that our trembling hands have transformed to hands of idolatry? Has our desire become an idol keeping us from true intimacy with God?

What exactly does it mean to take delight in the Lord? The word "delight" here is the Hebrew word "anag", which means "to take exquisite delight," but it also has another interesting meaning. It also means "to be bendable and pliable," like a green branch. Hmmm. Pliable in the hands of God. Letting Him bend our will toward His. Going further...the next verse says, "Commit your way to the Lord." This is the Hebrew word "gala," which means to "roll away" from us and onto Him. We are giving our way, with all of our heart's desires to Him and committing them to Him in trust. The word commit is actually a banking term. When we make a deposit into a bank account, we commit that money to the bank for safekeeping. We don't worry over it. We know it is safe. We don't go back five times a day to take it back out and look at it and worry over it.

Are you worrying about things that you have given to God for safekeeping? Are you allowing Him to bend your desires to make them like His?

Are you desiring God more than EVERYTHING else in your life, even that deep longing you are intensely praying about? God is trustworthy. Sometimes it takes years of aching from an unmet desire to realize that all of our desires can only be met in more of God Himself.

God may not be withholding your desires. He may be changing them.

REFLECT:

Look up the song "More Than Anything" by Natalie Grant. Can you say those lyrics are the echo of your heart? If not, can you ask God to help you with that?

If God were to answer one prayer for you today, what would that be?

Take some time right now to commit that deep desire you have to the Lord. Give it to Him for safekeeping, trust Him with it, and stop worrying over it. That doesn't mean you'll stop praying about it, but it does mean you will trust Him with the outcome.

Dear God, You are trustworthy and good. Help me to trust You with the deep desires of my heart, giving the outcome to You, even if the outcome isn't what I would choose. Bend my heart toward You to make me pliable to Your will. Amen.

WASHING THE
WOUNDS OF WORDS

"Now that I, your Lord and Teacher, have washed your feet, you also should wash one another's feet."

— John 13:14

IN HONOR OF NATIONAL MARRIAGE Week and Valentine's Day that both occur in February, I am sharing the story of my friend. Serving one another in humility is a crucial component of a healthy marriage. Sometimes it is hard. Sometimes we just have to obey and trust God to honor our actions.

**Note- I am in no way encouraging anyone to stay in a relationship that is abusive. The details of this friend's story are longer than I am able to include. Although her marriage has experienced healing, I am fully aware that this is not always the case for everyone. Having a spirit of humility does not mean subjecting yourself to abuse. If you are experiencing this, please reach out to someone for help- a women's shelter, church, friend, relative, even a health care provider. Google domestic violence help near you. There are also apps for your phone that can notify your contacts if you are in trouble. Please get help if you are in danger!*

. . .

She helped him out of the shower without a word. She was concentrating because it was hard supporting his weight during the transfer. He wasn't a skinny man. As she handed her husband a towel, she realized he was getting weaker. When he first had the stroke, he was able to walk well with his walker. Now his legs were so shaky.

Memories of earlier years flooded her mind. His alcoholism. The verbal abuse and cruel words. Tears from his hurtful remarks. She never brought friends home. Nobody could know her secret pain. How strong and capable she seemed to all her coworkers! They had no idea what she suffered at home. And she would never let her mask slip for them to see. She had not expected the drinking to stop in the manner it did. He was no longer able to drive to the liquor store. He relied on her for everything. Now she was the one in charge.

She is a dear friend of mine. Somehow during the course of our friendship, we both began to let our masks slip. We developed a kinship in Christ and began studying the Bible together. We grew together and learned from one another. She learned to study and apply Scripture to her life. I learned about humility, forgiveness, and serving.

It shook my soul to know how she served her husband. The very one who had hurt her the most in her life was the one to whom she now humbly ministered. She performed those menial tasks for nobody to see. Somehow in the process, her spirit was changed. A supernatural patience gave her the ability to suffer his gruffness with a softness she had not known before. She pitied his frustration at what his life had become due to his poor choices. He saw what hers had become through Christ.

What God did in the life of my friend is what Jesus taught in John 13. Walking along dusty roads in sandals caused feet to become dirty, so servants washed the feet of people as they entered the home. John 13:5-8 reads, "After that, he poured water into a basin and began to wash his disciples' feet, drying them with the towel that was wrapped around him. He came to Simon Peter, who said to him, "Lord, are you going to wash my feet?"

Jesus replied, "You do not realize now what I am doing, but later you will understand."

"No, said Peter, "you shall never wash my feet."

Jesus answered, "Unless I wash you, you have no part with me."

Peter did not understand why Jesus would degrade himself, performing the task of a servant. Jesus wanted to teach the spirit of submission to God even when we don't understand. Jesus was also teaching that we can walk more closely with Him by letting go of willful sin, allowing Him to cleanse us. Jesus was visually teaching the significance of humility as opposed to a proud spirit.

Would I be as willing to quietly serve, not where I am publicly lauded for my efforts, but in secret, where no one thanks me? Would I be willing to serve the one who has hurt me the most? This is humility. This is the spirit of Christ.

Matthew 6:1

"Be careful not to practice your righteousness in front of others to be seen by them. If you do, you will have no reward in heaven."

Philippians 2:3

"Do nothing out of selfish ambition or vain conceit. Rather, in humility, value others above yourselves, not looking to your own interests but each of you to the interests of the others."

REFLECT:

What humble act of service can you perform for someone?

Is God asking you to step out in obedience, but you are hesitant because you don't understand what He is doing?

Is there an area of your life that you need to relinquish to Jesus for cleansing?

—✝—

Dear God, thank you for the ultimate example of self-sacrifice by Jesus' death on the cross for my sin. Help me to live the example Jesus set for us by serving others with love and humility. Show me how to serve those who have hurt me and to serve out of love for you and not the praise of others. Amen.

—✝—

HOW IS YOUR PROGRESS?

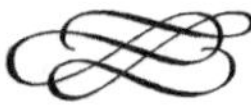

HAVE YOU EVER FELT THAT YOU WERE making no progress toward your goal? You pay off the credit card, then the washing machine breaks. You mop the floor, then the dog tracks in muddy footprints. We won't even talk about the endless mounds of laundry! Maybe you want a deeper walk with God and don't feel that you are making any progress. Seeing God do great things in the lives of others when we are faltering can be discouraging. How do we make progress in our relationship with God? How do we know Him better?

The people of Israel struggled with the desire to see God do great things in their lives as well. The first chapter of Joshua is where obedience and blessing meet to produce the manifestation of God's presence in a marvelous way.

As the new leader of the Israelites, Joshua had big shoes to fill after the death of Moses. There is nothing like a seemingly impossible task as your first assignment as leader! Almost to the Promised Land, the Israelites feared the obstacle of crossing the Jordan River. They were discouraged. They had traveled so long and so far, it seemed that as soon as they had made some progress, another hindrance lay before them.

I can relate to the feeling of taking two steps forward, then three steps backward, making no progress at all for my efforts. What barriers are you facing in your desire for progress? What can we do to move forward in our relationship with God?

God told Joshua how to conquer obstacles in order to make progress toward possessing the Promised Land. "Be strong and courageous. Be careful to obey all the law my servant Moses gave you; do not turn from it to the right or to the left, that you may be successful wherever you go. Keep this Book of the Law always on your lips; meditate on it day and night, so that you may be careful to do everything written in it. Then you will be prosperous and successful" (Joshua 1:7,8).

In a condensed version, God was saying, "Be confident, be cognizant, and be connected." Being strong and courageous is about putting our confidence in God's strength instead of our own. Obedience is about being cognizant and informed so that we not only know what is right, but we evaluate whether we are walking along the right path. Meditating on the Word of God is about being connected to God so that scripture takes root in our hearts to impact our lives. Being confident, cognizant, and connected will help us reach our purpose of a deeper walk with God.

Joshua told the people, "Consecrate yourselves, for tomorrow the Lord will do amazing things among you." I want to consecrate myself to His purpose for me and my progress toward that. And the Lord will do amazing things.

REFLECT:

Are you placing your confidence in yourself or in God?

. . .

If you're confident in God, what are you willing to pray for or do that you know can't happen without His help?

Are you being cognizant of what steps of obedience God is calling you to?

Are you staying connected to God through His Word and prayer?

Dear God, I admit that I sometimes lack confidence in You and trust instead in my own ability. May your will be done not only on earth, but in my own life as I learn to trust You more. Help me to obey and to stay connected to Your Word that helps me walk in that obedience. Amen.

SET FREE FROM THE STICKY TRAP BUT SO MUCH MORE

"We are heirs —
heirs of God and
co-heirs with
Christ."
— Romans 8:17

IT'S THAT TIME OF YEAR AGAIN...COLD. I know my northern friends are laughing at this southerner for not tolerating the cold very well. But there are others who don't like the cold either...tiny creatures. In the south we call them critters. This is the time of the year when critters like to find their way into houses to get warm.

One winter we had a mouse decide to take up residence in our house. I must say he was the most fortunate mouse in the world. Why? Because he just happened to come into a house in which my husband, an animal lover and most compassionate man, was the one who discovered him.

Instead of setting a regular mousetrap, Denny set out a sticky trap. Sure enough, it wasn't long until little mousie was stuck on it. Denny removed him with vegetable oil in order to set him free outside. BUT...it had just snowed, and we were having an unusually cold spell of negative temperatures. Because little mousie's fur was wet with vegetable oil, Denny was afraid the mouse would freeze to death.

So what did this compassionate man do? He made a little house for the mouse and fed him for three days until the weather warmed up. Once the temperatures were back into the 40's and 50's, he took his little mouse friend to the woods and set him free.

Denny showed great compassion by catching the mouse in a humane way. But he did so much more than just rescue what most people would consider an enemy or pest. He gave the mouse shelter from our cats. He kept him warm. HE FED THE MOUSE! WHO DOES THAT? LOL!

What a picture of what God does for us! As sinners, we were enemies of our Great Holy God. Like the mouse, we were on a sticky trap of sin, unable to free ourselves. But when we trust in Christ with a repentant heart, God in His great compassion, does so much more than just rescue us from that trap!

Psalm 103:3-5 describes the compassion of God in that He "forgives all your sins and heals all your diseases, [he] redeems your life from the pit and crowns you with love and compassion, [he] satisfies your desires with good things so that your youth is renewed like the eagle's."

God's forgiveness is such a great gift of mercy. But He does so much more than forgive us. He makes us His own children, "heirs of God and co-heirs with Christ" (Romans 8:17). He has given us His Spirit as a deposit, guaranteeing what more is to come (2 Corinthians 1:22).

Yes, there is more to come. God didn't just leave us as a free little mouse, forgiven and released from our trap but still destitute in the cold. Not even close! What is to come is unimaginable!

There are more generous gifts flowing out of His love and compassion. He has given us riches in heaven, an inheritance we cannot even imagine. He has given us the joy and glory of abiding with Him forever in complete harmony. He has given us the unfathomable treasure of being made perfect in His image.

We aren't just free paupers. We are rich heirs with all of the glories of heaven awaiting us. "See what great love the Father has lavished on us, that we should be called children of God! (I John 3:1) Set free from the sticky trap. Sheltered. Fed. Loved. Adopted and made heirs. Mr. Mousie has nothing on us!

REFLECT:

Are you simply grateful for escaping the trap of sin, or are you contemplating the glorious inheritance God has given to you?

How can you begin to live differently to reflect that you are a child of the King?

Take some time right now to thank God for the great love that He has lavished on us, even while we were His enemies. (Romans 5:8).

⁓✝⁓

Dear God, Thank you for Your incredible grace and mercy that I don't deserve. Thank you for the great inheritance I have in store and that I can call You my Father. Help me to live like a child of the King and not a pauper. Amen.

MARCH

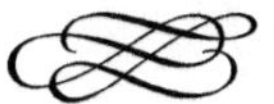

RESTING IN THE RHYTHM OF GOD'S FAITHFULNESS

My FEET POUND IN A RHYTHM WITH my breathing. The cold air leaves little puffs of condensation with each breath, but the work of my muscles warms me. I love running on this path. The sun is beginning to peek through the trees. I see you, God, shining down Your faithfulness in the faithful rhythm of the sunrise every morning. Your love letter is written in the trees and in the curious doe I saw, who stood at a safe distance to observe my intrusion on her space.

Lord, the rhythm of Your faithfulness teaches me to be faithful to You. In a world where everything seems unpredictable, You are unchanging. I admit that I have worried about the future of my children and grandchildren. I have wondered about the future of my country and the future of believers amidst hostile opposition to our values. I am calmed by your blanket of faithfulness that will cover future generations, just as it has covered me, just as it has covered Abraham, Moses, and other believers from the beginning of time.

Psalm 119:90 reminds me that "Your faithfulness continues through all generations; you established the earth, and it endures."

I, too, want to endure, Lord. Just as You are steadfast in Your faithfulness, I want to be steadfast in my faith. I want to cling to Your promises as those who have gone before me. Fortified by faith and confident in my convictions, I will put on the armor of God daily to stand firm when those around me scorn or oppose me. Respectful but resolved, I will speak truth when others oppose it. I will stand my ground with love, as Jesus loved unto the death. And I will stop worrying and start trusting. Resting in the rhythm of your unchanging nature, I put my concerns at Your feet, knowing You are still on the throne, knowing You can be trusted, and knowing You have a plan. You have always had a plan.

Your plan is for my good. Jeremiah 29:11 assures me that Your plans are to give me "a hope and a future." I hope in You, Jesus, as I place the future of all of those that I love into Your hands. No matter what happens in politics, no matter what happens in my country or my world, You are on the throne. This world is Yours. Your faithfulness will continue to all generations.

REFLECT:

Do you ever worry about the future of your kids, grandkids, or others? If so, what brings you comfort?

What does living a life of faithfulness to God look like to you?

What is something in your life that reminds you of God's faithfulness?

Did you grow up in a home with a strong legacy of faith?

· · ·

If yes, thank God for that and ask Him to help you to continue in that steadfast faith. If not, thank Him that His grace reached you and ask Him to help you start a new legacy of faith in your family.

Dear God, Thank you for your faithfulness through the ages. Help me to find comfort in the fact that You never change, even when I waver. I want to remain steadfast in my faith and to stand firm in a world that is ever-changing and drifting from You. Help me to leave a legacy of faith for future generations. Amen.

GOD IS YEARNING FOR YOUR RETURNING

PANIC SEIZED ME. MY SEVEN-YEAR-old daughter Emery had become separated from us at an amusement park. Our large group had gone in different directions and met back at an intersection. Instead of stopping when we stopped, Emery kept walking, distracted by the bright lights of the amusement sights. When Emery realized we weren't with her, she ran ahead, thinking we were ahead of her, but we were actually behind her. The fifteen minutes it took to find her seemed like an eternity. Thankfully, she went to someone she knew to trust, a security guard, and told him she was lost. He wiped her tears and encouraged her, assuring her that her parents would find her. He put her up on a high wall so that we could see her above the crowd. Lifting her up was a brilliant idea because we spotted her from a distance and were reunited.

There have been times in my life when I became separated from God. I don't mean in a spiritual sense of eternal standing, but separated from close intimacy with Him. Once we are believers, we are never separated from His love (Romans 8:38,39), and nothing we do can remove us from His hand because it is the divine power of Christ that keeps us secure, not our own works (John 10:28-30). There are, however, times when we wander, take our eyes off Jesus, and get lost, as Emery had taken her eyes off us and become lost. It could be the distraction of bright lights of amusement. It could be running ahead of the place God has for us. When we realize we are missing the fellowship of our Father, we wonder: how did we get here? How do we find Him again? Is He angry at us for our mistakes?

As Emery realized she needed help and found someone she could trust, we as believers can do the same. Finding an accountability partner, Christian friends, or a trusted pastor can help us get back on track. The body of Christ exists because we need one another. Hebrews 10:23-24 says, "Let us hold unswervingly to the hope we profess, for he who promised is faithful. And let us consider how we may spur one another on toward love and good deeds." One way to hold unswervingly, to stay on track, is to find a community of believers to spur us on.

As the security guard lifted Emery up on that wall, we can lift each other up by a wall of prayer. We didn't scold Emery when we found her. We embraced her. God does the same for us. Luke 15 tells three parables- the lost sheep, the lost coin, and the lost son, all showing the forgiveness of the Father who welcomes the wanderer back with celebration. He is relentlessly pursuing us, searching for our return because He loves us with an unfailing love. God is always yearning for our returning. May our wanderings become fewer and our intimacy become deeper as we keep our sights on Him.

REFLECT:

What bright lights of amusement distract you from the closeness of your Father?

Whom can you trust to encourage you to stay on track?

. . .

Whom do you need to lift up and encourage today?

Are you by His side, seeking your way back, or still wandering in the wrong direction?

—✝—

Dear God, I thank you for your compassion and unfailing love. Forgive me for the times I have wandered from your side. I don't want to be distracted by the amusements of the world. Help me to connect with others so that I can both encourage and be encouraged. If I wander, may I hear your voice calling me back so that I don't lose sight of you. Amen.

TO KNOW HIM

— *Matthew 16:15*

WHEN I WAS PREGNANT WITH EACH one of my children, my husband Denny and I compiled lists of baby names. We pored over baby name books, looked up different spellings, researched meanings, and lamented over names that reminded us of old flames or annoying people. Names are important. Our dog's name is Bear because he looks like a Bear. There is meaning attached to a name.

Perhaps that is why there are so many names for God. His names tell us about His character. They tell stories of how He worked in the lives of His people. Over and over in the Bible, when God performed a great act, He often revealed a new name for Himself. The more we pursue God, learn about Him, and experience Him in our lives, the more we understand the meanings of the many names for God.

Whenever I have struggled with a need, it has been an opportunity for me to discover a new aspect of God's character. If I had never struggled financially, I would never have known God as my Jehovah

Jireh, my Provider. If I had never been anxious, I would never have discovered Him as my Jehovah Shalom, my Peace. If I had never been sick or grieving, I would not know Him as my Jehovah Rapha, my Healer. I know God in a deeper way today because of the difficulties I have faced and the way He walked with me through each one of them, revealing His character.

Jesus asked a very important question in Matthew 16:15. "But what about you?" he asked. "Who do you say I am?" He was drawing out Peter's realization that He was the Messiah, the one true God. As you consider your points of greatest need, dear friend, who do you say God is? Who has God been to you in your tears? How have you come to know Him through your troubles?

I challenge you to look at your problems from a different perspective—as an opportunity to discover a new quality of God in order to know Him better. The more I know of Him, the more I desire to know Him even more. I pray that you continue to compile a growing list of His precious names!

To Know Him

Exalted One, Eternal God, The Beginning and The End,
Immanuel, Redeemer, King, My Hiding Place, My Friend,
The Name above all other names—so many titles show
Deep riches found in only Him for those who seek to know.
He is My Helper and My Peace, My Very Great Reward,
But He's a jealous God, The Holy One, The Only Risen Lord.
He's the One who judges righteously and tests the heart and
    mind,
Yet He's the Comforter and Shepherd, too, The Healer of the
    blind.
A Glorious Crown, My Mighty Rock, A God who does no
    wrong,
Creator, Maker, Ruler, Shield, My Advocate, My Song.
He is My Hope, The God of Grace, A Refuge for the poor,

*My Source of Strength, the Faithful God, The Way, The Gate,
    The Door.*
He is a Great and Awesome God. He sits upon the throne,
The Intercessor for our needs, Our Gift, The Living Stone.
Refiner, Purifier, Truth, The Son, Bright Morning Star,
*The Lamb of God, The Bread of Life, The One Who Bears My
    Scar.*
How sovereign is our God Most High, forgiving of our sin,
*Through Man of Sorrows, Christ the Lord, The Ransom for
    all men.*
*He is the Bridegroom, Teacher, Light, The One who hears my
    prayer,*
My Counselor and Master who will all my burdens bear.
The Resurrection and The Life, the Sure Foundation laid,
My Banner and My Victory, in whom my debt was paid.
*Wise Potter, Faithful Gardener—He shapes and prunes and
    molds;*
He's Provider God—The Great I AM, A Father who upholds.
For lack of knowledge of their God the people are destroyed,
*Yet when we know Him by His name, His power can be
    employed.*
O God, give me a thirst for You—To love, praise, and adore,
For as I see Your glory, Lord, I want to know You more.

— ©2005 BOBBIE PERKINS

REFLECT:

What name for God is special to you and why?

What have you learned about God's character through learning some
of His names?

. . .

Does anyone in your family have a name that has special meaning? Have you looked up the meanings of the names of people in your family? Try it for fun!

—✝—

Dear God, Oh, how I want to know you more! Thank you that there are so many ways my needs are met in You, showing me a new aspect of your character. Please give me a thirst for You so that I can know you better. Amen.

FAITHFULNESS FOR ALL OUR FEARS

THERE IS SOMETHING ABOUT THE unconditional love and faithfulness of a dog. When my grandson Bryce was two years old, he ADORED his dogs—Drake, a Golden Retriever, and Josh, a German Shepherd. Josh only had three legs, but he managed to run and climb stairs despite his handicap.

Bryce and his beloved doggies had an incident that was both sad and hilarious to me. My daughter was dropping the dogs off at the kennel before leaving town for a trip. Bryce didn't understand why she was leaving the dogs there. He thought they were LEAVING THE DOGS THERE FOR GOOD!

He began screaming and crying, "Mama, no! Joshie! Drake! Nooooooo!" He was hysterically crying the whole drive home. It was so pitiful because he thought he would never see his dogs again, but it was sweet to see the love between a boy and his dogs.

Aren't we just like that? We assume that the blessings of God have been taken from us permanently when our security is temporarily taken away. We begin to fear that we will never see the good things that we enjoyed again.

Financial stress brings fear of permanent financial ruin. Divorce brings fear of a lifetime of loneliness. Sickness brings fear of the future. We think God has deserted us because we don't understand what He is doing. We begin to cry, "God, no! This is too much! I can't do this!"

When we feel as if God has left us to fend for ourselves, in reality, He is ready to calm our fears with His presence. His love is unconditional, and His faithfulness surpasses any golden retriever! He promises in Deuteronomy 31:6, "Do not be afraid or terrified because of them, for the Lord your God goes with you; he will never leave you nor forsake you."

The word "forsake" in this passage is the Hebrew word "azab." It means to loosen ties with in a way to leave destitute and without hope. When God promises to never forsake us, He is saying that He never leaves us without hope. He assures us that He will fulfill His promises to walk with us through our difficulties. When I am scrambling to hang on to what is lost, Oh, how I need to learn to let go of what was lost and scramble for God instead!

Next time I am afraid, I will remind myself that I can trust His character of faithfulness. My fear is not conquered by knowing how my story will end. It is conquered when I realize that God goes with me into every unknown.

REFLECT:

Fill in the blank with a fear that you have: I will not be afraid or terrified because of ___________________, for the Lord my God goes with me; he will never leave me nor forsake me.

Can you remember a time when you worried about something that turned out to be only a temporary small problem? What did God teach you through that experience?

.   .   .

What would you say is one of your greatest fears?

—✝—

Dear God, Thank you that you never leave me, forsake me, or leave me without hope. Help me to put my hope in You instead of my circumstances. Thank you that I don't have to face the hard things alone, and that you use those times to strengthen my faith. Amen.

YOU ARE NOT INVISIBLE

PAIN CAN MAKE US FEEL INVISIBLE. WE don't want others to see us when we are in pain because there is something about being vulnerable to others that makes us uncomfortable. We don't think they will understand. They haven't been through the same experience. They might think we are just complaining needlessly. They might judge.

So we suffer in silence. We isolate ourselves. We keep that hurt bottled up inside of us until it becomes a weight that weighs down upon our soul. It can even lead to depression. Merriam-Webster online dictionary defines depression[1] as a "pressing down to a lower position." Think about how a footprint leaves a depression in the mud. Is your emotional heaviness weighing so heavily on your heart that you feel stuck in the mud, pressed down to a lower position?

---

1. Merriam-Webster. (n.d.) Depression. *In Merriam-Webster.com* dictionary. Retrieved March 3, 2021 from https://www.merriam-webster.com/dictionary/depression.

David suffered this type of anguish while he was fleeing for his life from King Saul. He was isolated from friends. In Psalm 88:18, he laments, "You have taken from me friend and neighbor—darkness is my closest friend." Isolation makes us even more depressed! I long for the company of friends if it's been awhile since I got to spend time with them. I miss the fun of being around big groups of people if I don't have the opportunity for fellowship.

David didn't only feel isolated from friends. He felt isolated from God. In Psalm 88:14, he cries, "Why, Lord, do you reject me and hide your face from me?" He was losing hope and felt that even God had abandoned him. Friend, do you feel as if God has abandoned you? Has your isolation made you feel unseen even by God?

There is also another person in scripture who thought she was unseen by God. She had suffered for twelve years with a bleeding disorder and had been told that no one could heal her. I think that after twelve years, I might feel that God had abandoned me, too. Jesus was her last hope.

The crowd was so huge around Jesus that scripture says they "almost crushed him." In her frantic yearning for relief, the woman squeezed her way through the throng, sandwiched between bodies that practically crushed her own frail frame. Can you imagine her desperation? She felt sure that Jesus was unapproachable by her, that she was unseen in the crowd and unseen by Jesus. Just a touch. Just a glimmer of hope. Though she couldn't get close enough to talk to Jesus, she reached out and brushed the hem of his garment with her fingertips.

And she was healed. She was not only healed, but she was also seen. Jesus immediately turned around and asked in Luke 8:45, "Who touched me?" Even the disciples were bewildered by his question and patronized, "Master, people are crowding and pressing against you." But Jesus knew he had bestowed power to someone who needed it. He saw her affliction and knew the anguish of her soul.

David, too, found the same relief for his soul. Psalm 31:7 radiates his relief with the words "I will be glad and rejoice in your love, for you saw my affliction and knew the anguish of my soul." Like the woman, like David, God sees you. He sees the affliction of your soul, the isolation of your spirit, and loves you fully. Touch the hem of his cloak, dear friend, but not with a casual touch. Reach out in desperation with all of the yearning in your soul and beg for healing. And I pray you will hear the words of Jesus in Luke 8:48, "Daughter, your faith has healed you. Go in peace."

REFLECT:

What struggles do you face that make you want to isolate yourself?

Do you really believe that there is hope in Christ? If so, how are you reaching for Him?

Do you think it took courage for the woman to approach Jesus? Was her bravery worth it? How can you be courageous in your own situation?

—✝—

Dear God, You are the healer of all things. Help me to have faith to bring to you the places that need healing in me. Help me to come to You for peace instead of isolating myself from You or other believers. Thank you for seeing me and loving me. Amen.

WHEN YOU DON'T FEEL GOD'S FORGIVENESS

HAVE YOU EVER THOUGHT, "I WISH I could go back in time and know then what I know now?" Or maybe it's more than just being wiser. Maybe the idea of starting fresh appeals to you because you are carrying a load of guilt. Sure, you know that the Bible teaches that God forgives, but you just can't seem to FEEL God's forgiveness. Crippled by feelings of shame and guilt, you are struggling to find healing from the scars that your own sin has left in your soul. I've been there.

There is hope for your burden. God sent His Son to free us not just from the penalty of our sin, but from the bondage of it. John 8:36 assures us, "If the Son sets you free, you will be free indeed." But how do we move forward to being truly free? How do we get to a point where we feel God has forgiven us? In Psalm 51 David not only receives deliverance from the emotional bondage of his sin, but he also comes forth with a testimony. Friend, your mistakes can be part of your testimony. But Satan doesn't want you to have that testimony.

He wants you to wallow in guilt because silencing your song of freedom is his best chance of crippling your impact on others. So, he continues to whisper lies to keep you chained to your guilt. I encourage you to take your Bible out now and read Psalm 51. Let's look at the steps that David took in being restored. (For background purposes, you can read about David's sin of adultery and murder in 2 Samuel chapter 11).

David's steps of restoration were confession (verses 1-6), cleansing (verses 7-9), creating (verses 10-12), and calling (verses 13-15). First David agreed with God about his sin and truly grieved over the fact that he had done wrong in the eyes of a holy God (Confession). Next, David asked God to cleanse him. Note that he didn't try to work for that cleansing. It came from God's mercy, not David's efforts (Cleansing). Then, David asked God to help him live a steadfast life by creating a pure heart within him and granting him a willing and obedient spirit (Creating). Friend, ask God to do the same for you. Then believe by faith that you are forgiven. Clean. Fresh. Verse 7 declares, "Cleanse me with hyssop, and I will be clean; wash me, and I will be whiter than snow." You can start fresh. You can be clean before God, because God's plan has always been forgiveness.

David revels in the fact that God was faithful to restore to him the joy of his salvation. Would you like to have the same joy that you experienced the moment after receiving the gift of salvation? That excitement and wonder at God's grace can flood your soul again. And that is what leads to David's last step-(his Calling). David celebrates in verse 13 that now he could "teach transgressors your ways so that sinners will turn back to you." His experience of restoration gave him a calling to help others. Is God calling you to help others? Your story is God's backdrop to show His grace. You don't have to conjure up a feeling of forgiveness. Walk by faith in the forgiveness that is being freely offered to you and come forth fresh, clean, and whiter than snow.

REFLECT:

Would you say your joy in the Lord is less today, about the same, or more than it was on the day Jesus became your Savior?

Is there a sin you need to confess to God in order to be restored to fellowship with Him? If so, do it now.

Can you think of how a season of sin in your life has led you to a calling to help others?

—✝—

Dear God, There is nothing like the joy of being in fellowship with You. Please help me to recognize, confess, and forsake sin before I let it form a barrier in my relationship with You. Thank you for your lovingkindness and patience when I stray from You. Please help me to point others to You by living a life of obedience. Amen.

HOW TO FIND THE HIDDEN TREASURE

MY HUSBAND HAS SEVERAL UNUSUAL hobbies. Other than the ordinary playing golf and watching sports, he is also very talented at arranging flowers and doing anything artistic. But one of his childhood interests that he continues as a hobby today is rock collecting. He had the best time foraging for precious gems in a large bucket of dirt on our last visit to Gatlinburg, TN. Frankly, I walked right by the big sign advertising the hidden gems. I wasn't interested because I was skeptical that there was anything good in that bucket of dirt.

Denny, however, was willing to roll up his sleeves and work to find those buried stones. Some children gathered around him to watch, and they began to squeal in excitement as each treasure was retrieved through the mucky sludge. Denny patiently brushed off the rocks, examining them closely to judge their value. He found treasures others had passed by because He made an effort to look. But the reason he made an effort to look was that he believed there was something of value in the dirt.

Do you believe there is anything of value for you in the Bible? I wonder how many Bibles are simply passed by, ignored by people who overlook the hidden treasures inside because they don't know the value. Perhaps they are skeptical that there is even anything of value inside. Or maybe they feel it takes too much work to find the treasure. Admittedly, some parts of the Bible are hard to understand if you have never studied it. But the Bible even gives us advice about how to understand The Bible!

Proverbs 2:3-5 says, "If you call out for insight and cry aloud for understanding, and if you look for it as for silver and search for it as for hidden treasure, then you will understand the fear of the Lord and find the knowledge of God."

Wow! I don't know about you, but I'd like to be full of the knowledge of God. But these verses explain that it doesn't just happen. If we really want to know God intimately and be filled with His wisdom, we have to do some things. First, we have to ask Him for that insight. The Psalmist basically says BEG HIM, using the words "call out" and "cry aloud." That's a pretty intense plea, spilling from a fervent heart's desire. Do you really want to know God better? Ask Him to teach you. Pray for Him to give you understanding and wisdom to understand His Word.

The second thing the Psalmist tells us to do is to expend effort in seeking out the wisdom of God. He says, "Search for it as for hidden treasure." That's the problem with treasure that is hidden. If it's not in plain sight, many people will pass it by, oblivious of its value. But those, like Denny, who are willing to take the time and make the effort to sit down and patiently search, patiently dig...those are the ones who find the treasure.

I have helped in a search for a missing person. Let me tell you this about a search...it is not a haphazard hunt! The search directors assigned designated areas for each team. When we finished an area, we spray painted the road in front of the woods to communicate that the specific area had been searched. There was a very organized plan.

Do you have a plan to read your Bible? If not, make one! Schedule it on your calendar. And just as a search party has a team, find your team! Ask for a friend's help to keep you accountable.

Is your Bible covered in dust? Forage through the dust in anticipation of finding precious jewels. Ask God to teach you, cry aloud to Him for understanding, and follow through on an organized plan. Find a team of friends to encourage you. May you find buckets of hidden treasure! He is like no other treasure!

REFLECT:

What kind of system do you have in reading your Bible? A) I have an organized specific plan. B) My Bible reading is a bit haphazard. C) I fluctuate between organized, haphazard, and not reading it at all. C) I'm really not reading my bible like I should.

If you're not reading your Bible, do you think it's because you don't expect to find a treasure? Have you tried praying and earnestly asking God to reveal truths to you?

If consistency is a problem for you, try joining a weekly Bible study group or meeting with someone regularly for accountability. Find a set routine to follow every day. Find a Bible study curriculum that interests you. Explore study tools and methods, such as concordances, commentaries, Bible dictionaries, word studies, or even do a study of how to study the Bible! Study a topic that interests you! How can you make it fun and interesting?

—✝—

Dear God, Your Word is a treasure greater than any diamond mine. Please give me a desire and love for Your Word that grows deeper with each day. Help me to be consistent and undistracted to find the hidden jewels in Scripture. Thank you that The Bible has answers to all of life's problems. Amen.

THAT ALL MAY COME
TO REPENTANCE

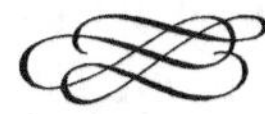

FLAGRANT, WILLFUL SIN. HAVE YOU ever been there? I have. It has a way of stifling the voice of God in our lives. But as damaging as it is to our growth as a Christian, there is another type of sin that is even more damaging. It's the sanctimonious judging of the sin in others while ignoring the secret sins of our own heart.

Flagrant sin is kind of out there. It's visible to others. We know it is there and feel the weight of God's conviction if we belong to Him. But the secret sin of self-righteousness...well, we might not even realize it is there. The fact is, Jesus had more to say about self-righteousness than any other sin.

In Matthew 23:27-28, Jesus condemns hypocrisy with "Woe to you, teachers of the law and Pharisees, you hypocrites! You are like whitewashed tombs, which look beautiful on the outside but on the inside are full of the bones of the dead and everything unclean. In the same way, on the outside you appear to people as righteous but on the inside you are full of hypocrisy and wickedness."

So, I have to wonder, what do I look like on the inside? Do I treat the drug addict with contempt, or do I grieve for the tormented soul who is living in chains? Jesus responded with compassion to those who were living in bondage. He said in Luke 4:18, "The Spirit of the Lord is on me, because he has anointed me to proclaim good news to the poor. He has sent me to proclaim freedom for the prisoners and recovery of sight for the blind, to set the oppressed free, to proclaim the year of the Lord's favor." Are we Christians proclaiming freedom to the prisoners, or are we tightening their chains with our hypocrisy?

What about the girl who is leaving the abortion clinic with scars on her soul? Do we rant about how anyone could do such a thing? Jesus is her hope of transformation, the One who removes her shame and bestows on her a crown of beauty instead of ashes (Isaiah 61). Are we telling her about Him? Or are we self-righteously viewing her as a hopeless, hard-hearted sinner?

In John 8:11, Jesus told the woman caught in adultery, "Neither do I condemn you." The word He used was "katakrino," which means to judge worthy of punishment. Although God is righteous and must punish sin, He doesn't want anyone to receive that judgment because He is merciful, "not wanting anyone to perish, but everyone to come to repentance" (2 Peter 3:9). Oh, that we were as merciful, helping others to come to repentance.

The problem is that we believers get in our little Christian circles and begin to judge sin with a sliding-scale. THAT sin is worse than our sin. I Corinthians 6:18 says to "Flee immorality." How many Christians judge the unmarried cohabitating couple according to this command, yet they themselves have been watching questionable content on television? What about coarse humor? Psalm 101:3 says, "I will not look with approval on anything that is vile." I admit that I love to laugh. I have to ask myself—What am I laughing at?

Romans 3:23 is clear: "All have sinned." Sometimes Christians like to classify sin; for example, gossip isn't as bad as robbery. And yes, our judicial system supports this idea by making "the punishment fit the crime." God, however, has a perfect standard, so there is no gradient. We either hit the target or miss it. And we've all missed it. Romans doesn't say some sinned little sins and some sinned big sins. It says all have sinned. Period. Romans 1:18 is also clear that God's wrath is "being revealed from heaven against ALL the godlessness and wickedness of people" (emphasis mine). All the godlessness. My godlessness. Your godlessness. ALL of our sin brings about God's wrath, not just the seemingly big sins. These verses in Romans don't categorize our sin according to severity. They put us all into the same category as being separated from God, falling short of His glory and in need of a Savior.

And there is such a Savior! Oh, dear one! Don't miss Him! If you don't know Him, please read Appendix B for help. There is nothing you could ever do that is beyond His reach of forgiveness if you come to Him with faith and repentance. To those who already know Him— let's take a look inside ourselves so that we can view others with the same compassion that Jesus did. He wants everyone to come to repentance. Even us.

REFLECT:

Do you relate more to the woman who was caught in adultery or to the people who were demanding that she be stoned?

Do you tend to look on some sins as more acceptable to God than others? Do you feel yours are more acceptable than those of other people?

What do you think is the best way to respond to a self-righteous person? Do you think they might learn from watching the humility of others?

Dear God, I ask You to search my heart and reveal self-righteousness I need to repent from. Help me to see my own sin as well as I see the sins of others. Thank you that You paid for all of our sin on the cross. Help me to live in a way that shares that grace and mercy with others. Amen.

ARE YOU LIVING AN EASTER LIFE?

> "I have been crucified with Christ and I no longer live, but Christ lives in me."
> — *Galatians 2:20*

ARE YOU LIVING AN EASTER LIFE? What does it mean to live a life that depicts the truths of this central Christian holiday? Easter is beautifully linked to the Jewish Passover, which is a commemoration of the Jewish people's freedom from slavery in Egypt. As Christians, we too, have been set free from slavery—our slavery to sin (Romans 6:18). Passover is also a time to remember the victorious protection from the death angel that killed every firstborn not having the mark of the blood of the lamb on their door frame. What a perfect depiction of the blood of Christ that delivers us from death! Not incidentally, the death and resurrection of Jesus occurred during the Jewish Passover (one of many flawless links between the Old Testament and New Testament).

Easter is a celebration of the gift God has given us of "new birth into a living hope through the resurrection of Jesus Christ from the dead" (I Peter 1:3). LIVING hope. The Greek word for living here is derived from the verb "zao," which means "not lifeless or dead; to be active, fresh, strong, efficient, powerful, efficacious." Efficacious means "having the power to produce a desired effect, like a remedy." What does that mean for us?

Jesus is the only remedy for sin, and we have the power to share the remedy! But are we doing that? Do those words describe our faith? Is it active, fresh, and strong, or is it stagnant and lifeless? We marvel at a newborn baby and celebrate that precious new life, but if we were to never offer the child nourishment, the baby would die. How many baby Christians are walking around lifelessly because they aren't receiving spiritual nourishment?

The salvation of our souls is a one-time event, but the process doesn't stop there. There is so much more. The growth, the learning to know and love God, the finding of Him in every joy and sorrow— THAT is the most exciting part! That is the LIVING part of our faith, a faith that grows. I have a friend who told me that her faith is boring because she doesn't have some great "turn-around" story. She grew up in church and doesn't have a dramatic testimony. Hallelujah! Even though it's encouraging to hear stories of God dramatically changing a life, if the most exciting part about your walk with Jesus is how you came to know Him, then you are missing the point! The most exciting part is LIVING that relationship day in and day out!

When Christ was crucified and raised to life, it wasn't just about His death and resurrection. It was about ours. "We were therefore buried with him through baptism into death in order that just as Christ was raised from the dead through the glory of the Father, we too may live a new life" (Romans 6:4). Paul goes on in verse 11 of this passage to use that same verb, zao. "Count yourselves dead to sin but ALIVE to God in Christ Jesus" (emphasis mine). Count yourselves alive—a NEW life. Don't let your past ever speak your name again. You aren't that person anymore. Galatians 2:20 states it clearly, "I have been crucified with Christ and I no longer live, but Christ lives in me."

Does Christ live in you? If you're not sure, please read the message in Appendix B. If He does, is that life flourishing? The wondrous thing about the new life in Christ is that it brings fresh grace every day.

Lamentations 3:23, one of my favorite verses, promises, "Yet this I call to mind [a deliberate action of intentionally focusing on something in our mind] and therefore I have hope: Because of the Lord's great love we are not consumed, for his compassions never fail. They are new every morning; great is your faithfulness."

Because of His great love we are not consumed by our mistakes. We are invited into a new life. Life that begins when His grace hits our soul and life that keeps growing. Even the secular icons of Easter carry an underlying spiritual message of this ever-growing life. Eggs signify the perpetuation of new life. The Easter bunny may bring a secular slant on a Christian holiday, but rabbits have a high multiplication rate! I think of how those twelve simple men, most of them uneducated dregs of society, multiplied their faith to reach all the way forward in history to bring knowledge of new life to me. I want to do the same. I want people I've never met—people who aren't even born yet— to find the Easter Life. Are you living an Easter Life?

Reflect:

Does the enemy ever try to remind you of past sin that has already been forgiven? Why do you think He would do that?

What does it mean that we were buried with Him through baptism into death and raised to walk in newness of life?

Are you walking in that newness of life?

—✝—

Dear God, Thank you for paying the penalty for my sin on the cross so that I am not only made righteous before You, but I am made new! Help me to walk in newness of life every day and not look over my shoulder at the past. Thank you for your promises that I can cling to when the enemy tries to bring up my past. Amen.

LET OTHERS BLESS YOU

A FRIEND BOUGHT MY LUNCH THE other day. It's a seemingly insignificant thing, but God used it to bring spiritual truth to my soul. You see, I argued with her for a minute. "No, I couldn't let her do that. No, it wasn't necessary." But then I felt the tug of the Holy Spirit telling me, "Let her bless you." So, I relented in my protests, surprising even myself that I didn't put up much of a fight.

I'm sure you have had similar arguments with friends or family over who is paying the check at a restaurant. But is it a pattern for you? Do you struggle to accept help, compliments, acts of service, or gifts from others? I think I have struggled with this because I feel undeserving of others' desire to bless me. It's as if I need to do something to earn that blessing. The light of realization creeps over me as I realize that I don't deserve the blessings God gives to me either. I definitely can do nothing to earn His blessings, yet He longs to bless me because He loves me.

God made an interesting promise to Abram (soon to be called

Abraham) in Genesis 12:3. God told him, "I will bless those who bless you." God was promising to send blessings to those who gave blessings. Hmmm. Perhaps if I refuse to let people bless me, I may be robbing them of a blessing from God. Maybe I need to think less about the awkwardness I may feel at receiving a blessing and more about the joy the other person may feel in giving it. Reflecting back on the times I have done something for someone out of sheer love for them, not expecting anything in return, I know that this is true. The joy of giving a gift to someone who is special to me far exceeds the joy of receiving a gift.

Jesus taught in Acts 20:35, "It is more blessed to give than to receive." I believe He meant several things by this statement. First, God looks upon a generous person with favor. Second, God will reward generous people. Proverbs 11:25 promises "A generous person will prosper." Lastly, there is an intangible blessing we receive from our generosity that stems from the satisfaction of giving someone else a little "happy" for their day.

So, does that mean our obedience guarantees blessings? Welllll… not necessarily in the way we might think. I know plenty of people who dishonor God and are surrounded by material blessings. Psalm 49:16 says, "Do not be overawed when others grow rich, when the splendor of their houses increases; for they will take nothing with them when they die." I think about the disciples who left everything they owned to follow Jesus. They may not have had wealth, but they were experiencing the greater wealth of walking daily amidst the glorious presence of Almighty God!

Do I obey Jesus because I want a blessing? Or because I love Him wholeheartedly? Am I looking for what I can get from God, or am I devoted to Him even if I don't see blessings of the particular kind that I have in mind? John Piper stated, "God is most glorified in us when we are most satisfied in Him."[1] One of my favorite bible teachers,

---

1. Piper, John. "God Is Most Satisfied in Us When We Are Most Satisfied in Him," Bethlehem Baptist Church, March 5, 2021 from https://youtu.be/eE-09ut2pzw?si= 8SKe22o4yCtwQefX

Jennifer Rothschild, explains his quote by saying, "That means even if you don't see a direct link between your obedience and God's blessings, you are the most blessed because your soul is most satisfied."

My soul is satisfied. I am blessed. And far be it from me to rob others of that same blessing. Let your friends bless you. You may be a conduit of God's blessings to satisfy their souls. Jesus said it. It is more blessed to give than to receive.

REFLECT:

Do you feel uncomfortable when others try to bless you? If so, why do you think you do?

Our salvation is the biggest way God has blessed us when we didn't deserve it and can't earn it. What other blessings has God unexpectedly given you? Have you thanked Him?

Who can you bless this week in some small way? Do it!

-✝-

Dear God, Thank you for the incredible blessings I have in Christ. Thank you that the satisfaction my soul has in You is greater than any material blessings. Help me to be sensitive to others and find ways to bless them unexpectedly. Amen.

APRIL

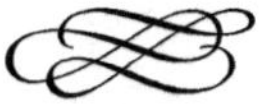

ARE YOU CONVINCED AND COMPELLED?

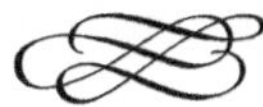

> *"I am the way and the truth and the life. No one comes to the Father except through me."*
>
> — John 14:6

One of my friends recently passed away with no warning. It sure did bring heavenly reality into focus because I never asked her about her faith. I'm sure she knew that I am a Christian. I am open about my faith. But I never directly asked her if she knew Jesus. And now it's too late to ask. The regret that I feel reminds me that God didn't call me to spend my life making sure my friends know about my faith. He called me to find out about theirs.

My life is not patterned after the love of Christ if I am not sharing the gospel with others. If I love them and love God, then I should be eager to talk to them about their faith. When Paul wrote in 2 Corinthians 5:14 "For Christ's love compels us because we are convinced that one died for all," the word compel means to "force" or "overpower in an irresistible way." In other words, we can't help but tell others about Jesus! The truth inside of us is bursting to be shared!

How often have you been to a great movie or restaurant and enthusiastically told your friends about it? Do we not have much greater news living inside of us that we should be bursting to tell others about? Then why are we so hesitant to talk to people about spiritual matters? I think it is because many people view spiritual matters as an opinion rather than a truth.

Our society largely embraces the view that truth does not exist. We must be "tolerant" of others' views to the point of believing that no truth really exists. We don't want to offend others, so we let them believe that "it doesn't matter what you believe, as long as you believe something." But all roads do not lead to heaven.

Jesus said in John 14:6, "I am the way and the truth and the life. No one comes to the Father except through me." Am I blocking others' path to Jesus with my own apathy? Truth does indeed exist. Paul was saying in that passage that he was convinced of truth, and that is why he was compelled. He felt an urgency to share the gospel because He knew it was true. He also said in Philippians 3:10, "I want to know Christ." His passion to know Christ flowed over to a passion to share Christ. I long to have that same urgency. I don't want to ever again have to say about one of my friends, "I never talked to her about Jesus."

Paul's Passion

Forget what's behind; press on toward the goal.
Take hold of that for which Christ took hold of my soul.
How I long for Paul's passion- such a deep inward burning
That I may gain Christ Himself and lose all other yearning.
Oh, Lord, please just teach me all things are a loss
Compared to the gain that I find at the cross.
For the little I know Him convinces me more
That He is worth any sacrifice there might be in store.
And what little I know of His glory and grace—
To think someday, intimate, I'll gaze in His face!
In the meantime, I'm driven—this one thing I do—
Strain toward what's ahead—there's a prize I pursue.
For I want to know Christ—that's the goal I run toward.

Christ in me, hope of glory, He is my reward.

— © 2002 BOBBIE PERKINS

REFLECT:

What hindrances do you have in sharing the gospel? Do you struggle with any of the following: I don't want people to be offended. I don't know the Bible well enough and am afraid they will ask me a question I can't answer. I have had a bad experience with it in the past. I honestly don't think about doing it. Which do you most relate to?

What do you need to do to address your reservations?

Read I Peter 3:15. How does that verse address some of the excuses we have?

—✝—

Dear God, I want to be so excited about You that I can't help but tell others about You. Please equip me to share the gospel in a way that draws people to You. Thank you for Your Holy Spirit who gives me the words to say when I need them. Amen.

COME TO THE CROSS

> "The Lord has
> laid on him the
> iniquity of us
> all."
> — Isaiah 53:5–6

DO YOU SOMETIMES FIND YOURSELF chasing the lies of this world more than you find yourself chasing eternal truths? It's easy to get so caught up in the day to day that we forget to have an eternal perspective. I never want to lose the wonder of my salvation and the fact that the One who created me also died for me. I'm glad that we have Easter as a reminder to center our hearts back to Him. I love the following quotes by C.S. Lewis, and I encourage you to think about how they impact the way we live.

"If you live for the next world, you get this one in the deal; but if you live only for this world, you lose them both." -C.S. Lewis

"If we find ourselves with a desire that nothing in this world can satisfy, the most probable explanation is that we were made for another world." -C. S. Lewis

Come To The Cross

Great Savior Christ, such pain you bore,
Blood shed on my behalf.
You're the One True Vine where my small branch
Was firmly made ingraft.
Oh, Chosen One, You chose me, too.
Such knowledge my heart stabs.
To think you traded royal robes
To wear my filthy rags.
Oh, Holy One, what gifts you give
This undeserving child—
Your Spirit dwelling in me,
Showing all that is defiled.
Remove those things and make me pure.
Remind me of my call.
Each day I give myself to You,
To be my life, my all.
May my redemption never be
Atonement won for naught,
But may my life reflect the price
With which my soul was bought.
So great a price! So great a love!
The gospel is the greatest story!
Jesus suffered unimaginable pain
To restore us to God's glory!
God's redemption reigns at Easter
In every heart that calls him Lord.
Don't miss the blessing of His gift
By chasing lies within this world!
He lives today! Come to the cross!
Come see the veil is torn!
The cross of shame brings life for us—
With an empty tomb on Easter morn!

— © 2018 BOBBIE PERKINS

But he was pierced for our transgressions, he was crushed for our iniquities; the punishment that brought us peace was on him, and by his wounds we are healed. We all, like sheep, have gone astray, each of us has turned to our own way; and the Lord has laid on him the iniquity of us all. -Isaiah 53:5,6

REFLECT:

Do you find yourself sometimes chasing lies of the world instead of Jesus? How can you incorporate the truths of those C.S. Lewis quotes into specific changes for your daily life?

Do you ever feel that the way you live is "atonement won for naught"? God doesn't feel that way! Thank God right now that His salvation is free and our works can do nothing to earn it. Remind yourself that we live in obedience out of love for Him, but not in order to earn His love.

⁓✝⁓

Dear God, Thank you for Your incredible plan of salvation for rebellious mankind who has turned from You. It's hard to think about the pain Jesus suffered, knowing that many people are still rejecting that gift. How great a love! I want to love You with an intensity that reflects that price. Amen.

HOW TO HAVE MORE PATIENCE

HAVE YOU EVER PRAYED FOR SOMEthing you later regretted? I did that recently. My drive to work is one of my prayer times. I always pray that God will put a guard over my mouth, a filter from which only thoughtful and kind words can pass. The Lord knows I need a filter! Praying this makes me a little more aware of my words, although I must admit that many times I could do better. I like to pray this, but recently I took it a step further.

Working in a hospital can be incredibly busy. It is stressful to have so many people and tasks all clamoring for my attention. Often my frustration levels rise as my patience with the endless demands plummets. I was driving to work and thinking about the probability of facing another crazy day. But maybe it would be a quiet day. We don't say the "Q" word at a hospital!

I began to pray, "Lord, help me to be patient today and to convey a spirit that displays your character." Then I thought for a moment. I continued in the next breath, "But please don't let anything happen to try my patience today. Let it be a good day." Whaaaaat???

Now, there is nothing wrong with praying for a good day. But on the heels of praying for patience, I'm sure God was laughing at me. God did answer my prayer. Not the second one. The first one.

It was a horrible day. I had a very difficult assignment that ran me ragged all day. I honestly could not keep up with all the tasks that needed to be done. Three babies with low blood sugars, a new mom with uncontrolled bleeding, several new patients and discharges, moms needing help with breastfeeding, two different hallways of running back and forth, and getting off a full hour late because I did not have time to chart. God was smiling at me in amusement. Have you ever heard the expression, "Be careful what you pray for"?

I'm glad I can be honest with God about how I feel, but I also have to admit I had asked for it! I had prayed for patience. How did I honestly expect patience to happen? If nothing happened to try my patience, then how could I exhibit patience? And I'll admit I did complain a little that my assignment was too much. But I did the best I could. And later (after it was over), I took a deep breath and thanked God for his obvious way of showing me that He hears my prayers. Even the ones I may regret praying!

James 1:2-4 says, "Consider it pure joy, my brothers and sisters, whenever you face trials of many kinds, because you know that the testing of your faith produces perseverance. Let perseverance finish its work so that you may be mature and complete, not lacking anything." This passage tells me that patience isn't something that is passively bestowed upon my character. It's not something I can just ask for. It happens only by pushing forward with faith and a will that is fully yielded to God. That is the part where I am to "let persever-ance finish its work." I can choose NOT to let it work in my life by continuing to respond in a way that dishonors God. And sadly, I have done that many times.

Developing patience reminds me about the process of developing muscle. I want to be more physically fit and develop muscle, but I don't enjoy the process it takes to get there. Working out isn't easy.

The development of patience in my life happens through God working in my spirit to develop it. And how does He work that in me? Through trials. Through struggles. Through frustrations. It definitely is not a fun process. But the end result is so worth it: "So that [I] may be mature and complete, not lacking anything." Wow! I have a long way to go. But I want God to work this into my life so that I can be mature and complete. So, although I'm not brave enough to pray for bad days, maybe I'll at least stop praying for good days. Jesus-filled days! Maybe that's what I need to pray for.

REFLECT:

Is patience hard for you? Next time you are feeling pressed in that area, try remembering the outcome that God is trying to produce. It makes it easier to respond in a way that glorifies Him!

Think of a recent time when you didn't respond in a way that would please God. What could you do differently?

Think of a time when you did respond in a patient way to a trying situation. What helped you be able to do that?

—✝—

Dear God, I know that patience is a fruit of the Spirit, so help me to be led by the Spirit more than being led by my flesh. Help me to make choices that bring glory to You, even in seemingly insignificant situations. Nothing is insignificant when it is conforming me more to the image of Christ. Thank you for Your own patience with me when I fail! Amen.

THE ME ON THAT HILL

I LOVE GOING TO SEE THE PASSION Play in our city during Easter week. It is a moving reminder of the suffering my Savior endured for me. It is also a clear example of how politics and corruption can impact society, and how people easily fall prey to following the crowd.

I've followed the crowd before, and it usually ended badly. It takes grit and a willingness to be shunned or even hated to stand for what's right in the midst of opposition. We see it frequently in political circles, but it happens in churches, schools, workplaces, and even among friends.

As I've watched the Passion Play, I've often marveled that the people turned on Jesus so quickly. One week they were singing His praises, and the next week they were clamoring for His death. But before I can be so quick to judge them, I wonder....how would I have reacted if I had been on that hill so many years ago? Would I have begged for His freedom? Or would I have demanded His death, as so many of his former followers did? How can I think I would have been any different from them? It's a sobering thought. It makes me want to take notice of times I am too quick to make judgements of others. Often those judgments are wrong. I am glad I was not one of the ones who was responsible for Jesus' death. But...really...I am. It was MY sin that put Him on that cross. "You see, at just the right time, when we were still powerless, Christ died for the ungodly. Very rarely will anyone die for a righteous person, though for a good person someone might possibly dare to die. But God demonstrates his own love for us in this: While we were still sinners, Christ died for us," (Romans 5:6-8). Jesus died for the very ones who were clamoring for his death. He died for the ones who were ripping the flesh off his back with a whip containing shards of glass. For if they had repented, salvation would have been granted to them, too.

Next time I'm tempted to judge someone else, I have to wonder....what would I have done if I had been on Golgotha's hill?

The Me On That Hill

If we had been there standing
On that hill at Calvary,
Would we even have defended Him?
Would we have cried out to set Him free?
I fear we, too, would be like Peter,
To deny Him before the dawn.
We might condemn Him like the others
Or with indifference just look on.
Why would we be any different,
When we kill in the same way?
As we passive people look aside,
We still crucify today.
We look past the grief of those we meet
Or drown out the cries for food to eat.
As indifference seeps into our lives,
We are a people who crucifies.

The nails are driven in deeper,
When only outward acts are good.
When my heart is like a white-washed tomb,
I drive more nails into the wood.
Lord, You took all my sin upon Yourself—
I want my whole heart clean inside!
Please change this ugly Pharisee heart
To have compassion without pride.
And as I ponder Your great sacrifice,
I submit to You my will.
Jesus, I'm so sorry for
The ME that was on that hill.
Lord, may I also think of others
And the truth You long for me to see—
"As you have done it to the least of these,
You have done it unto Me."

— ©2022 BOBBIE PERKINS

REFLECT:

Have you ever followed the crowd and regretted it? What motivated you to follow?

Are there areas of prejudice or pride in your life that God has put His finger on? Can you lay that at the cross and ask for help with that?

Can you think of a time when you prematurely formed an opinion of someone, and your assessment of them turned out to be wrong? What did that teach you?

⁓✝⁓

Dear God, I don't want to have a proud heart that looks at the sin in others without seeing my own. I don't want to follow the crowd. I want to follow You. Help me to keep my heart clean before You so I can hear Your voice better. Thank you for Your grace and mercy during the times I have failed to do that. Amen.

ARE YOU LEAVING RIPPLES?

EVEN THOUGH I AM TECHNICALLY A city girl, I do love the outdoors. Except swimming in lakes. Nope, my water has to be chlorinated. I am all too familiar with snakes to want to swim with one.

One of the outdoor things I never learned how to do was to skip rocks. I have since learned that I should have used rocks that were flatter instead of round. My round rocks would just plunk in the water, but I did think it was cool to see all the ripples they would leave behind. The ripples seemed to keep on going, spreading out in a beautiful, predictable pattern.

Our lives are kind of like those ripples. One life touches another, which touches another, which touches another, and on and on…. The impact we have on even one person can multiply into impacting many lives. I thought about this recently as I attended a funeral of a godly man who lived a beautiful life of integrity and faith. He impacted his family and friends to love God and serve Him wholeheartedly.

Even though I didn't really know this man very well, his life greatly impacted mine because the people he influenced made an impact on me. I am very close to his family. They are part of my faith story. They are some of those "ripple people" who changed the trajectory of my life by causing a ripple in my relationship with God. Like ripples in a lake, that man's legacy of faith had spread in a beautiful pattern, causing ripples in the lives of others.

The interesting thing is that people who leave a legacy of faith don't typically know they are doing it. They are building that legacy in the mundane activities of daily life, the consistent living out of their love for God. A monetary inheritance left for those we love will eventually be gone. The impact we leave upon the souls of other people is the only thing that will last for eternity. Is there anyone who will be in heaven because of your influence? Is there anyone who can say they know God better because of your impact? Then you've left some ripples.

In just a few short generations, there will be nobody left on this earth who will personally remember you. It's kind of a depressing thought! Those future generations who will never meet you will not have had a personal interaction with you, so how can you impact them? Simple. By impacting people today who will impact others, who will impact others. It reminds me of my favorite Christmas movie, "It's a Wonderful Life." One life touches many others.

I don't want my life to leave a barely perceptible undulation to make a faint ripple. I want to share the excitement of the gospel in a way that causes enormous waves! May our lives become colossal surfs that collide into the lives of others to form white-capped breakers! The tide is in. Let's take people surfing!

REFLECT:

Think back to the people who impacted you spiritually. They may not even know the difference they made in your life. If you are able, find a way to go back and thank them. Write some names down that God brings to mind.

. . .

Can you think of people you have left a positive spiritual impact on? Write their names down. If you can't think of anyone, write the names of people God may be leading you to impact in the future.

Try to begin approaching each day with the goal of uplifting someone even in a small way. It is more likely to happen when we are intentional about it. Who can that be today?

—✝—

Dear God, Thank you for the people You sovereignly put along the path of my life at critical moments in order to help me know You better. Please bless them for their faithfulness, and help me to do the same for others. Amen.

THERE IS NO GREATER LOVE

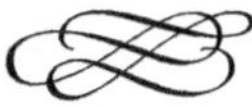

"See, I have engraved you on the palms of my hands."
— Isaiah 49:16

I'VE BEEN TO LOTS OF WEDDINGS. Maybe it's because it was the wedding of my youngest daughter, Emery. Or maybe it's because I'm older and have experienced more of life. But the words spoken by the minister in her wedding were the most touching and sweet of all the weddings I have ever attended.

I saw the tears welling up in my new son-in-law's eyes as the minister asked them to take each other's hands and look at them. He explained to my daughter that the hands she was holding would be the hands that would love her and work for her. They would be the hands that would protect her and comfort her. They would be the hands that would play with her children and lead her family. They were the hands she would hold as they prayed together. They would be the hands that would love her when she grows old.

In the same manner, my son-in-law looked at my daughter's hands to consider that those would be the hands that would love him and hold him after a long day. They would be the hands that would make their house a home. They would be the hands that would comfort him in his weakest moments. They would be the hands that would hold his children and wipe their tears. They would be the hands that would love him when he grows old.

There was something tangible about that reminder of love by looking at their hands. Hands can tell a story of the life they have lived. My dry, wrinkled hands tell that I have lived much (and washed hands a lot as a nurse!) My grandson's little hands are so soft and unspoiled by the world. Some hands are calloused or have grease stains from hard work. You can tell a lot about a person by looking at their hands.

Someone else had marks on His hands. I'm sure that as a carpenter, He had calluses and scars. But the greatest scars were those in his hands and side where He paid a debt that we could not pay. And the great mystery of that love is that my name is somehow etched in those nail prints. Isaiah 49:16 says, "See, I have engraved you on the palms of my hands." Etchings made by suffering and love and sacrifice. Planned before the creation of the world to redeem us. To save us from our own depravity.

Think about that. YOUR name is engraved on His palm as a constant reminder of His love for you. YOUR name is ever before Him. He will not forget you. When He looks at those scars, He sees you. And me. Unfathomable love. Love that creates, chooses, redeems, forgives, changes, keeps and so much more until that glorious day when we run our fingers over those scars engraved on His palm for us.

Be sure that your name is there. Know the One who is the true Bridegroom. Do you know why Jesus is called the Bridegroom? Because God created us for union with Himself, much as a bride and groom are united as one. This union of God with His creation is a jealous one. He wants preeminence over everything else in our lives. Just as a bride doesn't share her love with another man, believers don't let other things come before their relationship with God. The book of Hosea compares our idolatrous ways of placing other things before God to a wife committing adultery against her husband. He is a jealous God, not because He is domineering, but because He wants to bless us with the special relationship of great intimacy with Himself. Just as a bride eagerly anticipates her wedding day to be joined with her groom, we eagerly anticipate the return of Jesus, our bridegroom. What a sacred romance!

REFLECT:

When we love someone, we think about them often. Can you honestly say that you think about God a lot throughout the day?

Are you putting other things before your relationship with God?

Are you sure your name is engraved on His palm? If not, please read Appendix B.

—✝—

Dear God, thank you for Your love that is like no other. Help me to live in a way that shows I love You above all other things. Help me to grow in my intimacy with You. Amen.

THE TRUTH ABOUT REPENTANCE

"Repent, then, and turn to God, so that your sins may be wiped out."

— Acts 3:19

THREE-YEAR OLDS ARE WILLFUL CREA-tures. We can tell them not to do something, but the lure of the forbidden and their lack of self-control often spells disaster. Case in point…When my grandson Bryce was three years old, he had developed the habit of playing with the locks on doors. He had been told multiple times to stop touching them, but he willfully continued to play with them. Until THE incident.

On that particular night, Bryce had locked the back door as he and his parents went outside to play in the backyard. Nobody realized there was a problem until they were ready to go back inside. The door was locked, and they did not have a key with them to unlock it.

My son-in-law intensely labored to get into the house by jiggling the door, using tools, and doing anything he could to break in without damaging the door. Bryce knew his parents were upset. He knew he had done wrong. He kept saying, "I sorry. I no get a spanking. I sorry. I no get a spanking." It seemed suddenly he was ready to repent of his sin only after three things had happened. There were bad consequences. His parents were upset. And he felt the conviction to admit he had done something wrong.

After an hour, they finally did get the door open. As I later laughed about the incident, I realized how much like a three-year-old we can be as well. We step into sin, often willfully knowing we are in the wrong. And we often continue in sin until those same things that happened to Bryce happen to us. We suffer the consequences of our choices. We realize our Father is grieved. We know we have to agree with our Father that we have done wrong.

Have you ever willfully sinned, knowing that you were doing wrong? Of course. We all have. So what makes us repent? Is it the consequences? Sometimes. But being repentant is more than being sorry about the consequences. It is about being restored to a right relationship with our Father and being sorry that we have grieved Him.

God does indeed use consequences to bring us to repentance. The whole book of Judges paints the sad picture of Israel's cycle of rebellion, facing consequences of their sin, repentance, freedom, then going back to rebellion. I can think of times in my life when I was on that same merry-go-round. True repentance, however, not only wants to get off the merry-go-round, but it commits to leave the amusement park.

Consider these two people and how they responded to the same sin. Judas betrayed Jesus. And Peter betrayed Jesus. Same sin. But vastly different outcomes. Why?

Matthew 27:3-5 tells the sad story of how Judas was filled with remorse over his sin. But remorse is not repentance. We can be sorry about our sin but not repent. Even though Judas was remorseful, he never returned to Jesus for reconciliation. He never repented with a desire to be right again in obedience. And it destroyed him. He hung himself, dying without the forgiveness Christ offers to those who repent.

Peter, on the other hand, is beautifully reconciled to Christ in John 21:15-19. He affirms his love for Christ and his desire to serve his

Savior in obedience. He acknowledges that Jesus can see into his sinful heart. And Jesus not only welcomes Peter back, but He also gives him a ministry and a position of leadership, despite Peter's sin. And that is the difference repentance makes!

Forgiveness. Restoration. God made a plan even before the creation of the world to reconcile sinful man to Himself. Jesus didn't come to make us perfect; He came because we couldn't be perfect. God knew that we would fail so He planned to provide forgiveness. This forgiveness is not something God begrudgingly dishes out in small portions with the warning that we've met our quota for the day. Isaiah 30:18 says, "Yet the Lord longs to be gracious to you; therefore he will rise up to show you compassion." God longs to shower us with His compassionate forgiveness. But He can't do it unless we return to Him in repentance.

Have you gotten off the merry-go-round but are still hanging around the amusement park? Repentance is so much more than remorse. It brings peace to our soul by reconciling us to our Creator. "Repent, then, and turn to God, so that your sins may be wiped out, that times of refreshing may come from the Lord" (Acts 3:19).

Reflect:

Is there a particular sin you have struggled with or keep going back to? How can you "leave the amusement park?" Consider these: Having a friend hold you accountable, changing your routine or your schedule to not allow the opportunity for sin, memorizing Scripture to say to yourself when you are tempted, praying and reminding yourself of the strength you have through the Holy Spirit. Which of these do you think would be helpful for you?

What has God taught you in a season of your own rebellion?

. . .

Pick a Scripture that is helpful for you to memorize and write it down where you can see it often and commit it to memory.

—✝—

Dear God, I am sorry for the times I've turned to sin instead of You. Help me to learn from my mistakes and abide in You more faithfully. Help me to repent as soon as You convict me. Thank you that Your mercies are new every morning. Amen.

ARE YOU EMAILING GOD?

A FRIEND RECENTLY SHARED WITH ME how frustrated she was with her husband. He was going to have several days off work the following week, and instead of sitting down to discuss his plans for the upcoming days, he didn't bother to include her in the plan making. She had been looking forward to a date-night out. She eagerly anticipated a nice dinner and time with the one she loved. He did take her out to dinner, but because he had not communicated with her, it was to a restaurant she really didn't care for. To make matters worse, he told her wanted to hurry back home in time to watch the Grizzlies play basketball. I'm not hating on the Grizzlies because we also love basketball at our house, but she told me she felt like a second-place priority. The coup de grace was when he told her, "I have several golf games planned. I emailed you my schedule." Whaaaat?

He had actually emailed her his golf schedule! Like she was some unknown business associate! No face-to-face communication. A cold email with dates and times of HIS plans with no input from her. I applaud him for making the effort to communicate, but his means of communication showed a lack of understanding in the way women think! After she made her disappointment known, I believe he learned a little more about the needs of women.

Are you emailing God? Is your prayer time a little box you check off that you have completed your responsibility for the day? Is your time with God something you squeeze in so that you can rush off to some other form of recreation that you enjoy more? Are you consulting Him with your plans, or are you doing what you prefer to do? Are you even communicating with Him at all? Do you really want to spend time with Him?

David wrote in Psalm 63:1, "You, God are my God, earnestly I seek you; I thirst for you, my whole being longs for you, in a dry and parched land where there is no water." Most of us have never experienced this kind of thirst. We have an abundance of clean water and access to it. But this kind of thirst consumes the whole body. It's not just a dry mouth- every organ in the body longs for that hydration. I want to have that kind of thirst for God, when all I can think about is having that thirst quenched. Some days I believe I do. But there are days when I lose my focus, and I quench my thirst with other things that don't refresh my soul in the same way. Like drinking salt water that will only make me more thirsty, I fill my life with useless things that don't refresh my soul.

How hydrated is your soul? It all goes back to that communication...that CONNECTION with God. When we thirst for Him, he is the top priority. When He is my chief desire, I will choose Him over a basketball game or a trip to the nail salon. Not that I can't enjoy those things. But I make it clear which one I value more. What are you giving your soul to drink? Can you say, "Lord, earnestly I seek you"?

"Lord, I crawled across the barren desert to you with my empty cup, uncertain, but asking for any small drop of refreshment. If only I had known you better, I'd have come running with a bucket." -Nancy Spiegelberg

REFLECT:

What have you given your soul to drink that ended up being salt water instead of refreshment?

Do you look forward to your time with God, or do you feel like it's just another "to do" on your checklist?

If your time with God seems stagnant, which of these choices do you think would help bring new life to that time with Him? A) worship music B) Journaling C) Choosing a new Bible study curriculum/book to study D) Joining a group study

—✝—

Dear God, You are the only One who satisfies. Help me to recognize when I place other priorities over my relationship with You. Thank you that when I bring You my bucket of desires, You fill it to overflowing. Amen.

HOW TO LIVE A GODLY LIFE

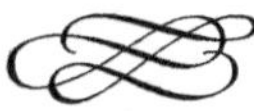

I DON'T UNDERSTAND WHY THEY DON'T come to class. They have been given everything they need but fail to access the wealth of resources given to them. Sometimes it's frustrating being a nurse, trying to educate new parents who don't prepare them- selves for the all-important job of caring for their new baby.

Our hospital provides prenatal childbirth classes, breastfeeding classes, lactation consultants, baby care classes, car seat education, infant CPR, support groups for new moms, parenting classes, and so many other useful tools to equip new parents to be ready for every scenario they may face.

Almost every day I still have new parents leaving the hospital clue- less about how to install her car seat or struggling with breastfeeding but had refused help when it was offered. Why don't they tap into the helpful resources?

2 Peter 1:3 reminds us that we also have been given a wealth of resources. "His divine power has given us everything we need for a

godly life." Living a godly life can be a difficult struggle, but it is impossible if I ignore the resources God has given to me to accomplish the task.

I am frustrated when my patients don't show up for class. But what about me? Am I showing up to church? For prayer? For serious study in the Word? What about developing my spiritual gifts through ministry? Serving others? Am I really showing up for the Christian life?

My salvation is not based on any of these works that I do. Jesus' payment on the cross with His blood is the only thing that could earn my redemption. I don't show up for these things to earn my salvation, but to grow into my salvation. To prepare myself for the all-important job of being a disciple of Christ. Like new parents, disciples need guidance, support, and help.

Sometimes a patient returns to have a second baby and excitedly tells me that I was her nurse for her first baby. It is especially heartwarming to hear that she remembers how I helped her with some breastfeeding struggles or how much she learned from me about baby care.

And because she showed up—she accessed the resources given to her, she shares that she is now able to help her sister, friend, or coworker by giving them guidance in the new adventure of parenthood.

Isn't that what discipleship is all about? Show up. Be hungry to soak in all we can about the Living God who lives in us. Scripture is the greatest gift we have been given to help us lead a godly life, and the Holy Spirit is the gift given to us to help us understand it. The Bible really does have all the answers on how to live a godly life! No, it doesn't tell us how to find a cure for cancer. But it tells us how to live with cancer in a way that pleases God. When we learn from His Word and add the qualities of mature faith to our lives, we can keep from being "ineffective and unproductive" in our "knowledge of our Lord Jesus Christ." (2 Peter 1:8). Then we are able to go help someone else do the same.

We are a part of those resources that others need. Are we showing up? Are we preparing ourselves for the all-important job of being a disciple? God has given us all we need for the task. But we need to open our Bibles!

REFLECT:

Score yourself from 0-10 on where you are in the following areas:

Bible Reading, Prayer, Church attendance, Witnessing, Serving, Giving, Obedience, Discipleship. What opportunities do you see for growth?

When you have a problem, do you turn to the Bible first for answers, or to other sources? What other things do you turn to?

Have you been able to pass along to someone else something that another believer has helped you with?

—✝—

Dear God, Thank you that You have given me everything I need to lead a godly life. Help me to desire to please You above all else. I commit myself to "show up" for class, using the resources You have given me in order to grow. Amen.

KEEP LOVING

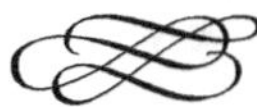

MY LEFT FOOT WOULD **NOT** STOP hurting. Right on the top, in front of my little toe and in the surrounding area. I couldn't see anything visibly wrong—no bruising or swelling. I didn't remember doing anything to injure it. I decided to be a little less active and skip my run/walk exercise time for a few weeks. I sure did miss being outdoors, but I figured that was the only way for it to get better.

But instead it got worse. I was perplexed and started wondering if maybe it was from the boots I had been wearing to church. Were they too tight? After two months of this, I considered seeing a doctor but ended up figuring out the cause on my own.

I'm embarrassed to admit the cause. Are you ready?....

I am pretty sure I am the only person in the world who could get a foot injury from reading! Yep! Lol! When I'm reading, I have this weird habit of bending my left knee and sitting on my foot. My foot was being stretched at an odd angle, and I had been doing a LOT of reading. Once I started using better body mechanics, my foot pain quickly subsided.

I remember thinking, "Oh, man! I missed the fun and connection with my running friends because I was trying to protect myself from pain, and running wasn't even the cause of the pain!

There have also been other times I've missed out on connection with others because I was trying to protect myself from pain. Emotional pain is a different type of discomfort, but everyone has experienced it. We may not want to share our struggles with others because we want to appear strong and confident. Self-protection can show up in a lot of different ways. Shutting down conversations when they turn to certain topics. Avoiding getting close to people. Hiding emotions. Not being open with others.

Self-protection can also affect our willingness to share the gospel. We might fear rejection or worry about offending someone. But self-protection is contrary to the gospel.

Self-protection puts self before others.

I don't mean we should make ourselves a doormat for others to abuse. But if we are to love others the way Jesus did, we should love them even at the risk of being hurt. We should love them even knowing there is a good chance we could be misunderstood.

A lot of people misunderstood Jesus. But that didn't stop Him from loving others. I imagine Jesus felt hurt as He watched the rich young ruler walk away from Him. I'm sure it was painful to offer salvation and see the young man choose riches instead.

I want to keep offering myself to others. I want to keep loving others. I want to keep sharing the gospel.

And I'll bring those hurts to Jesus.

Because sometimes the gospel offends. I just want to make sure that it is the gospel that offends people and not me or the way I'm presenting it. And I'm ok with being hurt by that.

REFLECT:

When you're having a faith conversation with someone, are you engaging them in the conversation, or are you doing most of the talking?

Obedience is ours. The results are God's. Does that statement make it easier to accept the outcome of faith conversations?

Are you able to lovingly accept those with different religious beliefs than yours but still have an engaging faith conversation with them, with both of you sharing your thoughts?

—✝—

Dear God, I want to be obedient to share the gospel, but I want to do it in a loving way that engages others. Help me to present the gospel in a way that doesn't offend them and in a way that pleases You. When others reject the gospel, help me to remember that the Holy Spirit is the one who draws them, not me. Amen.

MAY

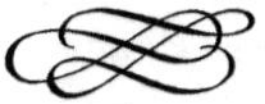

DO YOU NEED TO FEEL SPURRED ON?

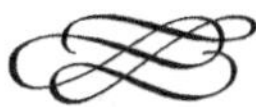

"Let us consider how we may spur one another on toward love and good deeds."

– *Hebrews 10:24*

Do you have precious friends who understand the true meaning of friendship? I don't mean the "let's get together and gossip about other people" type of friends. I mean the type of friends who don't have gossip as part of their makeup. These are the type of friends who will help you out on moving day or bring you dinner when you are sick. They will get out of bed at 5am to meet for prayer because that's the only time that works for your schedule. They will encourage you when you are broken.

Friends like these have an internal radar to sense when someone needs encouragement. That radar is called the Holy Spirit! The body of Christ beautifully goes to work to "carry each other's burdens," (Galatians 6:2). Encouraging. Praying. Sharing God's truth for a hard situation. Helping to shift a perspective. Having fun and laughing at life because sometimes laughter really is the best medicine.

The truth is—God doesn't need us. He wants us. But we do need God and each other. God planned it that way when he instructed us to "consider how we may spur one another on toward love and good deeds...encouraging one another" (Hebrews 10:24). He created the body of Christ to be there in the flesh for strength, comfort, accountability, and even just shared joy. There is a kinship in Christ that cannot be explained to an unbeliever. I am so grateful for these people in my life. I leave their presence feeling energized in my walk with the Lord, "spurred on," just as the Scripture says.

Do you have these types of friends in your life? I hope so. Many of my closest friendships have developed through a shared struggle or blossomed from a small effort I made to encourage someone, or someone else encouraging me. If you need encouragement, look for people in your life who need encouragement, and encourage them. The encouragement will come back to you.

Galatians 6:7 says, "A man reaps what he sows." If we sow superficial relationships, we will reap superficial relationships. If we sow love and compassion, we will reap love and compassion from others. Proverbs 11:25 says, "Whoever refreshes others will be refreshed." Friendship has a way of nourishing our soul and making us feel refreshed.

The Christian life is not meant to be a solo sport. Sometimes even our sufferings are not as much about us as they are for the benefit of others. Colossians 1:24 reads, "Now I rejoice in what I am suffering for you, and I fill up in my flesh what is still lacking in regard to Christ's afflictions, for the sake of his body, which is the church."

Wow! Let's read that again. Nothing is lacking when it comes to what Christ did on the cross. It is finished. Paul is saying that his suffering is less than what Jesus suffered. But He is also saying that his own suffering is for the benefit of the body of Christ. FOR OTHERS. When we suffer and handle it with grace, we are like a walking billboard, advertising the strengthening way God works in the life of a believer who suffers. Others see it and are spurred on to maturity.

I have seen this at work in the lives of others. I have had dear friends who have experienced cancer, lost a child, gone through divorce, experienced chronic health problems, or battled other painful experiences. I have seen these friends receive comfort from God, which they in turn, have been able to share with others who needed comforting.

"Praise be to the God and Father of our Lord Jesus Christ, the Father of compassion and the God of all comfort, who comforts us in all our troubles, so that we can comfort those in any trouble with the comfort we ourselves receive from God," (2 Corinthians 1:3,4).

God's design is beautiful to spur us on. I've heard it said before that we all need a Paul, a Barnabas, and a Timothy in our lives. In other words, we need someone who is a spiritual mentor for us (Paul), someone who comes alongside us in ministry, somewhat at the same spiritual maturity level as we are, (Barnabas), and someone whom we are discipling to help them to grow (Timothy). God has a beautiful plan to spur us on!

Iron Sharpens Iron

God sends in our lives certain people
To help us to grow and mature,
To help guide in our walk with the Savior,
To encourage our hearts to stay pure.
These friendships in Jesus are special—
Hearts bound by love that He gives,
Peace in His Spirit within us
And shared joy in a Savior who lives.
For we know He called us to be different—
To be light in a world dark and bleak,
To be accountable to one another,
To have boldness to step out and speak.
God knows that we need one another
When everything seems to go wrong,
And when we are part of the body of Christ,
We have others to help us stay strong.
It's easy to be mediocre,
But that's not what I want to be.
And my friends sharpen iron with iron,

And turn my gaze so it's Jesus I see.
I'm so glad God designed the body of Christ
That He knew with compassion to send—
Believers to be an example, a coach,
A mentor, a teacher, a friend.
I pray my friends keep loving Jesus.
And I pray they'll continue to grow
Because their light reflects Christ's love to others
And helps me more than they'll ever know.

— © 2021 BOBBIE PERKINS (DEDICATED TO THE
901 SOLE SISTERS)

REFLECT:

Who are the Paul, Barnabas, and Timothy people in your life?

Have you found that you have tended to add more "Timothys" as you have matured in Christ?

Think of an example of a friend whose suffering impacted you to grow in Christ.

—✝—

Dear God, Thank you that You designed friendship to be an important part of the body of Christ. Show me the Timothys I need to encourage. Thank you for the mentors you have brought into my life to help me grow. Help me to impact others for You. Amen.

FORGIVE YOURSELF THIS MOTHER'S DAY

"Therefore, there is now no condemnation for those who are in Christ Jesus."
— Romans 8:1

TODAY ON MOTHER'S DAY, I'D LIKE for you to give a gift to yourself. Give yourself the gift of forgiveness. Forgive yourself for all of your parenting mistakes, the times you were impatient, the times when you wish you had done better. We mothers pour ourselves into our children with the expectation that if we do everything right, our kids will be....well, maybe not perfect, but terrific.

And I do have terrific kids. But I know that they turned out terrific not because I was a great mom, but because they have a great God. I yelled at them sometimes. I may not have always been excited about huddling under a blanket in the cold rain to watch kids kick a soccer ball. I embarrassed them, annoyed them, and sometimes hovered a little too much. But I hope they have forgiven me for my mistakes. I had to learn how to parent. And just as I would get one stage of parenting down, then they would grow older and enter a new stage.

And I had to learn all over again how to parent this new, older version of my child.

If my children love me and forgive me for not being a perfect parent, I can forgive myself. And you should, too. In fact, you might be surprised to find that Scripture is full of Bible heroes who did a pretty sorry job of parenting. A few examples: Rebecca and Isaac played favorites with their twin sons, setting the stage for ongoing sibling rivalry. Eli the prophet did nothing to stop his evil sons from stealing meat designated for sacrifices, and he didn't stop them from sleeping with the young virgins who served at the house of the Lord. Amnon, David's son, raped his half-sister. David's other son Absalom set up a coup, attempting to dethrone and kill his father. Amazingly, David went to great lengths to protect the life of his traitorous son Absalom and grieved deeply when Absalom died in battle. Such is the love of a parent.

Now that my kids have children of their own, I think they can better understand the love of a parent. So, I can forgive myself, and I can also forgive my own parents for their mistakes. They were great in a lot of ways, but they made some big mistakes, too. Maybe you had an abusive parent or one who struggled with addiction. Can you grant them the same forgiveness for their mistakes that you need to grant yourself? In the long run, there really is only one perfect parent! And I hope that you know Him! If you don't, please read Appendix B! Have a blessed Mother's Day!

REFLECT:

If you could go back and do some things differently as a parent, what would they be?

What are some of your favorite memories of your parents?

What is your definition of successful parenting?

—✝—

Dear God, Thank you that I can look to You to see all the qualities of a good parent. I pray that my children will know how much I love them, and even more importantly, how much You love them. I pray that Your Holy Spirit will guide me as I lead my children and impact future generations. Amen.

10 WAYS THE HOLY SPIRIT
HELPS US REBUILD OUR LIVES

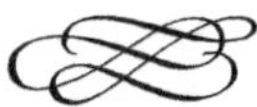

> "*I am with you,
> declares the
> Lord.*"
> – Haggai 1:13

MY MISTAKES LAY PILED IN DISARRAY all over my overwhelmed soul. How did I let my life become such a mess? How could I find hope for the future?

Even though I was a new believer, the enemy had invaded my thought life. Soon the voice of the accuser had drowned out the voice of my Creator. Sin had crept in unnoticed.

I surveyed the destruction in my life, much in the same way that the Israelites surveyed the destruction in Jerusalem upon their return from captivity. Rebuilding seemed hopeless. There was too much damage.

As God used the voice of the prophets to call His people to repentance, God was doing the same to me through His Word. He showed me that **hope for restoration and rebuilding could only come after that first step of repentance.**

"Yet I call this to mind and therefore I have hope: Because of the Lord's faithful love we do not perish, for his mercies never end. They are new every morning; great is Your faithfulness...**Let us search out** and examine our ways, and let us turn back to the Lord (Lamentations 3:21-23,40)."

I did have hope for my future because God is compassionate and full of mercy. He is faithful when I am faithless. He allowed me the pain of captivity just as He had with the Israelites, in order to bring me into greater freedom through repentance.

And as God gave instructions to the Israelites on how to rebuild, God was showing me how to **rebuild the rubble of my own life.**

In Ezekiel chapter 48, God named the new city "Yahweh Shammah," which means "The Lord is there." God was telling His people that they had hope during the rebuilding process because **the Lord was there.**

In the same way, God was rebuilding me and teaching me that **He would be there**, not just at church, not just at certain times, but in every part of my life.

I Corinthians 3:16 tells us that God sent His Spirit to dwell in us, "Don't you yourselves know that you are God's sanctuary and that the Spirit of God lives in you?" What a priceless gift to have the Spirit of the Living God living in us!

Jesus was limited by the constraints of His humanity. He couldn't be everywhere at once, but the **Spirit indwells every believer and fills us with His continual presence.** He assures us, "I will never leave you or forsake you (Hebrews 13:5)."

The Lord is there. Through the gift of the Holy Spirit, the Lord is there as we rebuild the broken down places in our lives. He promises us His presence just as He promised the Israelites, "I am with you," in Haggai 1:13.

The Spirit enables us to live a faithful, fruitful life as a Christian. That gives me great hope! There are numerous ways the Holy Spirit works in our lives, but here are 10 of my favorites.

10 Ways the Holy Spirit Helps Believers:

1. **The Spirit intercedes for us in prayer. (Romans 8:26, 27)**
2. **The Spirit comforts us. (2 Corinthians 1:3,4)**
3. **The Spirit produces fruit in our lives. (Galatians 5:22, 23)**
4. **The Spirit equips us to overcome sin. (Galatians 5:16)**
5. **The Spirit leads us into truth. (John 16:13)**
6. **The Spirit gives us the right words to say. (Luke 12:12)**
7. **The Spirit gives us power and strength. (Acts 1:8)**
8. **The Spirit convicts us of sin. (John 16:8)**
9. **The Spirit enlightens us to deep truths about God. (I Corinthians 2:10)**
10. **The Spirit gives us assurance of our salvation. (I John 5:13)**

The Holy Spirit would help me in the journey of rebuilding my life with God at the center of it.

God also gave an incredible promise to the Israelites when they were rebuilding. As they were comparing their simple temple built from meager resources to the former lavish temple of Solomon, they felt that the new temple could not compare. God reminded them that the beauty of the temple is not in the structure, but in **the glory that it brings to God.**

Haggai 2:9 promises, "The final glory of this house will be greater than the first." How could this paltry temple be more glorious than Solomon's? God's people did not understand that the temple's glory of which Haggai was speaking was not one that came from the splendor of its construction.

Over 500 years later, Luke chapter 2 reveals the glory of which Haggai was speaking when a young couple named Mary and Joseph brought their young son to be presented at the temple for consecration to the Lord.

Glory was present in that modest temple because God was there. He was there in the personhood of that young child—Jesus. God was revealing His plan of redemption. Redemption for mankind always brings God glory.

Just as it took over 500 years for the glory of that temple to be fully revealed, the glory of our present temple is but a shadow of what is to come, for we will receive our glorified bodies in heaven.

Christ is in us now bringing glory, but Colossians 1:27 points us to the future with "Christ in you, the hope of glory." **There is hope for yet greater glory ahead.**

As you rebuild the areas of rubble in your own life:

- **Remember** that God is there.
- **Return** to Him with a repentant heart.
- **Reject** the chains of captivity in your life.
- **Repair** the areas of damage as God reveals them.
- **Reconcile** your heart to an obedient state.
- **Realize** there is hope for glory ahead.
- **Rejoice** that He is there to bring glory to Himself through the temple of your life.

God is our Yahweh Shammah. **THE LORD IS THERE.** Even in the rubble.

REFLECT:

What rubble has God rebuilt in your life?

How has God brought glory to Himself in the rebuilding of your rubble?

What things that the Holy Spirit does for us are most special to you?

—✝—

Dear God, Thank you that there is nothing You can't restore. Thank you that You are with me always through the Holy Spirit, who empowers me to live in obedience. Help me to build my life around You. Amen.

HOW TO BRING LIGHT TO A DARK SITUATION

YES, I ALREADY KNOW. I DO A LOT OF goofy things. It's a good thing I love to laugh at myself as much as others may laugh at me. But this time—well, I am actually embarrassed to share what I did! It was just so thoughtless of me! But it brings spiritual insight… so here goes….

My husband's car had been in the shop. I picked it up while he was out of town, so I drove it for an entire week before we traded our cars so I could get mine back. I'm not used to his Mustang. All the controls are different, and I don't have to think about where things are in my Explorer.

The Mustang sits so much lower than the Explorer, and I noticed how hard it was for me to see at night. I complained to Denny that his lights don't sit as high, so I can't see the road far enough ahead. I had been having difficulty driving at night. I especially had trouble on a particular dark, curvy road.

When Denny got his car back, we looked at the lights together. He wanted to make sure everything was functioning properly and that it wasn't just the difference in how low or high the lights were in relation to the road.

It was then I discovered that I had been driving his car at night for an entire week with no lights on. Only the parking lights. On the dark, curvy roads. On the highway. To my defense, the mechanic had turned the automatic light setting off, and we always leave it on. I truly must have had guardian angels all around me because it's a miracle I didn't get hit in that black Mustang.

I had struggled and complained all week that I couldn't see, when all I would have needed to do was turn on the lights! And how many times have I struggled spiritually because I couldn't see the right path....all because I failed to turn to the light of God's Word to help me see more clearly?

Psalm 119:105 reminds me, "Your Word is a lamp for my feet and a light to my path." When I am struggling, God's Word helps me gain His perspective of a situation. It guides me to make better choices. It brings light to a dark situation. It shows me the path ahead with better clarity.

When our pathway is dark, sometimes we get used to living in the shadows. We make struggle a part of our lifestyle, not realizing how our lives could be different if we turned on the light. Are you struggling with something right now? God's Word is sufficient to provide answers to every problem we face. You may feel overwhelmed to the point that you don't feel you have time to study the Bible. I challenge you to spend more time reading it, not less.

Spending time in God's Word may not change our situation. But it changes us. It is the source of all wisdom, both spiritual and practical. Hebrews 4:12 tells us "the word of God is alive and active, sharper than any double-edged sword, it penetrates even to dividing soul and spirit...it judges the thoughts and attitudes of the heart."

But the verse right before it in verse 11 talks about entering God's rest—"Make every effort to enter that rest." It seems that there is a connection between having peace and rest and reading God's Word. His truth changes our perspective to relieve our fears and anxieties. Peace. Rest. Hope.

I pray you find peace, rest, and hope. I pray God illuminates your way when your pathways are dark. Just don't forget to turn on The Light!

In the Dust

Your Word is like a precious jewel,
Giving me my daily fuel—
To face the battles of the day,
To light my path and guide my way.
You are my heart's desire, my thirst.
Above all else, I'll love You first,
For, Lord, You've never failed to be
A help and hope and rock to me.
So often I have hit the dirt,
Lost and lonely, broken, hurt...
With friends on earth who can't quite be
The comfort that You've been to me.
But in those lonely times You've come,
Brushed off the dust, scrubbed off the scum
And bound my wounds with tender hands.
You are the One who understands.
How precious are my thoughts of You—
That You, God, care what I go through
And have it all in Your control
To mold my life toward You, my goal.
So teach me, Jesus, more of Thee
In any trial my life may see.
And when I taste the bitter dust,
I'll cling to You, whose hand I trust.

— © 2005 BOBBIE PERKINS

REFLECT:

When you are looking for answers, do you turn to the Bible first? Or do you turn to friends, the internet, or somewhere else?

Have you ever prayed for an answer to a problem, and God revealed the answer to you through Scripture? Did that make you want to read the Bible even more?

Can you think of a difficult time in your life when you immersed yourself in Scripture, and the Lord comforted you in such an intimate way that You felt His presence carrying you through that difficulty?

─✝─

Dear God, thank you for Your Word that never changes and is a source of wisdom, encouragement, and comfort for my every need. Help me to understand it better and use it to make wise choices in my life. Amen.

MAMA PRAYERS

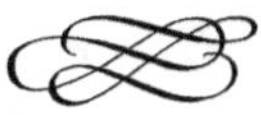

MOTHER'S DAY BRINGS ME MEMORIES of the past and hopes for the future. It's a day for me to honor my mother, who taught me how to love and serve others. She loved having her family gathered around a home-cooked meal. She loved meeting strangers and turning them into friends. She loved to laugh. I have her feisty, energetic nature.

I'm glad I have some of my mother's traits. Thinking about her makes me wonder about the traits that my own children might have gleaned from me. I pray that those traits are traits that are found in Jesus and that I have pointed them to Him instead of the world.

To be honest, I had no idea what I was doing when I was raising my kids! I was just learning to study the Bible for myself and to figure out who I was in Christ. When I brought those babies home from the hospital, I didn't know much about how to apply what the Bible says to the difficult task of raising children.

But I loved Jesus. And despite my mistakes, I believe my kids have grown up to love Him, too. That is the most important thing I could want for them.

But I know some of you are worried because you don't know where your children or grandchildren stand with God. You did your best as a parent to point them to Jesus, but now they are adults who just don't seem interested in spiritual things. They may even get annoyed at you when you try to talk with them about God.

There is still hope. Remember, Mama, that the story of their life is still being written, and you don't know what is on the next page.

Pray. Then pray some more. Then keep praying.

On Mother's Day, as I remember those little babies of mine who grew up too quickly, I also remind myself that their spiritual growth is as much a gradual process as my own has been.

Where I was when I was raising them is not where I am now. And I pray where I am now is not where I will be in ten years. And where they are now is not where they will be in ten years.

What I want for them, I have to remember, often comes only through the gradual accumulation of wisdom by searching the Scriptures for encouragement and instruction. It comes by trusting God when life hurts. It comes by walking those few steps of obedience in faith when the rest of the path is obscured. And that takes time. Growth takes time.

To live with the desire to bring glory to God and to enjoy a relationship with Him is my utmost desire for my children and grandchildren. And that is something I can lay a foundation for by sharing truth and modeling what walking with Christ looks like. But it is something that I cannot make happen. Both salvation and sanctification are works of the Holy Spirit.

But I can pray.

REFLECT:

Do you find it easier to spend more time instilling other forms of success (grades, sports achievements, etc.) for your kids or grandkids than instilling in them the importance of loving and following God?

. . .

What are your biggest desires/prayers for your kids/grandkids?

Do you make sure your kids and grandkids know you are praying for them and pray with them as well?

―✝―

Dear God, Thank you for the precious gift of family. Please help me to give my family my best, which is loving You wholeheartedly. Help me to persist in prayer for them, even when I don't see the prayers immediately being answered. I will trust You and trust Your timing. Amen.

TRUSTING GOD WHEN IT DOESN'T MAKE SENSE

"Since we live by the Spirit, let us keep in step with the Spirit."

– *Galatians 5:25*

TRUSTING GOD HAS OFTEN BEEN A struggle for me. He has grown me a lot in that area in the last few years. In 2021, I felt the Lord's direction to pursue studies to become a Biblical counselor. I feel strongly that Scripture is sufficient to give us help for EVERY life circumstance and that many of the problems people face today are because they don't know what the Word of God says about how to live life.

2 Timothy 3:16 says, "All scripture is God-breathed and is useful for teaching, rebuking, correcting, and training in righteousness, so that the servant of God may be thoroughly equipped for every good work." The Bible really does equip us for every task, to make wise decisions, and to solve problems.

As I looked at the information from seminary about costs and requirements for a master's degree in biblical counseling, I felt unrest. I didn't believe God would lead me to accumulate debt for an additional degree at my age, especially one that did not involve a change of career. I love being a nurse and plan to continue my nursing career. I was confused by what seemed to be clear direction from God but a direction that didn't make sense to me.

I prayed, prayed, prayed. I basically begged God to write it in the sky if this was from Him because I didn't want to pursue it without knowing for certain it was His will. He is so faithful. I got my answer, and there was no question about it.

It seemed every scripture, every sermon, every song, every conversation with other believers began to echo the messages of "Trust God and Obey. Take that leap of faith. When God calls you, He will equip you…etc., etc."

A dear fellow writer who knew nothing of my struggle even sent me an email about trusting God that had a video of Indiana Jones' famous leap of faith. (Check it out on You tube if you've never seen it by searching Indiana Jones leap of faith. It's less than 2 minutes long but has spiritual truth).

I knew God was painting it in the sky for me. I finally acted in faith to meet with some people from the seminary to discuss the requirements. That's when God did His wondrous work.

It was only by meeting with people from the seminary that I discovered that I didn't have to obtain a seminary master's degree in order to pursue Biblical counseling! They told me about a certifying organization called the Association of Certified Biblical Counselors.This was a path that I didn't know existed and didn't even involve going to seminary.

Through the Association of Certified Biblical Counselors (ACBC), there is a pathway that can be completed mostly online that is very affordable, rich with information, rigorous but not too difficult, and provides a solid foundation and training that leads to a certification for Biblical Counseling. That is the pathway I completed in a little over 2 years. It wasn't easy, but it was so rewarding! I spent hours upon hours in Scripture, learning how to apply the Bible to so many different problems in life. I loved every minute of it! (Except the paperwork!)

When you think about it, aren't we all counselors in some way? Don't we all give advice to friends, coworkers, and family members? I sure do want the advice I give to people to be rooted in truth from Scripture and not my own opinions.

Taking those faith leaps are beginning to get a little easier for me. When God has faithfully been there to catch me every time, it makes the next leap less formidable. What leap of faith is God asking of you? Is there something He is calling you to do that requires you to trust Him?

Dwight L. Moody said, "The world has yet to see what God will do with a man fully consecrated to Him. I aim to be that man." Yes! I want to be that woman. Fully consecrated and just waiting to see what God will do. I would hate to get to the end of my life and wonder what might have been different if I had trusted God more.

I guarantee that you will never regret trusting God. Dear friend, I pray you take your own leap of faith to whatever it is that the Holy Spirit is nudging you to do that is scary for you. Galatians 5:25 says, "Since we live by the Spirit, let us follow the Spirit's leading in every part of our lives." (NLT). Every part. Even the parts that don't make sense yet.

Trusting Him

I'm slowly learning to trust Him.
I wonder why it has taken me so long
To believe His will is best for me
When God has never been wrong.
I'm slowly learning to trust Him—
To stop fussing with my own schemes and plans,
But to quietly listen to what He has in store
And put each day in my Lord's hands.
I'm slowly learning to trust Him,
and I've found beauty like I've never seen
In the love between me and my Savior
By letting Him, and not me, reign as King.

I'm slowly learning to trust Him,
And whether doubts are many or few,
I know where to turn for my answers
Because the Word of God always stands true.
I'm slowly learning to trust Him,
And I don't have to understand.
In the end God works everything out for the good
According to His perfect plan.
I'm slowly learning to trust Him
In facing whatever unknown,
To keep praying He'll continue to nurture,
For He sees parts of me not yet grown.
I'm slowing learning to trust Him,
And though my way seems best as I'm wrestling,
I'll obey and step out of my safe zone—
Leaps of faith bring new showers of blessing.
I'm slowly learning to trust Him.
The Spirit's nudge I'll no longer resist.
I don't want to look back at my life with regret,
Wondering what adventures with Jesus I missed.

— © 2021 BOBBIE PERKINS

REFLECT:

Think of some situations when you had to trust God when it was scary. What did you learn?

What is God asking you to trust Him with at this point in your life?

Have you ever felt you couldn't trust God?

Dear God, You are righteous and trustworthy. Help me to take those faith leaps, even when I'm scared. I want to trust You fully and obey you completely. Help me to do that even when I'm not sure of the outcome. Amen.

WHERE ARE YOU PARKED?

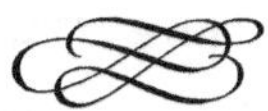

<blockquote>
"Not everyone who says to me, 'Lord, Lord,' will enter the kingdom of heaven."
— Matthew 7:21
</blockquote>

I HAVE YET AGAIN OUTDONE MYSELF IN doing something embarrassing and goofy. I would love to say I make these things up, but unfortunately, I actually do them!

My latest brain lapse was when I pulled into the parking space to pick up curbside delivery for Longhorn Steakhouse. I was looking forward to that steak and firecracker shrimp as I called the phone number and told them I was in the black Explorer in parking space number two.

They soon called me back and said that there was a white car in space two. I looked around and replied, "Well, there is a white car next to me in space one, but I am definitely in space two."

Soon a nice man was next to my car and asked about my order. I pulled up my email and showed it to him. "That's Longhorn," he replied, still waiting. "Yeeees???" I drawled in a bewildered voice. He gave me the patronizing look one would give a three-year-old. "Ma'am," he smirked, "This is Abuelos."

Yes, I really did pull up to Abuelos to pick up my Longhorn order.

Lol! In my defense, they are right next door to each other. But as much as I wanted that meal from Longhorn, and as much as I thought I was in the right place, I wasn't going to get Longhorn from Abuelos.

People right now are planning to spend eternity in heaven but have pulled up to the wrong parking space and are not going to get what they want. Wait. Isn't that awfully narrow-minded for Christians to think that their way is the only way?

Cultural catch phrases tell us that we should be tolerant and that it doesn't matter what you believe as long as you are sincere in your belief. It's the popular idea now that "whatever you believe is true for you, and whatever I believe is true for me."

But it didn't matter that I sincerely believed I was at Longhorn. I was wrong. The lie that people buy in today's culture is that there is no truth. But truth exists. If I were to point to a blue crayon and say that it is yellow, that would be false. My belief does not change reality.

Jesus clearly referred to Himself as the only way to heaven. In John 14:6 He stated, "I am the way and the truth and the life. No one comes to the Father except through me." That statement is not a subjective statement. It is objective—it is either true or false.

The Bible tells us everything we need to know about the truth of Jesus' identity and how to get to heaven. But the Bible does even more than contain information for us to learn.

When we read the Bible, which is called the sword of the Spirit, the Holy Spirit reveals to our hearts the truth about God and ourselves. John 16:12 says, "When he, the Spirit of truth comes, he will guide you into all the truth."

It is the Holy Spirit who draws us to know the truth, whether we are reading the Bible ourselves or hearing Biblical truth in a sermon or conversation. But truth definitely exists.

According to Lifeway Research, approximately 90% of Americans own a Bible, but more than half of those have read little or none of it![1] The truth exists whether they read it or not. I didn't read the sign

---

1. "Lifeway Research: Americans are fond of the Bible, don't actually read it," News.lifeway.com, April 25, 2017.

when I pulled up to Abuelos, or I would have known the truth that I was in the wrong place.

There are lots of people who are "good" by the world's standards, who are kind and loving, but who still won't go to heaven because they are in the wrong place. They are relying on works or knowledge or other wrong ways to know God.

In Matthew 7:21 Jesus said, "Not everyone who says to me, 'Lord, Lord,' will enter the kingdom of heaven." That's probably the saddest verse in the Bible. All those people who have created their own versions of truth will be missing out. Even those people who do lots of good things.

Those good works are like filthy rags next to God's perfect righteousness. God is a righteous judge, and our sin deserves death. But our Creator died for His creation.

Our Almighty God loves us so much that He laid aside the glory of heaven, took the form of a man, experienced sorrow and temptation and suffering just as we have, lived a perfect life, and died on the cross not to pay the penalty for His own sin (because he had none), but to pay for ours.

So we could be declared righteous. So we could know Him.

Knowing God isn't just knowing about Him and believing He existed. I know about Abraham Lincoln, but I never met him personally.

But I know God personally. I talk to Him every single day, multiple times a day. I love spending time with Him. He talks to me through the Holy Spirit revealing truth through the Bible, convicting me, correcting me, encouraging me, and guiding me. We are tight. We have a relationship.

I pray that you have that relationship. If you don't, please read Appendix B at the back of this book. And remember—there is truth. Don't park in the wrong parking space. You won't get what you want!

Eternity

Well, the day had finally come, and sooner than I'd thought.
I really wasn't ready. How off-guard I had been caught!
But the Lord is the one who claims our lives, so I stood in
*   misery,*
Not believing I had heard Him right when He said, "You don't
*   belong to Me."*
"But, Lord, I always went to church and usually did what's
*   right!*
I believed in You," I said defensively, "And I said some prayers
*   at night."*
"You're forgetting what you learned," He said, "Back in your
*   days on earth.*
The only thing I want to know is did you have a second birth?"
"Well, yeah, well, uh, I guess so," I stammered nervously.
"Jesus never was your Lord!" He broke in angrily.
"There are so many people," He added, "Who claim to know
*   the Lord.*
Yet how they live—it grieves me—no different than the world."
"Well, tell me then," I ventured, "Just how to be a Christian."
God said, "I told you how on earth, but you just would not
*   listen."*
He added, "People in your country see me in a funny way.
They say because they're not an atheist—They're 'Christian'
*   for living in the USA."*
"Some try so hard to do good," He said, a sad look on His
*   face.*
But no one will ever be good enough. Salvation's only by My
*   grace."*
He continued, "I want you in church—that's so. But heaven's
*   not found in church rolls by far.*
Just because you are sitting in a garage, does that necessarily
*   make you a car?"*
I listened as He talked on, explaining how to come to Him,

*And wished with all my heart that I could have a chance
    again.*
"Everyone has sinned," He said, "And sin can't see my face,
So fellowship with Me was broken. But Jesus took your place."
"That sin needed a payment—death from its ugly trap.
*But Jesus died in the world's place. You could say, 'He took the
    rap.'*
*Men can therefore have their fellowship with Me once again
    restored.*
Because Jesus rose up from the dead and is still alive as Lord."
*"They must place their lives in Jesus' hands and let Him
    control all.*
But the number willing to do that are sadly very small.
See, trusting is the answer. Believing is involved,
But believing entails trusting. The two must be resolved."
"Satan and his demons believe in Me, no doubt,
But one great factor's missing—it's trust they are without.
*You can believe a chair will hold you, and claim your belief is
    there.*
But proof of trust will not be seen till you sit in that chair."
*"When I, the Living God, dwell in a soul it should seem
    strange*
That in that person's life we see no evidence of change."
"What about those with real bad sins?" I interrupted Him.
*"Those who have done some awful things—do you forgive all
    of them?"*
*He answered, "Yes, some live in sin for years, but no matter
    what the sin,*
*I look in the soul and then forgive if the heart wants to be
    right again."*
He stopped, then finished, and I saw how stupid and how blind
*I'd been back when I lived on earth and said, "I change my
    mind!"*
"Lord, I see now and feel really bad of how foolish I have been,
But I am sorry and will repent if You'll only let me in!"

*He sent me then where I belonged, cast me out and closed the
     gate.*
He quietly said with a tear in His eye, "No, it is too late."

— © 1983 BOBBIE PERKINS

REFLECT:

Do you know Jesus like you know your best friend? Or do you know
Him like you know Abraham Lincoln?

Is your salvation based on something you did or are doing? Or is it
based on what Jesus did for you?

Think back to the time when you received that glorious gift of
salvation. Stop now and thank God for that. If you are not sure you
have done that, please read Appendix B in the back of this book
right now.

How has your life changed since Jesus became your Savior? How
would you like it to change? What can you do to help that growth
process?

—✝—

*Dear God, Thank you for the glorious rescue from sin that You have
provided through Jesus. Help me to continue to pursue Him as my best friend
and to grow more like Him in the process. Thank you that You are always
working to accomplish that in my life. Amen.*

MY REVIVAL FAUX PAS, GOD'S SENSE OF HUMOR, AND TRUTH

— *Ephesians 4:12*

WE'VE HAD REVIVAL SERVICES AT OUR church this week. It has been a spectacular time of hearing truth, worshipping through music, and bringing our hearts to God in prayer. Before I tell you how God got my attention, I must first tell you about my faux pas and how God has the best sense of humor.

The preacher was telling the story found in the fifth chapter of Mark of how Jesus brought freedom to the demoniac. I am usually careful to silence my phone before church, but somehow I had forgotten to do that. It was at that exact point in the message that my phone rang. Why is that funny? Well, my ringtone is the "Amazing Grace" version by Chris Tomlin, and the chorus starts with "My chains are gone; I've been set free…." So at that moment in the story when the preacher was saying how the demoniac had been freed, my phone blared out, "My chains are gone; I've been set free!" Lol! God has the best sense of humor!

But just as God brings laughter, He brings sobering truth. Truth that sears our souls to bring conviction, repentance, and a change in how we live. I pray that there are changes in how I live because of what I committed to God this week.

You see, I sat there for four nights this week, hearing truth and thinking about all the people who I wish had been able to come with me to hear the speakers. I thought of my friend who doesn't believe in God and is honestly hostile toward Him. I thought of my friend who says she is a Christian but doesn't read her Bible, make time to go to church, or seem interested in spiritual things. I thought about my friend who is a believer but struggling with difficult trials in her life.

And God poked me in the ribs and said, "You needed these messages just as much as any of them." I've heard the expression, "Revival needs to start in me," and I've even prayed for that. But it flooded over my soul this week as if I'd never heard it before.

I couldn't get those particular friends to come to church. But the church isn't the building. It is the body of Christ. I am the church. My friends may not come to the building, but they come to me every week in conversations, interactions, and divine appointments. And my excitement is what will intrigue them about Jesus.

So this was God's message to me this week:

Is my enthusiasm about Jesus really contagious? Or is my Christianity convenient and casual? Do I want others to know I am a Christian but make sure I "keep it under control" so I am not seen as a fanatic or weird? Paul said in 1 Corinthians 4:10, "We are fools for Christ." He was willing to look foolish and did not "tone it down" in order to win people over. On the contrary— his zeal teaches us that the way to impact others isn't by becoming like them. It is by standing out. Everywhere Paul went there was either a revival or a riot. He definitely didn't blend in.

Am I trying to cajole people to church so that the "professionals" can share with them? Or am I sharing my personal passion and my personal story about someone who can change their lives? Am I expecting the preacher to share with MY friends, whom God has placed into MY path for a reason? Or am I accepting my God-given role as the one who is to take His truth to them?

Churches have adopted business-type models on how to make decisions and run various functions. There are committees for everything, and this structure, though it lends to accountability, also lends to the thought that the pastor is more like a CEO and we are the customers.

The pastor's job is not just to teach us truth. His job is to teach *us* how to teach truth. His job is not just to minister. His job is to teach *us* how to be ministers. "So Christ himself gave the apostles, the prophets, the evangelists, the pastors and teachers, *to equip his people for works of service* so that the body of Christ may be built up," (Ephesians 4:11,12, emphasis mine).

It is my job to serve others and build up other believers. My pastor is just my coach, my trainer, in how to do that. Am I sitting on the bench? Or do I want to get in the game?

Oh, Lord, put me in the starting lineup! Revival can start with one person being obedient and sold out to God. Through the power of the Holy Spirit, it can spread like wildfire. May it begin in me.

Reflect:

Consider what keeps you from sharing your faith with others. What can you do to make that a priority?

Are you seeking to serve at your church? Or are you seeking only to be served?

If you're not currently serving, what are some ways in which you could serve?

—✝—

Dear God, Your Word says Jesus came not to be served, but to serve. I want to be like Jesus. Please show me where You want me to serve, and may I do it out of love for You and not to receive recognition from others. Amen.

FREEDOM FOR THE CAPTIVES

I WATCHED A FLOWER UNFOLD THIS week. It was a beautiful sight, and I felt privileged to witness it. The petals were hesitant, seeking the light, but unsure if the light would come. As the light spilled out, the blossom grew to its full beauty, reflecting the light that had changed it.

This flower was not in a garden, but in a counseling room. The stem was the body of a woman who had allowed a doctor to take the life of her unborn child. The petals were a face that had once been tear-stained in grief but was now tear-stained at the realization of God's forgiveness. She had carried that secret burden for over thirty years and had finally found freedom. The radical change in her countenance was truly like watching a flower unfold.

There are many women like her. In fact, in the United States alone, one out of every four women has had an abortion. Many women are silently keeping their secret so that no one will ever know. Often these women struggle to find forgiveness and are crippled by feelings of unworthiness.

I was one of those women. It took me over ten years after my abortion to truly grieve for my baby and embrace the freedom of God's forgiveness. You might be one of those women, too. If so, I am so sorry. I want you to know that your life can be different. You can be free from the shame and secrecy. Secrets make us sick. You can learn new ways of responding to the sorrow and guilt and find peace and yes... even joy…in the glorious gift of mercy! It is a journey that is best traveled with the support of others who have traveled the same road, using God's Word as your guide.

If statistics are accurate, even if you haven't had an abortion, then someone in your inner circle has. You can share with them that there is hope and a new understanding of God himself. Please see appendix A in the back of this book for helpful resources.

To Lillian Carroll

The years have passed, as years must do,
And often I have thought of you...
Thoughts of shame and deep remorse,
A cloak of guilt, my shame's recourse.
That cloak was heavy, hard to shed,
So Jesus took it to wear instead.
A royal robe He placed on me,
Declared me forgiven and set free...
Set free from condemnation, true,
But not from all my thoughts of you.
Yet now the thoughts of you I'm feeling
Have changed to ones of peace and healing.
The Lord has drawn me to His side
By all the tears for you I've cried.
Sackcloth and ashes thrown away,
I'm clothed with joy for each new day!
I've found how deep His grace could be

When my God poured it out on me.
So now, my child, though I regret
My choice, I'll have to say that yet...
I think you are smiling in heaven today
Because I've found Christ in a whole new way.
Lillian Carroll, I honor you.
I wish there were more that I could do.
Though your life on earth never came to be,
You'll always be living inside of me.

— © 1998 BOBBIE PERKINS

REFLECT:

Are you carrying a load of guilt that needs to be laid at the cross? Give it to Jesus now and accept His forgiveness. Take a few minutes to thank Him for His sacrifice that allows you to walk in that freedom.

Abortion is hard to talk about. Is there someone in your life who might need to confide in you but needs you to start the conversation? Pray about how to do that.

What lies does a woman have to believe in order to abort her baby?

⁃✝⁃

Dear God, Thank you for Your grace that covers all sin, including abortion. Help me to stand for the rights of the unborn while still loving the hurting women who make those choices. Give me wisdom as I share truth, and may I do it with boldness, gentleness, and love. Amen.

HOW TO LEARN TO LOVE YOURSELF

> "For whoever wants to save their life will lose it, but whoever loses their life for me will find it."
>
> — Matthew 16:25

"It will be so fun!" my friend gushed as I silently concocted excuses to get out of going. I usually love gathering with friends, but a ladies' tea? Kinda fancy style? If you don't know me very well, let me illuminate you...I am not a Fancy Nancy! I hate dressing up. Because I am comfortable with my little tribe of women, I will unashamedly show up to lead Women's Bible study in a tee shirt and jeans with no makeup. I'm the kind of gal you might find at a redneck campfire, not a ladies' tea! But I went to the tea.

And guess what? I had a blast! We enjoyed delicious food, breathtakingly beautiful decor and flower arrangements, sweet fellowship and the amazing gift of hospitality from the hostess. Her home is beautiful! So why did I initially not want to go? I really had to ponder that. I realized that I was remembering thoughts that I had struggled with in the past.

Thoughts of not measuring up. Of not being as beautiful as the other women, as sophisticated, talented, feminine, girly-girl...blah,

blah, blah…you get the idea. Thoughts that a tomboy like me always felt when I was around feminine women. Have you ever struggled with comparing yourself to others?

I began to realize, though, that while I was at the tea, I had none of the thoughts that might have plagued me in the past. Thoughts like: "Wow, her makeup is so on-point. I wish I knew how to make mine look like that" or "Her outfit is so cute, and I look like someone from *Little House on the Prairie*." I realized that the comparison game was finally over for me.

Oh, I still compare. I continue to admire other women for their beauty, poise, decorating skills, and other talents that I lack. But I can admire them now without feeling insecure. I don't feel that I have to be like them anymore. I realize how special God made me, and I have specific talents that He gave me in order to glorify Him. He could have gone a little lighter on the goofiness talent, but I haven't talked to Him about that yet….

What changed my perspective? The world tells us we need to love ourselves more in order to feel better about ourselves. Did I somehow lose my insecurity by gaining some extra measure of self-esteem? Did I learn to embrace my individuality by developing a deeper sense of self-love?

Nope.

Actually, it was kind of the opposite. I realized that I didn't need to think about myself so much because God doesn't want me to love myself more.

It's true. We are commanded to love God. We are commanded to love others. But there is no commandment to love ourselves. In fact, in Matthew 22:39, when Jesus says to "love your neighbor as yourself," He assumes that we all just naturally love ourselves! Loving oneself is just something that sinful people naturally do. But loving God and loving others is a work of the Holy Spirit.

When we are thinking about ourselves, we can't truly love others. And the converse is also true. When we are focused on loving others, we forget about ourselves and our insecurities. We are focused on building up the other person, not building up ourselves.

How freeing! Not focusing on myself enables me to actually love others and love myself in the way God wants me to. Not in a selfish, preoccupied way, but understanding that my value is only in relation to who I am in Christ. Because of who I am in Christ, I can live with God's glory as my goal, and loving others as Jesus loves them brings Him glory. And THAT brings soul satisfaction, the kind of self-love the world cannot understand.

"For whoever wants to save their life will lose it, but whoever loses their life for me will find it," (Matthew 16:25).

REFLECT:

When you are with others, do you tend to compare yourself in a self-abasing way?

List some of your special qualities or talents. Thank God for them now.

When you are gathering with friends, do you tend to think more about what they think of you or about how you can make them feel valued?

╾✝╼

Dear God, Thank you that I don't have to search for my value from other people because I find my value in You. Help me to love others unselfishly and point them to You, knowing that is the most loving thing I can do for them! Help me to give my insecurities to You. Amen.

JUNE

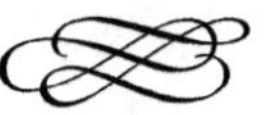

ARE YOU A FOLLOWER
OR A DISCIPLE?

> "Whoever wants to be
> my disciple must
> deny themselves and
> take up their cross
> and follow me."
>
> – Matthew 16:24

IT HAPPENS TOO OFTEN. I'M COOKING something out of my norm for dinner, and I'm in the middle of the recipe instructions when I realize I forgot to buy an essential ingredient. After a mad dash to the store, I remind myself that I should plan ahead before I commit to a new recipe.

You know, Jesus tells us to do the same thing before we commit to follow Him. In Luke 14, He tells us to "count the cost" or plan ahead for the changes in lifestyle that will come with being a disciple.

Jesus had many followers, but He only had 12 disciples. Why the disparity?

The word "disciple" actually means "learner" or "pupil." It carries the expectation of lifelong learning, of a deeper commitment than just a follower. A disciple was willing to follow Jesus to the unknown, to the discomforts, and even to the dangers that might lie ahead.

The followers in the crowd were content to follow Jesus up until a point, but not to do something difficult, to step out of the crowd and become a disciple. Jesus made it clear that He had stringent expectations for His disciples. Matthew 16:24 states, "Whoever wants to be my disciple must deny themselves and take up their cross and follow me."

As a disciple, I must be willing to DENY MYSELF— to humbly submit my will to God, to say no to myself or worldly pleasures in order to say yes to God. I have failed at this many times, but God wants to see that I am amenable and desire to learn this type of submission in my life. As a disciple, I must be ready to TAKE UP MY CROSS—to be willing to be uncomfortable, be hurt, or even to suffer in order to follow Christ. The cross was an agent of death. Am I willing to die to self? As a disciple, I must ungrudgingly FOLLOW HIM—to live a lifestyle of daily trust to whatever He calls me to do, even if it requires faith.

Am I really living as a disciple or just a follower? Am I willing to live differently, or would I rather follow Jesus only to a certain point? Do I want to follow just enough to make sure I have some fire insurance but not where I actually talk about Him to others? Am I willing to be viewed as one of "those" Christians, a radical for Christ, or do I leave that kind of Christianity to the "professional" Christians, such as the ministers, elders, or deacons?

Do others see me as a disciple? What about you? Are you in the crowd or have you stepped out? As my pastor recently said, "A convert checks the box; a disciple is all in." Are you all in for Jesus? He wants you to count the cost, but that cost is nothing compared to the gain you will find in Him.

In Luke 14:26, Jesus says a curious thing. "If anyone comes to me and does not hate father and mother, wife and children, brothers and sisters—yes, even their own life—such a person cannot be my disciple." Whaaat? Jesus wants us to hate our family? What does He mean?

Of course Jesus is not asking us to hate our family. He is making a point. In the Jewish culture of Jesus' day, family was valued above all else. Women who were unable to bear children even lived in disgrace and shame. In this passage, Jesus wasn't asking them to hate their family, but to evaluate what they valued most, and to put Him even above what they valued most, which was typically family. He was essentially saying, "Value me so much that the gap is so big that it looks like you don't value your family at all. It looks like you hate them in comparison."

I have to ask myself—what things do I value most in life? Do I put Jesus so far above them that it looks like I'm not even interested in those things by comparison? What insights would someone discover about what I value by looking at my calendar and my checkbook? Would they see that I am crazy about Jesus?

Jesus calls us to count the cost of discipleship because He knows what can happen in our lives when we fully commit all that we know of ourselves to all that we know of Him. If we don't count the cost, we aren't prepared for the sacrifice that grows our faith. He wants us to know what we are committing to because it is a deliberate choice of the heart to live in abandonment to Him.

Is Jesus on the fringe of your life or at the center of it? Don't be content to check the box. Go all in for Jesus! Commit to what He wants to accomplish in and through your life when He is the top priority. What soul satisfaction and limitless joy there is to be found in pursuing Him!

Missing Out

Did they know what they were missing
As they stood there in the crowd?
They listened to Him teach
With their hearts detached and proud....
Did she know He offered new life
To lift her from disgrace and shame?
She didn't trust Him with her sorrow,
So she left that day, unchanged.
There were others who believed His words.
They called Him "Lord" with high regard,
But commitment stopped when Jesus showed
A path austere and hard.

To deny themselves, To submit their will,
To take up a heavy cross,
And trust God with committed faith
To the point of suffering loss?
It seemed too much. So many left,
But as they made their journey home,
Did they realize they'd just passed up
The greatest joy they could have known?
Lord, I don't want to live like that—
To follow You from the fringe.
I want to live in full abandon where
On You all things will hinge.
I don't want to say I checked the box—
A convert on heaven's roll;
I want to live as a disciple
And commit every fiber of my soul.
I'm not content to simply know You.
Lord, be all up in my story!
My soul is satisfied in You.
You bring redemption, joy, and glory!

— © 2021 BOBBIE PERKINS

REFLECT:

On a 0-10 scale, how would you rate your level of commitment to Christ?

Have you ever known someone who stood out from the crowd because of their commitment to Christ? What made them stand out? Are you willing to be different, too?

What does taking up your cross to follow Christ mean to you?

—✝—

Dear God, Thank you for the joy I have in following You. The sacrifice You ask of me is nothing in comparison to the cross. Help me to die to self and live for You. Help me to live as a fully committed disciple instead of a casual follower. Amen.

HOW TO KNOW
YOUR FAITH IS REAL

"*Not everyone who says to me, 'Lord, Lord,' will enter the kingdom of heaven, but only the one who does the will of my Father who is in heaven.*"

— Matthew 7:21

I LOVE BEING A NURSE. I LOVE teaching my patients and talking to them about their lives. I love going the extra mile to make them feel special and cared for. I even love emergency situations where team-work results in positive outcomes for the patient.

But sometimes it is a different type of emergency situation. The nursing profession often leads to fatigue and burnout. When the pandemic began, nurses were apprehensive about caring for Covid patients. I saw one nurse actually cry before donning her Covid PPE that first time. Now nurses are more afraid of burnout than they ever were of Covid.

When the expectations for assessments, caregiving, medications, lab work, teaching, charting, admissions, discharges, and a myriad of other tasks seem impossible, I find myself letting my negative thoughts bubble over into negative words. Oh, I am sweet and encouraging to my patients. But I have felt entitled to complain to my coworkers while working in such frustrating conditions.

My complaining felt righteous, that is, until I read James 1:26 with new eyes. "Those who consider themselves religious and yet do not keep a tight rein on their tongues deceive themselves, and their religion is worthless." WORTHLESS?!

If you think like I do, sometimes the word "religious" can carry a negative connotation. I think of someone who follows rituals instead of having a relationship with Christ. But the word religious here is the Greek word "threskos," meaning "fearing or worshipping God." I do fear and worship God, but I also struggle with complaining when I feel overwhelmed. The Holy Spirit was tapping me on the shoulder, showing me how this verse applies to my own life.

It is interesting to note that what James says signifies true religion, true Christianity, isn't how well I can quote scripture or how many times I go to church. It isn't even about how kind I am to others or how many casseroles I take to the sick. No, the thing that communicates to others that my faith is real is how well I bridle my tongue. Ouch!

God is continually working on my heart. This verse reminds me that I have far to go! But I really do want to be obedient. I don't want my words to be uttered in haste with a negative attitude. My words will reflect my attitude, so the change needs to come, not from being deliberate about my speech, but being deliberate about my heart.

Matthew 12:34 says, "The mouth speaks what the heart is full of." Our mouth is like a bucket that brings water up from the well of our heart. If the heart isn't right, the water is putrid. I want others to have pure water to drink from the bucket of my words.

I have always been kind of an encourager. But God's Word reminds me to use my words in new ways to encourage people. That doesn't mean I have to ignore unacceptable working conditions. I can take my concerns to management. But my muttered words of complaining aren't changing my workload; they just make those around me miserable and contribute to an already low morale at work.

I have a new goal at work—to find at least one nurse every day to intentionally encourage. It may be in a small way, but I want people to feel edified, not defeated, from my words. What about you? Nurses aren't the only people who feel stress at work. How can you edify your coworkers with your words?

Ephesians 4:29 says, "Do not let any unwholesome talk come out of your mouths, but only what is helpful for building others up according to their needs, that it may benefit those who listen." I like the idea of being helpful and building others up.

Everyone needs a little grace. Me included. I know I will continue to battle bridling my tongue. But I thank God for His immeasurable grace! I pray for all of us to choose our words more carefully and hopefully become a little more like Christ in the process.

REFLECT:

How do you feel when you are around someone who is complaining? Do you want others to feel that way when they are around you?

Make it your goal to encourage one person every day this week with some words of encouragement. Did it boost your own morale?

How can the truth of Philippians 4:8 help us to choose our words more carefully?

—✝—

Dear God, Please forgive me for my words when they don't glorify You. Help me to spread joy instead of misery and to encourage others with my words. Help me to filter all my words through the Holy Spirit. Amen.

SPIDERMAN WISDOM

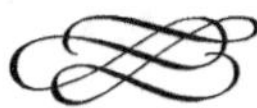

> "I have learned to be content whatever the circumstances."
> — *Philippians 4:11*

He used to love Spiderman. In fact, he was OBSESSED with Spiderman. His red and blue markers were the first to run out of ink. The refrigerator was covered with pictures of his favorite superhero.

So in typical Nana fashion, when he was four years old, on one of his visits I bought him a Spiderman book that came with a flashlight. He pushed every button, enjoying the sound effects and lights. Four-year-olds are easy to please.

As I drove him back to his parents on the last night of his visit, I glanced at his face in the rear- view mirror. He was holding up the flashlight, admiring it. "Thank you, Nana, for my new toy. I really like it!" That began our discussion about how some kids don't have any toys to play with. He didn't understand, so I had to explain that toys cost money, and some parents don't have enough money to buy their kids toys. He was silently considering this new information. "That's kind of sad," he solemnly announced. "But do you know what?"

"What?" I wondered what great revelation he was going to share with me. Bryce is always full of interesting revelations. I thought he might talk about sharing and generosity. He is kind and eagerly shares with others. I waited for his words of wisdom.

"Wellll," he drawled in his cute southern accent, "They really don't need toys to have fun," he spoke with authority. "They can run outside and chase each other. That is fun."

I laughed as I thought about how much that boy loves to run. He had already completed two 5k races with me and earned a third place medal.

"And, Nana, you know...I love my new toy, but really...the hugs are the best thing. The hugs are better than the toys."

My heart thoroughly melted. Simple truth from a Spiderman lover. Bryce could have talked about generosity, but he was talking about something just as important...Contentment. Joy in relationships instead of things. He had learned something that some adults have yet to learn.

Adults who are collecting toys. Accumulating things. Nice houses. Fancy cars. A boat that will keep them out of church and at the lake on Sundays. Expensive toys for their kids. Then comes financial stress and weariness from having minds filled with the things of the world instead of the peace of God. They haven't learned that "they don't have to have toys to have fun. The hugs are better than the toys."

And I wondered how many children are missing those hugs because their parents are so busy working and accumulating things that they never spend time with their kids? I wonder how many parents feel they have to buy their children the newest gadgets, when what their kids really want is some quality time together? We all need material things, but sometimes material possessions get in the way of higher priorities, like relationships and having an eternal perspective.

Jesus gave a strong warning in Luke 12:15, "Watch out! Be on your guard against all kinds of greed; life does not consist in an abundance of possessions."

The hugs are better than the toys. I love four-year old wisdom. I learn so much from him. Like Paul, he was telling me the truth of

Philippians 4:11. "I have learned to be content whatever the circumstances." I'm still learning, Bryce. Thank you for teaching me.

REFLECT:

Think back to some happy memories of your childhood. Are they about things or about time spent with people?

Do you tend to think more about tangible material goals or about spiritual goals?

Do you think your kids or grandkids would enjoy a day spent with you doing something fun as much as they would enjoy a new toy?

—✝—

Dear God, Thank you for life's simple blessings of fellowship with the ones we love. Thank you for providing for all my needs. I want to remember the difference between a want and a need. Help me to be a wise steward of my material possessions and to be content in all circumstances. Amen.

WHAT IS THE ARMOR OF GOD?

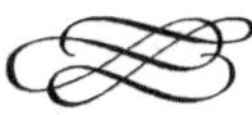

> *"Put on the full armor of God, so that you can take your stand against the devil's schemes."*
>
> – Ephesians 6:11

WE WALKED OUT OF THE RESTAURANT, laughing with our friends with whom we had just enjoyed a wonderful dinner. As I approached the passenger side of our car, I stopped dead in my tracks. Not again! Seriously?

The rear window had been shattered, as our new car had been broken into for the SECOND TIME in two weeks! What an anticlimactic experience after such a fun evening! Memphis is a high crime area, but this seemed a little much!

The police officer explained that a large gang of about twenty thugs were stealing Chargers and Infinitis. And of course, our new car just happened to be a Charger. Thankfully, the car had not been stolen, but we realized that we were not prepared for this kind of unseen formidable enemy. We needed additional protection.

The car now has a top-level security system on it. It warns us if anything is amiss, and if the alarm is activated, the car cannot be started. It has GPS tracking and many more features. It is also helpful that we can access the security system app on our phones, which are usually with us at all times.

As believers, we are also fighting an unseen but very real enemy. Spiritual forces of darkness lurk in the unseen realms. Ephesians 6:12 states, "For our struggle is not against flesh and blood, but against the rulers, against the authorities, against the powers of this dark world and against the spiritual forces of evil in the heavenly realms."

A gang of twenty thugs is small compared to the devil's army. Satan is the prince of darkness, and his goal is to steal and kill and destroy (John 10:10). He wants to destroy our faith and trust in God. He wants to destroy our thought life, our families, our health, our witness to others, our relationships, and our future. He wants to destroy us because we are the object of God's love, and he hates God.

Satan wants us to live as defeated Christians, but God has equipped us to stand up to his tactics by taking up "the shield of faith, with which you can extinguish all the flaming arrows of the evil one" (Ephesians 6:16). The shield of faith is like a security system on steroids. But that isn't all. God has given us a whole array of weapons against our adversary.

Ephesians 6:10 doesn't say to put on some of the armor of God. It says to put on the "full armor." Why? "So that you can take your stand against the devil's schemes." Exactly what is meant by the full armor of God? Verses 10-17 explain each piece that God has given us.

1. THE BELT OF TRUTH- Oh, how our culture clamors that there is no truth! "What's true for you may not be true for me" and situational ethics are the philosophies of our world today. Scriptural truth reveals blatant lies and stealthy deception of the enemy.

2. THE BREASTPLATE OF RIGHTEOUSNESS- God has called all believers to personal holiness. The more we stand up to temptations in our lives, the easier it is to continue to choose righteousness.

3. THE GOSPEL OF PEACE- The enemy uses anxious thoughts and fear to destroy our peace. This ploy distracts

us from seeking God, even planting seeds of doubt that God is good. The gospel brings peace— peace that we have been reconciled to God for eternity. Peace that we can trust God with our lives. Peace that He will never leave us. We can choose to walk in worry or choose to walk in the peace that comes to us through the gospel.

4. THE SHIELD OF FAITH- The shield of faith protects us from fear. We don't have to be afraid of attacks from the devil because God has provided us a way out of every temptation, and the Holy Spirit gives us strength (I Corinthians 10:13). Does that mean I deliberately put myself in temptation's way? Of course not! Sometimes the best way out of temptation is to avoid it altogether! It is by faith we believe God's promises and trust His power to protect us and help us through difficult circumstances.

5. THE HELMET OF SALVATION- How can I claim the King's power over the enemy if I don't know if I belong to the King? In order to defeat the enemy, I must be certain I am in the right army! Salvation is the key to using ALL of the pieces of armor. Our entrance into God's army is by grace through faith. God has given us security in our salvation that as believers, there is nothing we can do that will separate us from His love (Romans 8:38; John 10:29). ***If you have questions about salvation, please read APPENDIX B in the back of this book.

6. THE SWORD OF THE SPIRIT- This is the only offensive weapon we have been given—Scripture. God's Word was inspired by the Holy Spirit and speaks to our hearts through that same Holy Spirit's revealing its truths to us. The Word of God is "living and active and sharper than any two-edged sword" (Hebrews 4:12). If God's Word is my offensive weapon, am I making sure my weapon is fully loaded? How much time am I spending in His Word?

It remains to be seen if the car will have any more mishaps. The car security system isn't foolproof, but I feel better knowing that I always have my phone security app with me. And in the spiritual realm, my Great Protector, the Holy Spirit, is always with me as well. He is constantly protecting me from the enemy and exposing darkness in the world. I commit to do my part of vigilance by donning every piece of the armor God has given me!

REFLECT:

Which piece of the armor of God do you struggle with consistently wearing?

Do you think others can look at your life and know which army you belong to?

Are you loading your offensive weapon by spending time in God's Word?

Dear God, Thank you that You have given me the resources to stand firm against the attacks of the enemy. Forgive me for the times I have not been vigilant or have even been too lazy to put on the full armor You have given me. Thank you that I don't fight alone— that You have Your own army in the spiritual realm. Amen.

YOUR LAST NIGHT ON EARTH

I GENTLY WASHED THE BLOOD OFF OF her. She looked up at me, embarrassed. "I bet you hate this part of your job," she said, "Giving birth isn't very glamorous."

I smiled at her as I decided to let her in on my secret. "Actually, I love this part of my job. Every time I do it, I think of Jesus washing the disciples' feet. If Jesus could wash the disciples' feet, then I can certainly wash some bloody bottoms!"

My patient laughed and began to relax. "Well, that's a different way of thinking about it."

I wanted to say, "Yes. Jesus makes us different," but I just silently continued the task that I've probably done over 20,000 times throughout the almost 40 years of my nursing career. That's over 20,000 times of thinking about Jesus and His lesson on humility and service.

But my pastor made a point recently regarding this portion of scripture that I had never even considered before. His point was this:

If you knew you were about to die…that it was your last day on this earth…how would you spend it? I would probably spend it having fun with family and friends. Most people don't know when that day will be. But Jesus knew it was His last night on earth. And Jesus spent it serving others. He didn't spend it preaching. He didn't even spend it healing. Knowing He was at His appointed time to die, Jesus spent His time washing the feet of His disciples. Serving others with humility is so high on His priority list, that He spent His last night on earth teaching the disciples how to serve with humility and setting an example for them to follow.

And that's why I love that part of my job. Jesus thinks it is important. Am I willing to serve others even when the act of service is something that some people may deem as unpleasant? Jesus did. Washing dirty, stinky feet. Ponder the thought for a moment. The Almighty One performing an act of service that others would find degrading. A strong statement about humility. About others before self. About love.

Another way to serve others is to love them when they aren't very easy to love. I have had patients who were dubbed as "difficult" by hospital staff because they were hostile and seemed to hate everyone. Instead of dreading caring for them, I like to look at them as my personal challenge for the day! It makes my day if I can get a smile out of them, a little lowering of the wall they have built. I want to show them the unconditional love of Christ, who loves them at their most unlovable. Christ loved me when I didn't love Him. I want to love others with this kind of love. "While we were still sinners, Christ died for us," (Romans 5:8).

Nursing isn't the only way to serve others. You don't even have to be in a "service" profession to serve others. I recently hired a man to do pressure washing for me who was so nice and helpful that I felt as if I had gained a new friend. He truly served me by doing an "above and beyond job," and we began to talk about Jesus together. When he left, I felt uplifted and encouraged spiritually. What a testimony this man has to be able to do that, not as a pastor or teacher, but as a pressure washer!

How can you serve a stranger today? How can you serve your family and friends? It isn't the task that matters. It is the attitude of our hearts. We can perform amazing sacrificial acts of service and still not glorify God if we do it with the wrong attitude. But with the attitude of Christ, to humbly serve in love brings glory to God and immeasurable joy to our hearts.

To spend our last day on earth as Jesus did...not knowing when that day will be...perhaps we should begin to serve like this today.

REFLECT:

How can you approach others with the attitude of Christ in all of your interactions today?

How has someone served you like Christ?

How would you like to spend your last day on earth?

Dear God, Thank you for Scripture that shows us the humility of Christ and reveals our own selfishness. Help me to have a servant's heart to serve like Jesus. I want to live every day as if it is my last and bring glory to You in all I do. Amen.

ONE VOICE

THERE WAS A SEA OF PEOPLE, AND MY 4 foot-eleven-inch self (ok, yes, I rounded that up) could not see over them. Too many other parents were standing in front of me. I would have to use my ears instead of my eyes. The fun week of summer camp had ended, and all of the children were excitedly crowding toward the door as their parents arrived to pick them up.

It was my 4th grade daughter's first church camp, and the 4th graders were the youngest ones there. I hoped she had enjoyed the week and prayed she had grown in her walk with God.

Enthusiastic voices echoed from the high rafters of the barn-style gathering room. I could hear animated snippets of conversations—" And we made puppets....I won the talent show....I asked Jesus to be my Savior...." Beautiful children were eagerly telling their parents about their week, and I strained my ears to hear the familiar voice I was looking for.

As I concentrated, trying to filter out the clamor of the others, I heard her. "Mama, I'm over here!" As I peered through the armpits of the parents ahead of me (this is the life of a short person), I saw my sweet daughter's face peering back at me.

We found a quieter corner so she could tell me about her week. She shared about the fun she had experienced and told about the new friends she had met. She was exhausted but beaming with a heart that had been drawn closer to Jesus. I am so glad I took that moment to step away from all the other voices so that I could hear what she had to say.

I have to do that with God, too. So many voices clamor for my attention, and if I don't step away for some quiet moments with my Savior, I hear the voices of other people instead of His voice. In my busy world of juggling a full-time job, household duties, ministry, family, recreation, writing, counseling, and other things, sometimes it's hard to hear the voice of my Savior over the din. What's even worse, sometimes I let the voices of others drown out His voice in my life.

Negative comments. Disapproval. Unwelcome suggestions. Voices criticizing me or the people whom I love. People-pleasing. The opinions of others sometimes drown out the voice of God in my life. I don't ever want to let what others think of me overshadow what God thinks of me. But it can happen. It is a favorite tool of the enemy to distract me from God's call in my life.

I've allowed it to impact me many times. It's hard to be wounded by the words of others. It takes concentrated effort to focus on God's voice over the voice of others.

But it is so worth it to go find that quiet corner so I can hear His voice of truth. The rewards of finding that One Voice amidst the clamor of all the others is like a life-changing week at camp. It helps me to remember that I live to please God, not others. I have to repeatedly examine my heart to see if I am valuing the opinions of others more than the opinion of God.

Paul recognized this struggle when he said, "If I were still trying to please people, I would not be a servant of Christ," (Galatians 1:10, NIV).

One Voice

I'm juggling things I feel I should do,
But my Savior is calling...He's the One I pursue.
I want to hear Him, but the bustle and noise
Sometimes drowns out the sound of His voice.
Lord, help me to filter the things that don't matter,
All the critical comments and negative chatter.
Teach me to retreat to that still, quiet place
To stop looking at others and instead seek Your face.
Lord, help me to seek you in times when it's hard
And not look to others for my self-regard.
You are the only One I need to please,
No matter if everyone else disagrees.
My Redeemer, I know there's no person on earth
To whom I should rely on to gain my self-worth.
So why do I listen to others with fear
When Your Voice alone is the one I should hear?
Following You is the goal that I'm after
Undivided in heart, eyes on Jesus, my Master.
Teach me to stop looking to the left or the right
And instead keep Your call in the field of my sight.
When I retreat from the clamor, I can drown out the din
And follow Your Spirit who is living within.
You've established my worth by the cross and its price...
I'm not following people....I'm following Christ.

— © 2024 BOBBIE PERKINS

REFLECT:

Whose voice is loudest in your life?

Whose opinion matters the most to you?

. . .

Whom do you serve?

Are you pleasing people or pleasing God?

—✝—

Dear God, Help me to remember my worth to You when others are criticizing me. Help me to get away from all the other voices so I can hear Your voice clearly. I want to follow You faithfully and value your opinion above all others. Amen.

POTHOLE BLESSINGS
AND FLAT TIRE RICHES

IT WAS ANOTHER HOT DAY. IN TYPICAL Memphis fashion, the sun was piercing through my windshield, and the A/C in my car was struggling to keep up with it. A smoothie sounded good. As I advanced toward the drive-thru to get a smoothie, my car rocked back and forth, protesting the huge craters in the parking lot. Massive potholes! I was muttering about how ridiculous the parking lot was and complaining to myself about how they needed to repair it. Then I saw the birds.

Feisty little sparrows were rejoicing in those potholes. The recent rain had left behind several little pockets of water, perfect little swimming pools for the birds. They were chirping excitedly, gleefully flapping and having a bird party in the water, oblivious to my consternation over the potholes.

Jesus told us to look at the birds, and he taught life lessons from their behavior. As I amusedly watched their antics, I saw the clash between their joyful flitting about and my grumpiness over the heat and the potholes. No wonder there are almost 300 references to birds in the Bible! They just seem like joyful creatures. The Holy Spirit nudged me to a more sunny disposition. I can choose to brood over annoyances, or I can find the hidden blessings in those same annoyances. In fact, I think God wanted so much to impress this upon me, that He gave me another example of it the following week....

I was driving by myself to Branson to meet my husband and the rest of our family for vacation. I was in high spirits, listening to some praise music and was about halfway there when I noticed my low tire pressure light was on. I was in the middle of nowhere, but I figured I would stop to check it when I reached the next town.

I didn't make it to the next town. Soon I felt the familiar off-balance sensation of a flat tire. Great! I'm alone in the middle of nowhere. I have a AAA membership, but it might take quite a while for a tow truck to come to this deserted stretch of the highway. I made it to the next exit and saw nothing but a gravel road in the country that led to a building. As I pulled in, I saw a large trailer and people with horses. Maybe it was a horse business of some sort, and they could let me come inside away from the heat while I waited for AAA to arrive.

It turned out that the people with horses were also travelers, and they had just stopped to let their horses move about and get some water. The building was locked with no sign of life. The husband, wife, grandmother, and two young boys were friendly and concerned about my predicament. I assured them I would be fine as I waited for AAA to arrive.

They would not hear of it. The kind gentleman, whom I only know as Kevin, insisted that I allow him to remove my flat and put on my spare tire. He expertly had it completed in about fifteen minutes. I was extremely grateful for his kindness toward a stranger because I would have probably waited a couple hours or more for AAA to arrive. He would not even allow me to pay him for his help!

As Kevin worked, I talked to his wife and boys, learning that the boys had qualified for a national competition in rodeo riding. The boys excitedly told me about their hobby, allowing me to stroke the muzzles of their beautiful horses—such a treat for a horse-lover like me! I laughingly told them that my life goal as a child had been to become a horse trainer. Back in those days, while my friends had posters in their bedrooms of the latest heartthrob singers, my bedroom walls were plastered with horse posters.

As we parted ways, I thanked this sweet family for their help and wished the boys well on their competition. I was smiling as I drove the ten miles to the tire shop for a new tire. I marveled about how an annoyance like a flat tire ended up being such a blessing of kindness and shared fellowship. It reminded me of the week before when my annoyance over potholes was curtailed by the happy songs of the sparrows.

And I wondered…how many blessings have I missed because I was focusing on the negative instead of looking for the hidden treasures that God was giving me in the midst of those annoyances?

"I will give you hidden treasures, riches stored in secret places, so that you may know that I am the Lord, the God of Israel who summons you by name," (Isaiah 45:3).

Riches in secret places like potholes and flat tires. And I know that He summons me by name.

REFLECT:

Have you ever gotten a blessing out of something that started as an annoyance?

Have you ever helped someone in a time of difficulty to make their experience a blessing instead of an annoyance?

Would you say you are a "cup half full" or "cup half empty" kind of person?

—✝—

Dear God, Help me to have joy even in the midst of life's annoyances. Help me to bring encouragement to others and trust You in all things. I thank you that the joy I have in You isn't based on circumstances. Help me to live in a way that reflects that. Amen.

LIFEJACKET LESSONS

> *"The Lord is my strength and my song; he has become my salvation."*
> — Psalm 118:14

I AM MODERATELY GOOD AT A FEW things. Some of my skills are kind of weird, like being able to identify snakes. (When you are a runner, you want to know if that moving stick is a good guy or a bad guy!) However, some skills that are easy for other people are hard for me. Like swimming. Yes, I really cannot swim! Oh, I can dog paddle and float, but I truly do not swim well and even refused to own a pool. I was afraid that a child would fall in, and I wouldn't be able to save the child.

When we were on vacation, we rented a boat and spent a peaceful day on the lake. I wore a lifejacket and all was good. Until I got hot. I wanted to get into the water to cool off a bit. I didn't plan to go far from the boat, so I removed my life jacket so I could go under the water to get my hair wet in order to cool off. I figured I would be able to tread water for a minute then get back into the boat. But I didn't consider how choppy the water was.

I went under water to wet my hair, then tried to come back up, but the choppy water pulled me back under. I came up again only to be pulled back under again. The third time I came up, I gulped, "Help," before going back under. I felt my son-in-law's strong arms pulling me up, and he guided me back to the boat. I was okay, but I realized how foolish I had been to take off my lifejacket. I had misjudged my own ability and strength. And I had misjudged the strength of the water.

I have a friend who made a similar mistake. Only her near-drowning was not in water, but in drug addiction. She was clean for a long time. Then she misjudged her ability and strength. She had experienced some victories and told herself, "I'm strong enough to handle it just this once." That was the beginning of her spiral right back into addiction.

Before she went back into rehab, I talked to her about it, and she asked me to pray for her to be strong. Thinking of my water mishap, I didn't want her to feel strong. Trusting in our own strength can be fatal. We are never strong enough to combat sin in our own strength. She needed to know her weakness.

The apostle Paul understood this concept when he wrote in 2 Corinthians 12:9 that he would boast about his weaknesses so that "Christ's power may rest on me...For when I am weak, then I am strong." Paul understood that his own strength paled in comparison to that of an Almighty God. He joyfully embraced his weakness, so he would rely on God's power rather than his own.

We drown relying on our own strength. It may not be lake water or drugs for you. Maybe it's controlling your anger or your tongue. Maybe it's about trying to save a marriage based on the world's counsel instead of God's. Maybe it is about trying to pull yourself out of the pit of depression. Friend, your own strength isn't enough for those deep waters.

There is no shame in wearing a lifejacket. There is no shame in going to rehab or counseling. But there is shame when we are drowning in sin because we keep weakly fighting our own battles instead of turning them over to the strength of an Almighty God.

Whatever it is that you are trying to do that is not working for you…friend, please ask God for help. He will give you answers in His Word. And feel His strong arms lifting you up, carrying you to the place where you are safe.

It's one of the first songs many of us learned. Why is it so hard to live as if we believe it?

Jesus loves me, this I know, for the Bible tells me so.

Little ones to Him belong; THEY ARE WEAK, BUT HE IS STRONG.

Yes, Jesus loves me! Yes, Jesus loves me! Yes, Jesus loves me!

The Bible tells me so. [1]

"The Lord is my strength and my song; he has become my salvation," (Psalm 118:14).

"Let us then approach God's throne of grace with confidence, so that we may receive mercy and find grace to help us in our time of need," (Hebrews 4:16).

Strength

I watched them play outside my door,
The children playing tug-of-war.
The chubby hands would grasp and grope
To get a grip on the piece of rope.
Their laughter rose above their fun;
They'd see which side was the stronger one!
The rope went back and forth again;
It was hard to tell which side would win.
Then the advantage went to the farther side;
"Hey, we're winning!" They shouted in pride.
Then I heard the sound of a heartier voice,
And a father's voice chuckled, "Need some help, boys?"
He took the rope from the losing end
And tugged till they had the advantage again.
Then they planted their feet, and he stood back to see
As

---

1. Anna Bartlett Warner, "Jesus Loves Me," 1859. Public Domain.

they pulled and tugged till they had victory.
Both teams then surrounded the child's amused dad—
Of course they could win with the strength that he had!
It was all in good sport, and they laughed before long,
Knowing the father made the winning team strong.
As I turned from the doorway, I thought of their game
And realized as a Christian my life's much the same.
We are constantly pulled between battles within,
And often we wonder which nature will win.
For though through Christ Jesus we have been made new,
We still have our old nature tugging us, too.
In watching those children, I could then clearly see
Just how in our battles we can have victory.
For just as that father had helped in their game,
Our Heavenly Father will do just the same.
We need only to ask Him for His strength that is great.
It's not from ourselves; it's God's power to create.
So next time in the battle, remember just where
Your strength is to come from— your Father does care!

— © 1989 BOBBIE PERKINS

REFLECT:

Are you bringing your battles to the Lord in prayer? Are you asking for others to also pray for you?

The Word of God is a mighty weapon. Try memorizing 1 Corinthians 10:13 to help you in times of weakness.

Can you think of a time when you overestimated your own strength? What did you learn from that experience?

—✝—

Dear God, Thank you that I can approach Your throne with confidence to find help when I'm in need. Please help me to set aside my pride and recognize when I need help from others and from You. I want to win battles and walk in the victory You can give. Thank you for the cross that makes that possible. Amen.

REDEEMING YOUR EGYPT: HOW TO GET OVER YOUR PAST

ANNIVERSARY DATES. DRIVING BY THE clinic. Seeing the white crosses displayed at a church. For the women I counsel who have abortion in their past, there are so many things that bring the trauma of abortion back to pierce their hearts once again.

It may not be abortion for you. It may be the location of a car accident that took someone's life. It may be another painful memory. A sight, a word, or a date can elicit a reaction in us that takes us catapulting back to the abyss of grief.

It doesn't have to be that way. God can redeem even those places or things that bring painful reminders of our past. He can make those reminders a reason to celebrate rather than a reason to mourn. Impossible? He did it for the Israelites when He told them, "This is what I covenanted with you when you came out of Egypt" (Haggai 2:5).

EGYPT! Why was God talking to them about Egypt? Just the thought of that place brought back dark emotions. Memories of slavery, oppression, toil, and tears. They had no good thoughts about Egypt.

Yet God reminded them in that same verse that Egypt represented more than just their pain. Look back at the verse again. "I covenanted with you." A covenant is a promise. God was reminding them of His promises. God keeps His promises, dear one. He is faithful. In the midst of those painful memories, the Israelites were being reminded that God is faithful, and that He had a plan for them.

God has a plan for you, too. The second half of Haggai 2:5 says, "And my spirit remains among you. Do not fear." God doesn't want those painful memories to stir up fear or grief. He wants those reminders to bring us to the realization of the glorious redemption He has provided for us. He is reminding us that His spirit is alive in us, freeing us from the past, giving us new life through the shed blood of Jesus. He is reminding us that He promises to always be with us, walking with us even in those difficult places.

"My spirit remains among you. Do not fear." What a marvelous promise when we look at our own Egypt. Our God walks with us through all of our difficult places.

I often go to a particular place that used to stir up ugly memories. When I would drive by it, I would remember my life without Christ and feel the taunting from the enemy about the things that happened there. But do you know what? It is my absolutely favorite place now. It symbolizes to me the glorious salvation I have received, the great rescue that my Savior provided for me because He loves me so much. It reminds me that I am not who I used to be. I can't be in that place now without my heart swelling in worship and thanksgiving. God redeemed my Egypt and made it a glorious place for me.

Where is your Egypt? Can you look at it through the lens of His salvation and faithfulness? Can you grasp the promise of His presence as you walk through it? Your Egypt doesn't have to bring grief. Let it bring a celebration of His rescue, a trust in His promises, and a glory in His presence that will never leave us.

"Then my soul will rejoice in the Lord and delight in His salvation"

(Psalm 35:9). Oh, yes! I rejoice. I delight. And I celebrate. Especially when I see my Egypt.

REFLECT:

Where is your Egypt? Can you use it as an opportunity to praise God for His deliverance?

If it's hard for you to go there, choose a worship song to listen to while you are there. What song is special to you?

What did God teach you from your Egypt?

—✝—

Dear God, Thank you for your glorious deliverance. Thank you that I have a reason to celebrate even the broken places because You have redeemed and restored me. Help me to live in that reality and never forget that You go with me, building new memories of joy. Amen.

HOW TO PROTECT
YOUR MENTAL HEALTH

I HATE MOSQUITOES. THEY ALWAYS seem to find me! Not only that, but my body seems to release an extra amount of histamine, making the bites itch terribly and swell more than they do for most other people. This time there were only two bites on my ankle. I had definitely experienced worse damage on other occasions after being outside, so I didn't think much about it.

Those two little bites sure did itch though. While I was at work, I was mindlessly rubbing my opposite foot against them to scratch while I was working at the computer. My shoe was rubbing against those little pinhole bite openings in my skin. That shoe had no telling how many germs on it from the hospital floors, grocery stores, and the running path I traverse. Kind of yucky thinking about it now.

Yep. I got a nice infection from those two measly mosquito bites. My ankle swelled double its normal size and became red, inflamed, and painful. I developed a raging case of cellulitis. All because I had a breach in my skin's defense, and I had mindlessly allowed dirt to enter it.

I've done it with my heart, too. The struggles of life can bite us. Difficulties pierce our hearts, breaching our defense and bringing an onslaught of thoughts and emotions that lead to "stinking thinking." Thoughts can lead us away from the truths of Scripture and infect us with lies. Those lies turn our hearts away from peace and away from the One Who is our peace.

Satan is called the father of lies in John 8:44, and lies are definitely his specialty in drawing us into sinful responses to our emotions. When life bites us, if he can get us to believe his lies and doubt God's truth, then leading us into poor choices is a piece of cake. All sin starts in our thoughts. The Bible actually calls it our "heart," which is the seat of our will, thoughts, and emotions. We feel what we feel... because we do what we do... because we think what we think. It's a complicated cycle because our emotions, thoughts, actions, and experiences are all a tangled web of interconnectedness that affect one another.

In the United States alone, our psychologized culture spends in the HUNDREDS of billions of dollars on "mental and emotional health." It is obviously a big problem for countless people, affecting the quality of life for many with various types of struggles. But what keeps our thoughts and emotions healthy? And do we have any control over it, or are we at the mercy of whatever thoughts and emotions flood our brains?

"Above all else, guard your heart, for everything you do flows from it," (Proverbs 4:23). If those lies infect our heart, it affects our entire life, everything we do. How do we guard against this?

The very first lesson I learned in nursing school was about hand-washing and cleanliness. As beginning nurses, we learned the importance of keeping out impurities in order to maintain optimal health. Purity of our thoughts is just as important for our spiritual health.

"Whatever is true, whatever is noble, whatever is right, whatever is pure, whatever is lovely, whatever is admirable—if anything is excellent or praiseworthy—think about such things," (Philippians

4:8). That is my all-time favorite verse! It changed my life years ago when I was struggling with the enemy's lies. So, what is true and right?

"The precepts of the Lord are right, giving joy to the heart," (Psalm 19:8). Joy to the heart! There we are talking about emotions again! It is by thinking right thoughts from God's Word that we experience joy and protect our hearts from being infected by lies that lead us away from God.

"But I can't help how I feel. I don't have any control over my feelings or thoughts. I only have control over my actions," you may say. Welllll...that's not what Scripture teaches. "We take captive every thought to make it obedient to Christ," (2 Corinthians 10:5). The Bible teaches that we can, by an act of our will, bring even our thoughts into obedience to Christ by focusing on right thoughts. Right thoughts are truths found in Scripture.

Scripture memory is a reliable way to remove those lies from our hearts and replace them with truth. Consider these:

- LIE: "I have a lot of things in my past I'm ashamed of. I keep confessing them over and over, but I don't feel forgiven."
- TRUTH: "If we confess our sins, he is faithful and just and will forgive us our sins and purify us from all unrighteousness," (1 John 1:9).

- LIE: "My son is struggling in school. I have been praying for him to succeed, but there is no use in praying because God doesn't seem to hear my prayers."
- TRUTH: "I love the Lord, for he heard my voice; he heard my cry for mercy. Because he turned his ear to me, I will call on him as long as I live," (Psalm 116:1,2).

- LIE: "I am crippled by anxiety. I just can't seem to find peace."
- TRUTH: "I sought the Lord, and he answered me; he delivered me from all my fears," (Psalm 34:4).

. . .

- LIE: "These health problems are ruining my life. I have no
  purpose or reason for joy anymore."
- TRUTH: "And we know that in all things God works for the
  good of those who love him, who have been called
  according to his purpose," (Romans 8:28).

- LIE: "My life is hard right now. It seems like God keeps
  kicking sand in my face and loves other people more than
  He loves me. He doesn't care if my life is successful or if I
  accomplish my goals."
- TRUTH: "For I know the plans I have for you," declares the
  Lord, "plans to prosper you and not to harm you, plans to
  give you hope and a future," (Jeremiah 29:11).

I encourage you to find verses that directly relate to the particular
kind of problematic thoughts and emotions you tend to struggle with.
Memorize some of those verses. Listening to an audio Bible helps me
to reinforce verses I have memorized. I also write verses on flashcards
and keep them in my purse. When I'm standing in line somewhere, I
can put the wait time to good use by reviewing them. Every time the
enemy tries to feed you lies, repeat those truths from Scripture
instead.

Scripture memory was my lifeline as I was learning to grow in
Christ and break free from old patterns of thoughts and behaviors.
My go-to weapon was Romans chapters 6, 7, and 8. Memorizing them
helped me to understand them better. And understanding them better
helped me to live them better. Another great chapter is Ephesians 1.
You don't have to tackle entire chapters. But find those verses that
confront the lies that the enemy has tailored just for you.

Notice I said, "Tailored just for you." Believe me, the enemy does
use calculated planning in his attacks because he knows where each
one of us is especially weak. Ephesians 6:10 calls his actions against us
"schemes." The subsequent verses give us a detailed counter-attack

plan. It can be summed up as putting on God's armor. This armor is walking in the wisdom of God's Word. It is walking in the power of the Holy Spirit, who inhabits all believers—with the same power that has already defeated Satan! This is all tied together with prayer (Ephesians 6:18-20) because prayer relies on the Lord, rather than ourselves.

It's surprising how quick infections can set in. I want my mind to stay clean and renewed, free from the infection of lies. Satan is a liar. Don't let him hijack your thoughts and emotions. "Submit yourselves, then, to God. Resist the devil, and he will flee from you. Come near to God and he will come near to you," (James 4:7,8a). According to those verses, the first step is not to resist Satan. The first step is to submit ourselves to God. It is God's wisdom through His Word and His redemptive power through the Holy Spirit that changes our hearts (minds, thoughts, and emotions). This is what helps us to resist the devil and brings us closer to the likeness of Christ. And having a mind more like Christ sounds like the best mental health I could ever have.

"Do not conform to the pattern of this world, but be transformed by the renewing of your mind. Then you will be able to test and approve what God's will is—his good, pleasing and perfect will," (Romans 12:2).

"Create in me a pure heart, O god, and renew a steadfast spirit within me," (Psalm 51:10).

"...be made new in the attitude of your minds...put on the new self, created to be like God in true righteousness and holiness," (Ephesians 4:23,24).

REFLECT:

What "stinking thinking" thoughts does the enemy like to use to discourage you?

Find a Scripture that defeats that stinking thought. Write it down and memorize it.

. . .

Do you spend more time thinking about your physical health than you do your spiritual/mental health?

—✝—

Dear God, Thank you that you have made me a new creation in Christ. I want my thoughts to be made new to reflect Your truth. Please help me to tear down the old wallpaper in my mind of stinking thoughts and put up new wallpaper of truth from Scripture. Amen.

JULY

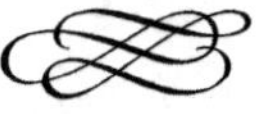

AMAZED BY YOU

I love this picture of my grandson Bryce. It shows the utter amazement on his face while watching fireworks in our driveway. It wasn't the first time he had seen fireworks, and they weren't even the best fireworks he had ever seen. But from the look on his face, you would think he had never seen such beauty before. He is amazed by the simplest things.

Lord, help me to be amazed in the everyday, simple things. Help me to be amazed by You. I am amazed by the beauty of the changing seasons as I take a morning run. Sometimes a deer will watch me curiously. Birds hop around, busily gathering food that their heavenly Father provides for them. They don't worry over it. They don't complain that they have to work so hard to gather food every day. They sing their praises to the Almighty and give joy to others.

Lord, help me to be more like the birds. Help me to not complain or worry. Help me to sing praises to You every day in my heart.

I am amazed at how God made our bodies to sleep and how sleep is such a mystery to me—almost like a precursor to death. While we are in this less responsive state, our brains are busy remembering snippets of things to give us dreams. Sleep refreshes us and gives us energy for the new day.

Lord, help me to come to You for refreshment so that I can perform the tasks You have for me each day. Help me to die to self, relax more, and fully rest in Your presence.

I am amazed at the sacrificial love of a parent for a child. How most parents would without hesitation suffer or even die for their children because God made us to have that kind of love. Our Father has that kind of love for us. Jesus, the God-Man did that for us.

Lord, I am amazed by Your love that I don't deserve. Help me to love others in the same way. Help me to live a life more worthy of the sacrifice You made, even while knowing I will never come close.

I am amazed by the intricacies of the universe. That the oceans are so deep we can't descend that far. That there are stars and celestial bodies that we don't know about. That if the earth were closer to the sun we would burn to death, but if it were farther, we would freeze. That there are spiritual forces in the heavenly realms we don't yet see.

Lord, I am amazed by Your power and sovereignty. Help me to trust You more and remember that "In him all things were created: things in heaven and on earth, visible and invisible, whether thrones or powers or rulers or authorities; all things have been created through him and for him. He is before all things, and in him all things hold together," (Colossians 1:16,17).

Lord, help me to release my control and remember that I don't have to hold all things together because You do. Help me to be more than thankful.

Help me to be amazed by You.

REFLECT:

What complexities of life amaze you? Allow those things to point you back to the Creator of them all.

. . .

Psalm 66:5 says, "Come and see what God has done, his awesome deeds for mankind!" He did those deeds for whom? Think about that!

What amazing things have helped you to gain a deeper understanding of God?

—✝—

Dear God, You are an amazing God, great in power and worthy of my praise! Thank you for the incredible creation You have made and will someday make new for us for eternity. Help me to be amazed by You every day. Amen.

I SALUTE LAURA INGALLS WILDER

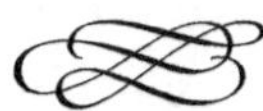

> "Give thanks in all circumstances; for this is God's will for you in Christ Jesus."
>
> – 1 Thessalonians 5:18

I WHOLEHEARTEDLY SALUTE LAURA Ingalls Wilder! She had to go fetch the water, then heat it over a fire just to take a bath. Nope. Nope. Nope. I am admittedly spoiled by indoor plumbing. Our hot water heater went out last week, and because we have a home warranty company that is never in a hurry to do anything, we are now on day six of no hot water. I must admit that I am frustrated over the delay. We are thankful for the showers available at our YMCA but are eager for the phone call we are expecting today about scheduling the repair.

Have you ever been anxiously waiting for something, and it seemed that it was taking too long? Perhaps you are praying for a wayward child or a troubled marriage. Maybe you are begging God for relief from financial difficulties or health problems. Waiting for something that we are eagerly anticipating can be frustrating. Sometimes we wonder if God hears our prayers or cares about our struggles.

Friend, I assure you that God cares. Even David, who was called the apple of God's eye, had times when he felt God was distant and uncaring. David asked in Psalm 10:1, "Why, Lord, do you stand far off? Why do you hide yourself in times of trouble?" I don't know why God made me wait for certain things. But I do know that during some of the times of His seeming silence in my life, it caused me to seek Him that much more fervently. It taught me to trust Him. If He had immediately answered every prayer, it wouldn't have taken much faith or trust on my part. I would have definitely missed out on precious times of growing. As David sought God in the writing of that Psalm, he later affirmed his trust in God with Psalm 10:17, "You, Lord, hear the desire of the afflicted; you encourage them, and you listen to their cry."

God hears your cries. Keep praying. He is trustworthy. His answer is for your good, even if His answer is different than you might expect. "The one who calls you is faithful, and he will do it," (I Thessalonians 5:24). What is it that He will do? The preceding verse says, "May God himself, the God of peace, sanctify you through and through." That sanctification process of making us more like Christ often happens in that waiting room.

REFLECT:

Are you in a waiting room right now? If so, what are you waiting for?

Do you pray expecting that God will hear and answer?

Have you ever felt as if God were far away or uncaring?

Which desire is greater—the desire for the thing you are praying for or your desire for God Himself?

✢

Dear God, I want to bring You all my needs, and I want to trust You with Your answers. My faith is in You, not in the strength of my own faith. I am willing to wait if that waiting room is a time You have given me to grow. Amen.

THE MARKS LEFT ON YOU

> *"For those God foreknew he also predestined to be conformed to the image of his Son."*
>
> — Romans 8:29

WHEN MY DAUGHTER HANNAH WAS little, she had a beloved blanket, much like Linus in the Peanuts cartoon. She snuggled with "strings" (as we affectionately called the worn fabric) when she watched tv or was sick. She would cling to the blanket when she was afraid of a storm. She would hold it closely and bury her face into it when she was tired. She had to have it for every nap and every night at bedtime. That blanket was familiar and comforting to her.

Some mornings Hannah would stumble out of bed with a mark on her face from the pattern of the blanket making an imprint on her. Her face had been pressed so hard against it, little swirls from its design were visible against her cheek or forehead. Like a temporary tattoo, what she had clung to had left its mark on her.

It works the same for us, you know. We become like what we cling to. Have you ever thought about what you are clinging to? What do you hold close when you are afraid of the storms of life? What brings you comfort when you are sick in body or soul? What gives you peace and rest when you are tired? Because what you cling to will leave its mark on you.

We could turn to the comfort of a big bank account, and it will leave marks of pride and greed. We could turn to alcohol, and it will leave marks of addiction and broken relationships. We could even turn to friends. Some of them will point us to Jesus, but others will point us to the world.

Life gets hard sometimes. I have a friend who at this moment is going through a difficult, scary experience on the heels of another difficult, scary experience. As I prayed for her, I couldn't help but wonder, "Why, Lord? She loves you and serves you and wants to glorify you. Hasn't she been through enough?"

And then I remembered the blanket. Suddenly it all made sense. We become like what we cling to. My friend is clinging to Jesus. She is clinging hard. I think He must have her taped to His side! She is running to Him for peace in her storm. And the more she clings to Him, the deeper the imprint He is making on her. He is making her like Him. Glory! Isn't that our ultimate goal?

When you are tired, Jesus will give you rest. When you are afraid, Jesus will give you peace. When you need comfort, He is The Great Comforter. He is the familiar, the beloved, the One I want to cling to so that His imprint is seen in my life…making me more like Him. "For those God foreknew he also predestined to be conformed to the image of his Son…" (Romans 8:29).

"Let perseverance finish its work so that you may be mature and complete, not lacking anything," (James 1:4).

"Come to me, all you who are weary and burdened and I will give you rest," (Matthew 11:28).

My Earnest Prayer

Lord, take me and mold me to make me like Thee.
Be the Light for my soul when the darkness I see.

Let me rest unshaken in Your perfect peace;
As I draw nigh to You, may all struggling cease.
My Jesus, for me you suffered such pain,
Yet You stood at my heart, an entrance to gain.
I lift my eyes to the cross where I gaze at Your face,
And know it is I who should hang in Thy place.
So, God, in great awe I now yield You my soul.
No longer mine, but Your Spirit control.
All that is there by Your grace to renew,
Submitting in prayer, my stubborn will to subdue.
Oh, more like Jesus is my prayer to be—
Naught else my seeking but longings for Thee.
I have no want for the world's passing ways—
My goal— to see Jesus and lift Him my praise.
My heart's desire rings out true and clear—
To tell of my Savior so others may hear.
As I put off the old me and put on the new,
Lord, please mold my heart to make me more like You.

— © 2001 BOBBIE PERKINS

REFLECT:

Have you ever clung to things that hurt you instead of helped you?

Can you think of a time when walking a hard path brought you closer to God?

What would you say you are clinging to most in life?

Dear God, Oh, how I want to cling to You so that others can see the imprint of You on my life! Help me to turn away from worthless sources of comfort and cast my burdens on You, my only source of rest and peace. Amen.

VULTURE PRAYERS: 10 QUESTIONS TO IMPROVE YOUR PRAYER LIFE

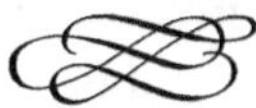

I HAVE A DEAR FRIEND WHO, LIKE ME, loves to run, although she is a much faster runner than I am. One of our favorite things to do is to run together and pray while we are running. Praising God just comes naturally when we are enjoying the beauty of His creation.

One particular day on our prayer run, we spotted several huge vultures up in the trees above us. We began thanking God for His incredible forethought to create vultures to clean up the gross mess of decaying animals! I had definitely never thanked God for vultures before, but isn't God amazing?

At that very moment, we were unaware that one of our running friends was on the same trail running behind us. She spotted us but didn't know we were praying. She started yelling a greeting to us and excitedly pointing to the vultures. When she caught up to us (because she is a faster runner than BOTH of us…lol), she realized we were praying. She immediately started apologizing and telling us how bad she felt that she had interrupted our prayers.

I was bewildered for a moment when I realized how different my perspective was about that. You see, I expect my prayers to be interrupted. I want to have such frequent conversations with my Father that life just interrupts that communion sometimes. And that's ok! Don't our conversations with friends often get interrupted by other things? Why wouldn't that happen with our conversations with God, too?

I can't imagine going through even one day without prayer. Sometimes I have times of more intense, focused, private prayer. But many times I am praying in the middle of my day, while others around me are totally unaware of the conversation in my heart.

I have silently prayed for wisdom in finding the right words to say to a discouraged friend while the friend was talking to me. I have been busy at work taking care of patients who had no idea I was praying for my daughter who was miles away, suffering her second miscarriage. Romans 8:26 was happening that day, "The Spirit himself intercedes for us through wordless groans."

When my children were little, I tried to teach them this same idea of praying throughout the day. One day they were in the car with their aunt, and an ambulance passed them with lights and sirens blaring. My daughter, who was about five years old at the time, said, "We need to pray for that sick person," and began praying. I smiled when my sister told me about it. That is what the Bible tells us to do.

The Bible encourages this lifestyle of praying frequently: "Pray continually," (I Thessalonians 5:17). "Seek His face always," (I Chronicles 16:11). "Pray at all times in the Spirit," (Ephesians 6:18). But the Bible also talks about praying in a more focused way, praying fervently. "I have cried out by day and in the night before you," (Psalm 88:1).

Scripture also reminds us that the conversation isn't one-sided. When we are praying, we should be listening as much as we are talking. Psalm 119:145 says, "I call with all my heart; answer me, Lord." Are we waiting for God to answer, or are we spouting off a grocery list of requests? Here are just a few of the many verses that talk about waiting for the Lord—Micah 7:7; Psalm 27:14; 33:20; 37:7; 40:1.

The Bible has so much to say about prayer, that I will be dividing this devotion into 4 parts.

In the next 3 parts, I will talk about 10 reasons we should pray, but today I would like to encourage you to take inventory of your prayer life with the following 10 questions:

REFLECT:

1. Are you waiting for God to answer when you pray? Are you listening for His guidance and direction through time spent in His Word?
2. Are you praying in all kinds of circumstances? Are you making prayer part of your daily conversation with God? Can you say that you are abiding in Him by weaving prayer throughout your day?
3. Are you taking time for more focused, fervent, persistent prayer? Could you say that you are crying out to God about something the way the Psalmist did?
4. Are you prioritizing prayer? Do you put it off until the end of your day, or do you wake up anxious to talk to God? I love this quote by Anne Graham Lotz: "Why tune the violin when the symphony is over?" Making prayer a priority as we begin our day helps us to respond Biblically to the challenges we will face throughout our day.
5. Are you using prayer as a weapon for spiritual warfare?
6. Are you persistent in prayer? Do you keep praying even when you don't see the answer?
7. Are you obedient to pray? Do you tell someone you are praying for them but then forget to pray? (I usually try to pray right away when others ask me to because I have been guilty of forgetting!)
8. Do you see prayer as something you are "supposed to do" or something you "are privileged to do?"

9. When God answers your prayers, do you thank Him for His answers?
10. Have you ever tried keeping a prayer journal? Writing prayers has helped me to focus, and it is such a blessing to read those prayers years later after you have seen them be answered!

Keep praying! But I bet you won't be praying about vultures!

—✝—

Dear God, Thank you that You encourage us to come boldly to Your throne with our needs. What a privilege it is to have access to You any time we want! Help me to remember that truth throughout my day, not just during times of planned prayer. Amen.

10 REASONS WE SHOULD PRAY (PART 1 OF 3)

> "*Because he turned his ear to me, I will call on him as long as I live.*"
>
> – Psalm 116:2

THERE IS SO MUCH TO TALK ABOUT in regard to prayer! So much that I am dividing this devotion into three parts!

Prayer is a spiritual discipline that is spoken of MULTIPLE places in Scripture. We know we should pray, but do we know the myriads of reasons WHY we should pray?

When I was young, my little rebel-headed self didn't like doing things unless I knew the reason why, and the reason why had to make sense to me. At least I'm better about being a rule-follower now that I am older, but the Bible does tell us lots of reasons why we should pray!

1. WE PRAY BECAUSE GOD LISTENS.

I was astounded by how many verses mention the fact that God listens to us. Think about that! The creator of the universe listens to us when we talk to Him. He cares about what we have to say. There were too many verses to list, but here are a few of my favorites.

Isaiah 65:24- "Before they call I will answer; while they are still speaking I will hear."

Psalm 116:1,2- "I love the Lord, for he heard my voice; he heard my cry for mercy. Because he turned his ear to me, I will call on him as long as I live."

Psalm 17:6- "I call on you, my God, for you will answer me; turn your ear to me and hear my prayer."

2. WE PRAY BECAUSE OUR PRAYERS ARE EFFECTIVE TO CAUSE GOD TO ACT.

Our prayers are like flipping on a light switch to release not electrical power, but the very power that created the electricity!

2 Chronicles 7:14- "If my people, who are called by my name, will humble themselves and pray and seek my face and turn from their wicked ways, then I will hear from heaven, and I will forgive their sin and will heal their land."

James 5:16- "Therefore confess your sins to each other and pray for each other so that you may be healed. The prayer of a righteous person is powerful and effective."

Matthew 7:11- "If you, then, though you are evil, know how to give good gifts to your children, how much more will your Father in heaven give good gifts to those who ask him?"

3. WE PRAY TO BE CLEAN BEFORE GOD.

Confession is the first step in repentance. What is confession? To admit our guilt to God and agree with Him about our sin. We use prayer to acknowledge our sin to God and to ask for His forgiveness.

I John 1:9- "For if we confess our sins, He is faithful and just to forgive us our sin and cleanse us from all unrighteousness."

Psalm 51:1,2- "Have mercy on me, O God, according to your unfailing love; according to your great compassion blot out my transgressions. Wash away all my iniquity and cleanse me from my sin."

Psalm 32:5- "Then I acknowledged my sin to you and did not cover up my iniquity. I said, "I will confess my transgressions to the Lord. And you forgave the guilt of my sin."

4. WE PRAY BECAUSE OUR PRAYERS PLEASE GOD.

Oh, how I want to please God! God is pleased because He loves to spend intimate time with us. But He is also pleased because He knows that prayer brings some wonderful things into our spiritual life.

Proverbs 15:8-"The Lord detests the sacrifice of the wicked, but the prayer of the upright pleases him."

Psalm 141:2- "May my prayer be set before you like incense; may the lifting up of my hands be like the evening sacrifice."

2 Corinthians 5:9- "For we make it our goal to please Him..."

I hope these verses encourage you in your prayers! We will continue in the next two devotions to talk about reasons we should pray.

REFLECT:

Which of these reasons to pray stands out to you the most?

Do you have a certain time or place for prayer? Sometimes establishing a habit helps us to be more consistent.

What could you do to make your prayer life better? A prayer journal? Praying with a friend regularly? Praying Scripture? Think about it!

—✝—

Dear God, When I think about all of the reasons You want us to pray, it makes me want to pray more. Thank you for always listening and caring about what is on my heart. I want my prayer life to be pleasing to You. Amen.

10 REASONS WE SHOULD PRAY (PART 2 OF 3)

"Let us then approach God's throne of grace with confidence, so that we may receive mercy and find grace to help us in our time of need."

— Hebrews 4:16

I HOPE YOU HAVE HAD SOME SWEET prayer time! Today is part two of a three-section devotion. We are continuing to talk about the ten reasons we should pray (although I'm sure we could find many more than ten reasons!)

5. WE PRAY BECAUSE PRAYERLESSNESS IS SIN.

Prayer isn't just a good thing to do. It is a commandment to follow. We are actually commanded to pray many places in Scripture! Praying is part of obeying God.

I Samuel 12:23- "As for me, far be it from me that I should sin against the Lord by failing to pray for you" (I Samuel 12:23).

Matthew 6:9- "This then is how you should pray..."

James 4:17- "If anyone, then, knows the good they ought to do and doesn't do it, it is sin for them."

6. WE PRAY BECAUSE PRAYER DEEPENS OUR RELATIONSHIP WITH GOD AND HELPS US TO KNOW HIM BETTER.

The story of Hannah is a beautiful example of this truth. Hannah fervently prayed and wept before the Lord, begging Him for a child. It wasn't until after that time of prayer that God granted her Samuel, but He also did something else for her. He granted her a better understanding of His own character! Her prayer of praise to God, telling how she came to know Him in a deeper way is found in *I Samuel 2:1-10. Here is an excerpt from verse 2: "There is no one holy like the Lord; there is no one besides you; there is no Rock like our God."*

Jeremiah 29:12-14- "Then you will call on me and come and pray to me, and I will listen to you. You will seek me and find me when you seek me with all your heart."

Psalm 145:18- "The Lord is near to all who call on him, to all who call on him in truth."

Psalm 17:8- "Keep me as the apple of your eye..."

That last one intrigues me. Despite his track record of heinous sin, David had a special bond with God. Do you see that in Psalm 17:8 he had prayed for that bond? I love that we can pray for a special intimacy with God because I always want to know Him better!

7. WE PRAY BECAUSE PRAYER CHANGES US AND GIVES US SPIRITUAL WISDOM.

James 1:5- "If any of you lacks wisdom, you should ask God, who gives generously to all without finding fault, and it will be given to you."

Psalm 16: 7- "I will praise the Lord, who counsels me; even at night my heart instructs me."

Psalm 17:6- "I call on you, my God, for you will answer me; turn your ear to me and hear my prayer. Show me the wonders of your great love..."

Think about that last one. When was the last time you just pondered on the great love of God and reveled in the glory of His Spirit who lives in you? It is a true wonder! David is asking for God to show him the deep wonders of God's character.

8. WE PRAY BECAUSE PRAYER HELPS US AVOID TEMPTATION.

Yes, we have been set free from the power of sin, but not from the presence of it. We still battle the flesh and the enemy, winning that battle not by our own strength, but by the power of the Holy Spirit. Prayer connects us to His power and focuses our thoughts on Him.

Matthew 26:41- "Watch and pray so that you will not fall into temptation. The spirit is willing, but the flesh is weak."

Hebrews 4:16- "Let us then approach God's throne of grace with confidence, so that we may receive mercy and find grace to help us in our time of need."

2 Corinthians 10:4- "The weapons we fight with are not the weapons of the world. On the contrary, they have divine power to demolish strongholds."

REFLECT:

Can you think of a time when you called out to God about something, and He so clearly answered you that you came to know Him better through that experience?

How can the Lord counsel you through prayer?

. . .

How does the statement, "The spirit is willing, but the flesh is weak" relate to your own experiences with prayer?

—✝—

Dear God, thank you that I can ask You for wisdom because I don't want to rely on my own wisdom. Like Hannah and David, I want my prayers to help me to know You better and grow in my intimacy with You. Amen.

10 REASONS WE SHOULD PRAY (PART 3 OF 3)

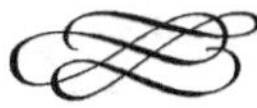

THIS IS THE LAST PART OF THE THREE-part devotion on prayer. Today we will talk about two more reasons why we should pray! I could keep adding more reasons because there are so many more, but I still stop at ten!

I love this quote by Corrie Ten Boom: "The wonderful thing about praying is that you leave a world of not being able to do something and enter God's realm where everything is possible. He specializes in the impossible. Nothing is too great for His Almighty power. Nothing is too small for His love."

9. JESUS SET US AN EXAMPLE THAT WE SHOULD PRAY.

Jesus is the perfect example for us to follow. If in His perfection, He saw the need to pray, how much more do we need to be praying?! Sanctification is the process of our being made more like Christ. Are we praying in the pattern that Christ set for us? Are we following His example out of obedience and to become more like Him?

Luke 5:16- "But Jesus often withdrew to lonely places and prayed."

Mark 1:35- "Very early in the morning, while it was still dark, Jesus got up, left the house, and went off to a solitary place, where he prayed."

Luke 11:1- "One day Jesus was praying in a certain place."

A certain place. That's what the Bible says about where Jesus was praying. It wasn't just any place. It was a certain place He repeatedly went to for prayer. Repeated actions lead to habits, and prayer is definitely a habit we want to establish! Do you have a certain place for prayer? I encourage you to find your own special place to meet with God!

10. WE PRAY TO WORSHIP GOD AND HAVE FELLOWSHIP WITH HIM.

When we love someone, we look forward to spending time with them. We will even rearrange other things on our schedule in order to spend time with that person we love. Do we put that priority on spending time with God, the person we should love above all others? Our actions reveal what we think. It kind of raises red flags when people say they love God but never make time to spend with Him in prayer. God loves spending time with us! God doesn't need us, but He wants us because we bring Him pleasure. He created us for the purpose of having a relationship with Him and to glorify Him through that. When we seek intimacy with Him and worship and praise Him through prayer, we are accomplishing our very purpose in life and bringing Him pleasure!

Isaiah 43:7- "Everyone who is called by my name, whom I created for my glory, whom I formed and made."

John 15:14, 15- "You are my friends if you do what I command. I no longer call you servants, because a servant does not know his master's business. Instead, I have called you friends, for everything that I learned from my Father I have made known to you."

Ephesians 1:5,6- "He predestined us for adoption to sonship through Jesus Christ, in accordance with his pleasure and will to the praise of his glorious grace, which he has freely given us in the One he loves."

As we finish this last part of the discussion on prayer, MY prayer is that you will look forward to that special time with God, both through the continual uplifting of your heart throughout the day and by a planned, intimate time with God in more concentrated prayer. God has sent you an exciting invitation to meet with Him. Are you going to RSVP? Or are you going to miss the party?

The Invitation

An invitation has been given for me to come before
A Holy God, the Risen One, my Savior, Christ the Lord.
What joy awaits unspeakable! And wisdom yet to gain!
What comfort to my heart He brings when I call out His
*　　name!*
What strength to fight the tempter's guiles and boldness to go
*　　tell...*
The way to life is narrow, but how broad the road to hell!
As I lift my heart in worship, I am drawn in deeper still
To know Him and to better see His good and perfect will.
My prayers rise up like incense and my heart bows in
*　　surrender*
To Him, my Mighty Rock, My Peace, My Joy, and Great
*　　Defender!*
Amazing love that ushers us to come sit at His feet
And enter in communion— there's no other joy so sweet!
O Lord, each day remind me there is cause for celebration
When I meet You as You've asked me to, a most treasured
*　　invitation!*

— © 2000 BOBBIE PERKINS

REFLECT:

Try this the next time you are listening to worship music: Don't just sing the words. PRAY the words to the Lord.

Evaluate your prayer life in these areas:

How often you pray.
The attitude of your heart in prayer.
Minimizing distractions.

Persistence in prayer.
Praying to worship and enjoy time with God.
Praying for your country and city.
Praying for others, such as your pastor, church, missionaries, family, and friends.
Praying to confess sin.
Praying for God's will to be done, being willing to surrender your own will.
Praying to gain wisdom and knowledge of God, not just to give Him a grocery list.
Praying with thanksgiving.

—✝—

Dear God, I am sorry that too many times I have "stood you up" in the invitation you have given me to meet with You. Help me to grow in my prayer life, which will help me to grow in my relationship with You. Amen.

GOD ISN'T DONE YET

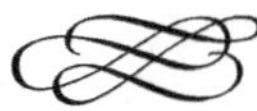

I LEFT FEELING ENCOURAGED AND uplifted. Nope...it wasn't a party. It was a funeral! Virginia lived a full life of 81 years, and to most people, she would appear to be nobody special. She didn't have a college degree. She spent her life as a homemaker and didn't do a lot of the things that impressive people do. BUT...she DID do a lot of things that most people never do.

Her daughter Sheila shared how her Mama used to read the Bible to her so often, painstakingly pointing to each word, that Sheila already knew how to read when she started school. Virginia's other daughter Rita shared what a prayer warrior her Mama was. She told how her Mama would kneel in front of the couch in prayer so much that her knees would become red. Rita laughingly confessed that she would copy her Mama, not so much to be praying, but to make her knees red like her Mama's. She shared how she and Sheila would be lying in bed at night and hear their Mama praying for them in the den, especially on a day when they had bad attitudes. There's nothing like lying in bed, convicted of your sin, hearing your Mama sick Jesus on you!

But Virginia didn't just impact her immediate family. Cousins, nephews, and others talked about the impact she had left on their lives...How she and her husband Jerrell had opened their home to them, told them about Jesus, talked to them about Scripture, and taught them what was right.

She greatly impacted me, too. My family lived across the street. Rita and I were friends, and as a child, I spent many hours at their home. My family didn't go to church, so I heard my first hymns at their house. Virginia had a beautiful voice and loved to sing with her daughters. I was intrigued by the strange lyrics that didn't quite make sense to me. All this talk about the blood of Jesus...what was that all about? But I loved the songs about God's love and how He cares for us.

I remember one day getting excited about what I was learning at my friend's house and going home to tell my parents some of the things our neighbors were telling me about God. But my parents laughed it off. BUT....GOD WASN'T DONE YET.

The seeds of the gospel had been planted in my heart as a child by those sweet neighbors, but it wasn't until years later that other people came along and watered those seeds. When I was 16 years old, I went to a Young Life meeting and finally understood what those songs about the blood meant. I finally understood that Jesus died on the cross FOR ME in order to take the punishment that I deserved, so that I could be declared righteous before God and have a relationship with Him forever. I received the glorious gift of salvation that night, but I knew that God had first begun tugging on my heart when I was a child, listening with a heart full of wonder to my friend's Mama telling me about this God that I did not know. AND GOD WASN'T DONE YET....

God did a great work, but not just in me. My mother later attended Bible study with me and eventually came to know Christ.

She began studying the Bible on her own and became active in church, serving in various capacities. When she got older, she would tell me, "I talk to the Lord all the time." And I would smile as I'd hear her asking Him to help her find something she had misplaced. Eventually her dementia took her mind and her life. But I know where she is. I know I will see her again. And I wonder if that is only true because a neighbor planted some seeds.

So, even though I felt uplifted and encouraged by this funeral, I also felt convicted. I want to have a heart for souls like Ms. Virginia did. I want to care about whether my neighbors and their children know Christ. And I want to plant seeds. Lots of seeds. There are other lives where GOD ISN'T DONE YET.

I was also convicted because I wish I had been that kind of mother to my own children. I wish I had set the same kind of spiritual example to persevere in prayer as Ms. Virginia did. But, you know, it's never too late. And I have grandchildren now to teach. AND... MAYBE...JUST MAYBE...GOD STILL ISN'T DONE YET.

REFLECT:

Is there a neighbor or friend who left a great spiritual impact on you? Why don't you thank them for it?

What kind of seeds can you plant in the lives of your neighbors and their children?

Can you be patient with God's timing—that you may be the one to plant the seeds, while someone else may be the one to reap the harvest?

—✝—

Dear God, Thank you for the people You have sent into my life to impact me spiritually and help me grow. I want to have the same impact on others. Please open my eyes to those opportunities around me and give me the right words to say to draw others to You. Amen.

MORE SPIDERMAN WISDOM

While I was visiting my daughter for the birth of Haven, her new baby girl, I spent a lot of time with my then four-year-old grandson Bryce. We were coloring, which I enjoy, but then Bryce asked me to draw a picture of Spiderman. Confession time…I have absolutely no talent in drawing. NONE! My Spiderman ended up looking like an alien who had surgery.

Bryce solemnly assessed my sad attempt and announced, "Nana, you are not a very good draw-er. But it's okay. You can hold my marker while I draw Spiderman, and I will teach you." I laughed at his honesty, and then the Holy Spirit gave me one of those "Aha!" moments.

The truth was…Bryce had already discovered that most people don't learn by being TOLD how to do something. Instead, he offered to model it for me and let me copy him. When I was homeschooling, I read about learning styles and discovered that the majority of people learn best not by being told how to do something, but by WATCHING OTHERS. I began to think about how much I try to tell my grandson about Jesus and how to live in a way that brings glory to God. No matter how much I verbally teach him, it is by watching how I respond to everyday life that actually teaches him the most about how a Christian should live.

What a sobering truth! Paul knew this when he instructed the church in Corinth to "Follow my example, as I follow the example of Christ" (I Corinthians 11:1). I have always thought that sounded quite bold of Paul to have that much assurance in telling others to follow his example. Doesn't that sound a little overly self-confident? But that's exactly what we are supposed to do with our kids and grand-kids! And they are learning by following our example.

We don't just teach them Bible stories and simple prayers. We love God in ways they can see. We explain that we make certain choices because we want to please God. We model the behaviors but focus on the heart that makes us choose those behaviors. We love and serve others, even those who aren't easy to love. We teach children the spiritual disciplines and habits that help us to grow in Christ. We show humility and ask forgiveness when we don't do it right. We admit we don't know all the answers but explain that the Bible has all the wisdom we need to live a godly life. We trust God when life hurts. And somehow through our imperfect lives that are slowly being changed to be more like Christ, we pray that our children and grandchildren get it. I pray Bryce, Nora, Haven, Lana, Evan, and any other future grandchildren will get it. And I must remember they are following my example.

Yes, church is an important place of learning for a believer. But the family is the primary place of spiritual teaching. It's where we live life. It reminds me of a song by Phillips, Craig, and Dean called, "I want to Be Just Like You." I encourage you to listen to it online because it will encourage you to point your kids to Jesus. The chorus says:

"Lord, I want to be just like You

'Cause he wants to be just like me.
I want to be a holy example
For his innocent eyes to see.
Help me be a living Bible, Lord
That my little boy can read.
I want to be just like You
'Cause he wants to be like me." [1]

Oh, Lord, I want to be just like You. And do a better job at it than I do at drawing Spiderman!

REFLECT:

Are there ways you would live differently if you knew your kids or grandkids would be copying what you do?

What basic truths do you think are most important to teach to your kids or grandkids?

—✝—

Dear God, Help me to live a holy life so that I can leave a positive influence on those to whom I am an example. I want others to be able to look at how I live and know that You are the most important priority in my life. Help me to be more like You. Amen.

---

1. Phillips, Craig and Dean, "I Want To Be Just Like You," Songwriters: William Daniel Dean/Joy D Becker, Dawn Treader Music, 1994.

DRIVING, DIRECTION, AND DECISIONS

OUR FAMILY LOVES TO REMINISCE funny memories of things our kids did or said when they were small. Hannah was (not sure if this is really past tense) our goofiest child, so a lot of those stories stemmed from her antics. One in particular happened at Walt Disney World when she was about five years old.

We were riding Mr. Toad's Wild Ride (it has since been remodeled into The Many Adventures of Winnie the Pooh). The ride featured little cars that traveled along a self-propelled track with crazy twists and turns. Hannah was sitting in the front, clutching the steering wheel, totally stressed out from all the crazy turns. We were talking to her, and she frantically yelled, "Leave me alone! I'm trying to drive!"

We thought it was so funny that she was anxiously working so hard at turning that steering wheel that didn't work. She was so frazzled that the car was moving in the opposite direction of her turns to the steering wheel. Once she understood that the car was in control, she was able to relax, let the car do the work, and enjoy the ride.

Have you ever done that with the Holy Spirit? I sure have. I have this incredible resource of strength, wisdom, and power actually living inside of me, ready to steer me in the right direction if I will only give up the steering wheel. I am a logical thinker, so many times when problems arise, I think I have to figure out all the answers myself. In my own foolish pride, I have often tried to find a solution to a problem that God already had a solution for. Scrambling to fix things, I am white-knuckling the steering wheel and getting more and more off course.

It's a wild ride trusting God. But when I've done it, it's more exhilarating than any roller-coaster I've been on. Even now, God is leading me down a path of trusting Him with a difficult decision. My knee-jerk reaction is to think logically through the pros and cons about which decision is best. But sometimes God calls us to do things that don't seem logical. Sometimes He calls us to trust Him to work out the details when we are looking at that "cons" list. And sometimes He wants to see if we will obey that tiny flicker of light at our feet that shows only the next step before He will illuminate the rest of the path. "Your word is a lamp to my feet and a light to my path," (Psalm 119:105).

I don't know what decision I will make yet. I know that there are Scriptural principles to cover all circumstances of life decisions. Sometimes God gives us more than one equally legitimate option that is within His will. I am praying for the wisdom that God promises to give. "If any of you lacks wisdom, let him ask of God, who gives to all liberally and without reproach, and it will be given to him," (James 1:5). I don't want to make an emotional decision based on what I think I want if that isn't God's plan for me. But I also don't want to make the decision that seems the safest and miss out on seeing God work. I know that I can trust God because He is trustworthy, and He loves me. He will steer me through the twists and turns when I come to Him in prayer with my hands off of the steering wheel.

Through your own twists and turns, who is holding your steering wheel?

"Trust in the Lord with all your heart, and lean not on your own understanding; in all your ways acknowledge Him, and He shall direct your paths," (Proverbs 3:5,6).

REFLECT:

Think of a time when you stepped out in faith. Did it help you learn to trust God more? Did it make it easier to step out in faith the next time?

Who does more of the steering in your life—you or the Holy Spirit?

Has God ever led you to choose the least logical choice in something, but it turned out to be the best decision?

—✝—

Dear God, I want to trust You even when it requires me to step out of my comfort zone. Thank you that you have a good plan for my life. I want You to always be in the driver's seat! Amen.

AUGUST

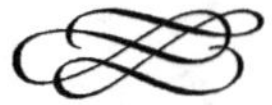

CRACKER CHICKEN TEARS

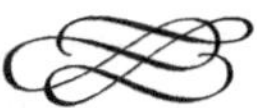

My grandson Bryce, who at the time of my writing this was almost 5 years old, did it yet again. Oh, that sweet boy just warms my heart! He and his Mama were eating leftovers for lunch. Not just any leftovers. Bryce's all-time favorite—cracker chicken! Most people know this as poppyseed chicken casserole, but when a kid says something funny, it sticks.

Bryce quickly cleaned his plate, then asked if he could have some more. Hannah replied, "Well, we don't have any more, but you can have the rest of mine. "No! Mama, no!" He protested with horror, "I can't eat your lunch!" Hannah told him it was fine; she could eat something else. But he didn't understand that she was going to get some other kind of leftovers for herself. As she placed the plate of cracker chicken in front of him, Bryce began to cry.

He cried because he didn't want his Mama to sacrifice something for him. Now, let me clarify…ain't nobody in our family missing any meals! That is obvious by looking at all of us! But that sensitive little boy cried because he thought his Mama might be hungry and was giving her food to him. Wow! How convicting about the sensitivity of my own heart!

If Bryce was shedding tears over his Mama possibly missing one meal (which she wasn't), then how would he react if he realized how many children battle hunger every day? I know my thoughtful, sympathetic grandson would be very upset. Upset enough to want to help them. Probably upset enough to cry.

Bryce does understand that some children are less fortunate, and he has been excited to donate some of his toys to children in need. But he has no idea of the horrors that some children experience. Unfortunately, I see it too often. As a nurse, I have rocked newborn babies who were screaming from the pain of drug withdrawals due to being born to a drug-addicted mother. I often wonder what their lives will be like in the future. I pray for a loving adoptive or foster home for them or for their mother to be able to conquer her addiction. I pray they are able to know their value to God.

There are hungry children in my own city. There are children who are left alone with no food in the house, while their mother is out meeting her drug dealer and their father is in jail. It's not about whether these parents are trying hard enough or making poor choices. It's about children who didn't have a choice. Children who didn't get to choose their life circumstances.

It's a hard world. I pray that this hard world doesn't make me have a hard heart. Jesus ministered to the poor and needy more than any other aspect of the population. I'm not wealthy, but I have enough to share with others and to help others. I pray that God will open my eyes to where, when, and how. I want to care about others. I want to be like Bryce.

Well, no. I want to be like Jesus. But Bryce is reminding me how.

"Speak up for those who cannot speak for themselves, for the rights of all who are destitute. Speak up and judge fairly; defend the rights of the poor and needy," (Proverbs 31:8,9).

The Children

Rejoicing, I knelt down to pray
For my kids the other day.
The ones who give a slobbery kiss,
Weeds picked for me clutched in their fist.
Who spill their milk, draw on the wall,
And throw a tantrum in the mall.
Who pick at dinner, wet their pants,
Are spoiled by me at every chance.
Who race their bikes and skin their knees,
And "need a kiss on boo-boos, please."
Who fuss when told to clean their room
And sing their songs way out of tune.
Who time and time again hereafter
Are quick to frustrate me to laughter.
And likewise, through these growing years,
They've often amused me to tears.
Weeping, I knelt down to pray
For the kids I saw the other day.
Who stared at me through empty eyes,
Longing for someone to sympathize.
Who rarely get a hug or kiss.
Who learn of hate and prejudice.
Who have no bike to ride and race,
And no one who cares to wash their face.
Who will stand tall and learn to fight,
Yet their stomachs growl in bed at night.
They have no rooms to go and clean.
Their little eyes see things obscene
In places I won't dare to go.
This is the only life they know.
Their boo-boos are on the inside.
They patch them up with fierce-like pride.
Yet they'll attach themselves to anyone

Who'll listen to the things they've done.
And one thing that they do not lack-
If you'll only love them, they'll love you back.

— © 1996 BOBBIE PERKINS

REFLECT:

What are some ways you can help the less fortunate?
Consider some of these:

Find your closest food bank at FeedingAmerica.org- you can
donate food, and you can also volunteer!
Volunteer to be a tutor or mentor for a neighborhood child, a
child through YMCA, United Way, or a local school.
Donate through your local utility company to help pay for utilities for those in need.
If you see someone at the grocery store who appears to be
struggling, offer to pay for their groceries.
Get involved in your church's community missions opportunities by donating or serving as a volunteer.
Prayerfully consider becoming a foster parent or adopting a
child who needs a forever family.
Donate clothing, toys, and other items for foster children.
Donate or volunteer at the Salvation Army.
Consider going on a mission trip or helping fund someone
who is going.
Donate money, services, or baby items to a pregnancy resource
center.

"Inasmuch as you did it to one of the least of these My brethren, you
did it to Me," (Matthew 25:40).

—✝—

Dear God, I am grateful for the blessings you have given me. Help me to remember those who live in poverty and have other needs that I could help meet. Give me the compassion of Christ for others and eyes to see the needs they have. Amen.

BACK TO SCHOOL WISDOM

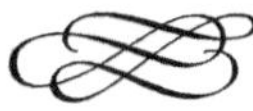

"I sought the Lord, and he answered me; he delivered me from all my fears."

— Psalm 34:4

I LOVE SEEING ALL THE BACK TO school pictures on social media! It's a time of excitement and new beginnings. But it can also be a stressful time for both parents and kids. Buying school supplies and packing lunches. Organizing schedules and changing bedtimes. Helping little ones be brave on their very first day or helping older ones adjust to new schools.

The school year often comes with concerns about keeping kids safe and worries of kids falling behind or getting along with their peers. I will tell you this: your worries won't go away when your kids are grown. You may have thought you will worry less when your kids are "grown-up," but the truth is, you will still worry—you will just have different things to worry about. It is simply our human nature to struggle with worry and fear. It is certainly no coincidence, then, that the words "Fear not" appear in the Bible 365 times! Once for each day!

So how do we calm our fears? David wrote about how he conquered his fears in Psalm 34:4. "I sought the Lord, and he answered me; he delivered me from all my fears." But if you back up a few more verses, David actually started seeking the Lord by praising the Lord. "I will extol the Lord at all times; his praise will always be on my lips. I will glory in the Lord; let the afflicted hear and rejoice. Glorify the Lord with me; let us exalt his name together."

Praising God reminds us of His glorious character—that He is trustworthy and powerful beyond measure. It reminds us to stop scrambling for control of our circumstances and rely on Him. There is just something about seeking the Lord through praise that lightens our mood and our burdens, helping us to release our fears to Him.

Before I switched to homeschooling, my oldest daughter did go to school for a couple of years. I remember worrying about her as she went off for her first day of kindergarten. I had the typical thoughts and worries of a nervous Mama. While she was learning new things in kindergarten, I was learning new things about trusting God with my children. God loves my kids even more than I do. It's hard to imagine, but it's true.

God not only loves my kids, but He also has a plan for their lives to accomplish His purposes in their lives. Psalm 139:16b says, "All the days ordained for me were written in your book before one of them came to be." The word "ordained" means planned, and the Hebrew word "written" here is "kathab," which means "to write," but also means to "prescribe," like a doctor writes a prescription. Doctors write prescriptions for our good, to make us better! I had to let that truth sink in— that God has a good plan for my kids, even better than my plan.

The important thing to note here is that what God sees as good may not always be what I see as good. The hard part is in learning to trust God's good more than my own idea of good. I don't want my kids to struggle to succeed in something. In my eyes, that's not what is good for them. But what if struggling teaches them tenacity? I don't want my kids to have their feelings hurt by other kids, but what if that develops a sensitivity and kindness in them toward others who might feel left out? I want to trust God with them, even when what He chooses is not what I would choose. Because God is always good.

So keep posting pics and praying for your precious kids! The college-age ones, too, because they probably need your prayers the most! And keep releasing them to a faithful God, who loves them even more than you do!

First Day of School

It's your first day of school. I can't believe how you've grown,
But the day had to come. Growing up won't postpone.
Your hair bow is straight. Don't get your dress mussed.
Here is your lunch. Did you get your teeth brushed?
As I watch you get ready, my mind starts to stray,
And I think back to a memory of another first day.
The first time I held you with wonder and pride,
That maternal devotion was born deep inside.
Your fuzzy head snuggled up under my chin,
I knew you were knit to my heart even then.
That love has grown deeper as you've grown through the
*   years,*
And though I'm proud of this milestone, I'm the one plagued
*   with fears!*
Will you be able to keep up with the things you will learn?
Will your teacher encourage you? Will she be patient or stern?
Will you be shy or afraid? Will you come home in tears?
Will some child hurt your feelings? Will you get along with
*   your peers?*
And I can't help but wonder as we get in the car—
How can some strange teacher know how special you are?
The clock ticks by slowly as you're gone, and I wait.
Was it yesterday you kicked me, as I awaited my due date?
Growing up seems to happen overnight in a flash,
But as I pray, the Lord whispers, and I loosen my grasp.
I let go, and I realize that as you go everywhere—
Though I can't always be with you— your God will be there.
I can teach you and guide you to avoid each mistake,

But as you get older, your own choices you'll make.
I pray that those choices will keep you from sin—
That as your love for the Lord grows, you will glorify Him.
I release you today on my knees deep in prayer
To a God all-sufficient in mercy and care.
I guess all moms feel this same protective concern,
But I knew on this school day, I had a lesson to learn!
As I arrive to come get you, does it show on my face?
That God lovingly pruned my new branches in place?
Now I see your hair flying as you run to my side.
"I had so much fun!" you exclaim, your eyes wide.
I glance at your teacher as I hug you so close.
With a nod and a smile, she knows who learned the most.

— © 1997 BOBBIE PERKINS

REFLECT:

Have any of your children ever had a hard experience at school that taught them an important life lesson? Have you?

Can you see the value in letting your children make some mistakes in order for them to learn, or are you constantly rescuing them?

How can you maintain a balance in protecting your kids but also give them room to grow?

—✝—

Dear God, What a comfort it is to know that You have a plan for my kids that is better than anything I would have planned. Help me to have a balance in protecting my kids but also giving them room to make mistakes and grow. I release them to You, trusting You with their future. Amen.

PRO-LIFE ARGUMENTS
AND PRO-CHOICE FRIENDS

> *"Have nothing to do with the fruitless deeds of darkness, but rather expose them."*
> — *Ephesians 5:11*

THE OVERTURNING OF ROE V. WADE was a monumental moment in history. Those of us who value life celebrate the decision that there is now no constitutional right in the United States to have an abortion! But it is also necessary to continue fighting for life because the Supreme Court decision does NOT make abortion illegal. Yes, in some states it is illegal, but even in those states, at this time it is still happening in clandestine ways. In other states, it is not only legal, but also celebrated and flaunted.

Did you know that numerous research studies have found evidence that babies in utero have the structures to feel pain as early as 7 weeks gestation, only 1 week after most women first discover they are pregnant? Did you know that fetal surgeons actually use methods for pain relief when performing surgeries on unborn babies? This is just one of the many bits of evidence that emphasizes that an unborn baby is alive and has rights. (There are many articles, but a particularly good one is "Fetal pain in the first trimester," by Bridget

Thill. It was first published in 2021 and is available from journal-s.sagepub.com).

I could make this an educated argument against abortion. But that isn't the only message I feel burdened to share here. Frankly, my heart IS burdened for those babies. In thinking of that, I want to tell you a story that gave me chill bumps. A friend of mine shared with me the last words that her grandmother said just before she stepped into heaven. Right before she died, this dear woman looked up, widened her eyes, and said, "Look at all the babies!" Then she died. Wow! Have you ever thought about all of the babies that are in heaven? Since abortion became legal in 1973, over 63 million babies have lost their lives through abortion. 63 million!!! Heaven is full of these babies who never saw this earth but are still greatly loved by their Creator.

But the babies are not the only ones I am burdened for. Abortion hurts women. How do I know? Because it hurt me many years ago. Praise be to God that He released me from the chains of that guilt and grief because "He does not treat us as our sins deserve or repay us according to our iniquities. For as high as the heavens are above the earth, so great is his love for those who fear him; as far as the east is from the west, so far has he removed our transgressions from us," (Psalm 103:10-12). I can truly say that I am free from that burden. But, oh, what a heavy burden it was! For many years the guilt and shame of it choked my growth as a Christian. So, dear sister, if abortion is one of the burdens you carry, I encourage you to bring that burden to Jesus. "Come to me, all you who are weary and burdened, and I will give you rest," (Matthew 11:28). Please see Appendix A for helpful resources.

There are other groups of people in the abortion arena who also burden my heart. I pray for the politicians and judges, the doctors and nurses, the clinic owners and employees…but the burden that especially overwhelms my heart is the number of friends I have who support abortion and truly believe they are doing what is right in supporting it. How do I respond to them? That is a question that must be answered by all of us in the pro-life arena. How do we respond as Christ would to the pro-choice world?

"Have nothing to do with the fruitless deeds of darkness, but rather expose them. It is shameful even to mention what the disobedient do in secret. But everything exposed to the light becomes visible—and everything that is illuminated becomes a light," (Ephesians 5:11-13).

What does that verse say about how we should respond to sin? Expose darkness. Bring light. When we bring light, the darkness becomes visible, and when it is illuminated, it changes to light. We must bring people to the light of Christ because the light of the Holy Spirit is the only true means of change for the human heart. I have to ask myself if I am fighting as hard for the souls of people as I am for the pro-life agenda. Yes! Fight for life! But I must not forget the souls within the people I am speaking to. So as I have conversations with people, I have to be careful to speak truth both boldly and in love. For that is how Jesus always confronted sin.

Roe v. Wade

The pro-choice crowd clamors and tries to convince,
Planting fear and confusion over recent events.
They claim to care about women and to be their ally,
But women's rights never means that their babies should die.
We can protest and argue till we're blue in the face,
But at the end of the day, when each side has made its case,
Are we just fighting and causing a wider divide?
Do we poison the gospel with our hatred and pride?
We don't have to be silent! We must fight for what's right!
For darkness fades only when exposed to the light.
We should refuse to be bullied by those who oppose us,
But are we still telling others of the love that God shows us?
If opposers spew hatred or are simply misled,
Do we respond in like manner or with Christ's love instead?
The reason for babies being murdered and tossed
Is that hearts have no knowledge of the work of the cross.
We can't expect for the lost to see the truths that we do

When their lens to the world has no God in its view.
I'll keep fighting for life and speak truth even more
But examine my heart's goal to love and restore.
Dobbs versus Jackson is a victory- that's true!
But abortion is still legal in many states to pursue.
Our fight isn't over; this is where the work starts!
We battle in courtrooms, but the war is won in hearts.
I want to think on this issue with the mind of my Savior
With words fitly spoken for His glory and favor.
At the cross Jesus looked on the repentant assassin
And offered him paradise with love and compassion.

— © 2022 BOBBIE PERKINS

Reflect:

Do you feel you can make an educated argument to defend the sanctity of life? If not, See Appendix A for resources.

How can you defend the unborn yet respond to abortion supporters the way Jesus would?

What do you think would help change a person's mind about life if they are currently in favor of abortion?

What are some things you can do to take a stand for life?

—✝—

Dear God, Forgive us as a nation for our complacency in the face of evil. Help me to do my part to protect the unborn by educating myself and supporting pro-life legislation. Help me to approach those who support abortion with both boldness and love, knowing the gospel is the greatest changer of hearts. Amen.

ONCE AND FOR ALL

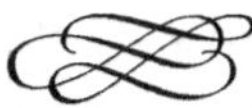

IT WAS JUST A TINY CORNER. NOBODY else even knew about it. But God did. He asked me for it, but I didn't want to give it to Him. And I'm ashamed to say that this was not when I was a teenager. It was about eight or nine years ago. But God got my attention in a way that only He can …

I love music. And I like all different kinds of music. I have thousands of songs on my phone- from about every genre…. you could name a song, and I probably have the song on my phone. My husband hates listening to my playlists because he says they are too schizophrenic. His brain can't change gears that fast from "How Great Thou Art" to "Play that Funky Music White Boy." Lol!

A long time ago, I had removed a lot of songs from my collection because they contained elements that I didn't feel were pleasing to the Lord, whether it was language, subject matter, or the artists themselves. But I held onto a few select songs that I should have deleted. I rationalized that I really liked the beat in those particular songs because they were great for when I was exercising. I self-justified that they weren't that bad, and I had at least gotten rid of the worst songs. Besides, those worst songs were still tamer than other people's music. But God kept asking me for those few other songs. And I'm stubborn and willful and didn't want to give them up. Enter now…. God's sense of humor.

I was driving to the gym to exercise. I wanted to listen to some of those upbeat songs to get my energy level boosted. But for SOME reason, I couldn't get my car to play those particular songs from my phone. It kept giving me an error message, saying, "indexing device." Frustrated, I yanked the phone cord out of my car. It immediately switched over to the radio, which was on the K-Love Christian radio station. And for the first time, I heard Lauren Daigle's song "Once and for All," knowing it was God's special message to my heart. This wasn't about music. It was about the idol of autonomy in my heart. I had to ask myself some questions, and I encourage you to ask yourself the same questions.

Who or what rules my life? Is it God, is it me, or even something else? Is there anything in my life that I put before God? Am I willing to obey God even when I don't want to? And if I don't want to, why is that? Do I compare myself to others so that my sin doesn't look so bad, or do I look to Scripture for my standard? Do I live in a way that shows God has called me to a holy love, or does He have just a corner in my heart? Does my heart exalt Him as worthy of my complete devotion? Is there anything I partake of that I would not partake of if Jesus were sitting next to me in the flesh? (Because the truth is, He is present everywhere, all the time…in fact, He lives in me through the Holy Spirit).

John makes an interesting closing statement in 1 John 5:21. He says, "Dear children, keep yourselves from idols." That seems random because nowhere in John's letter does he talk about carved images. What are the idols of which he is speaking? There is no mention at all of pagan gods, such as Baal worship, etc. in the book of I John. Using Scripture to answer Scripture, we find a clue: "…the Israelites set up idols in their hearts…" (Ezekiel 14:4). A closer look at I John reveals that John was indeed talking about idols of the heart. He wrote about righteousness, habitual sin, and the enemy who wants to control us. If Satan can get us to worship anything other than God by setting up false idols in our hearts, then he has accomplished his goal in our lives. Idol worship isn't just bowing to a statue. Worship is from the heart, and anything that turns our hearts away from obeying and glorifying God, anything that takes preeminence over Him in our lives—THAT is an idol. I have often had to do battle with the idol of rebellion in my heart—the desire to make my own rules. What seems so trivial can be the root of something pervasively sinister.

It's probably not music for you, but I'm sure you've struggled with your own idols of the heart. Maybe you are overly concerned about the opinions of other people, being liked and accepted by them. Society calls that codependency. The Bible calls it sin. "Fear the Lord your God, serve him only..." (Deuteronomy 6:13). Maybe it's having a proud, argumentative spirit. Society calls that being assertive. The Bible calls it sin. "Sin is not ended by multiplying words, but the prudent hold their tongues (Proverbs 10:19). Maybe it's addiction to Facebook, TikTok, drugs, alcohol, pornography, shopping, food, ANYTHING that you are not willing to lay down for the sake of God's glory in your life—that, my friend, is an idol. "So whether you eat or drink or whatever you do, do it all for the glory of God," (I Corinthians 10:31).

I had to lay down my silly idol. And the funny thing about it? I don't even remember the names of those songs that I clung to. But I do remember the song God used to convict me...see the lyrics below. (Isn't it funny that God used music to convict me about music?)

Once and For All

God I give You all I can today
These scattered ashes that I hid away
I lay them all at Your feet
From the corners of my deepest shame
The empty places where I've worn Your name

Show me the love I say I believe
Oh Help me to lay it down
Oh Lord I lay it down
Oh let this be where I die
My Lord with Thee crucified
Be lifted high as my Kingdom's fall
Once and for all, once and for all
There is victory in my Saviors loss
And in the crimson flowing from the cross
Pour over me, pour over me yes
Oh, let this be where I die
My Lord with Thee crucified
Be lifted high as my Kingdom's fall
Once and for all, once and for all.
Oh Lord I lay it down
Oh Lord I lay it down
Help me to lay it down
Oh Lord I lay it down
Oh let this be where I die
My Lord with Thee crucified
Be lifted high as my Kingdoms fall
Once and for all
Once and for all
Oh once and for all
Once and for all. [1]

I still have a variety of music on my phone. After all, I grew up in the 80's, and we had all the greatest rock bands! But the songs I tend to keep adding to my phone are Christian songs because those are the

---

1. Lauren Daigle, "Once and For All," Songwriters: Lauren Ashley Daigle/Paul Brandon Mabury/Paul T. Duncan, Capital CMG Publishing, Essential Music Publishing, 2015.

lyrics that especially speak to my heart. My heart...that is gradually being more and more overtaken by His rule, as my kingdoms fall. Once and for all. Once and for all.

"But in your hearts revere Christ as Lord..." (I Peter 3:15).

REFLECT:

Is there an idol in your life you need to lay down?

Has God ever used a creative way of convicting you about sin?

Are you able to look back on your life and see how God has brought conviction about things that in the past would have seemed insignificant, but that now show His gentle process of refining in your life?

⁓✝⁓

Dear God, Thank you that You don't leave me like I was when you saved me and that You are so gentle with the gradual process of conforming me to the image of Christ. I have so far to go, but I am grateful for the glimpses You show me of the progress. I want to lay it all down before You, once and for all. Amen.

HOW CAN WE HAVE
HOPE IN SUFFERING?

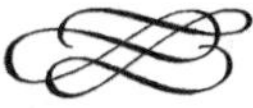

"And the God of all grace, who called
you to his eternal glory in Christ,
after you have suffered a little
while, will himself restore you and
make you strong, firm and steadfast."

— 1 Peter 5:10

"Suffering is either having something you don't want or not having
something you do."
-Elisabeth Elliot

As believers, we often have trouble reconciling suffering. In looking at the horrific suffering of a fellow believer or experiencing it personally, have you ever struggled with these types of thoughts?— "God is fully in control, so if He's allowing this, He is cruel and can't be good." Or "God must not love me or is punishing me." Or "I know that God is good. So this suffering must be from the enemy because God wouldn't allow this to happen to someone who loves Him."

It is true that all suffering began from the enemy. Man's decision to rebel in the garden opened the floodgate of suffering, pain, and death for all future generations. So, in that sense—yes, suffering is from the enemy. But it's not true that God doesn't allow suffering in the lives of people who love Him. The enemy uses this lie to make us question God's love for us. We only have to look at the lives of early believers to see that they endured unimaginable suffering. The apostle Paul describes his suffering and tells us, "In fact, everyone who wants to live a godly life in Christ Jesus will be persecuted...but as for you, continue in what you have learned and have become convinced of..." (2 Timothy 3:12-14). What is it that they were convinced of?

They were convinced of the sovereignty of God. They were convinced of the goodness of God. And they understood that those two things can coexist even in the midst of suffering. They understood that God very often uses suffering for our ultimate good.

Joseph is one of my favorite people in the Bible. His unwavering faith despite difficulties shows that He understood that God uses suffering for His divine purposes. Joseph was sold into slavery by his own brothers. His integrity won him favor, and he became an attendant of Potiphar, one of Pharaoh's officials. Yet he experienced numerous trials, including false imprisonment. He was eventually released from prison and given charge over all the food sources, which saved the lives of many people during a famine. Despite the injustices he experienced, Joseph held no animosity toward his brothers and trusted God throughout his trials. He understood the concept of God using our suffering for good as he told his brothers, "You intended to harm me, but God intended it for good to accomplish what is now being done, the saving of many lives," (Genesis 50:20).

You may think, "Well, that's great for Joseph. But what about me? What about my loved one? I don't see any good coming out of our suffering. Does God not see me? Does God not care? Where is the good? How can I have hope?"

We CAN have hope in taking these things to a God that we can't fully understand. There is nothing wrong with taking the questions and cries of our soul to God. It may seem sacrilegious to bring our doubts and questions to God, but it is actually an act of faith to do it. We are acknowledging that God is trustworthy with our deepest doubts and sorrows. We want to be like Joseph, to SEE the good that is coming from our suffering. But God doesn't promise that we will see it. God doesn't always give us the reason why. There is no indication in the Bible that Job ever found out why he endured such suffering. It is presumptuous for us to demand from God the answer to the why. Some things are not meant for us to know. It was that thirst for forbidden knowledge in the garden of Eden that brought suffering to mankind in the first place. "The secret things belong to God," (Deuteronomy 29:29).

Instead of focusing on the why, let's focus on the Who. God is sovereignly in control over even our suffering. Even when we don't know why, we can trust that God is good and trustworthy because Scripture gives us truths about His character. Instead of searching for the why of suffering, next time search for the promises that help us walk through the suffering. Search for the extra measure of God's presence that walks with us in a deeper way as we turn to Him in our suffering. God wants us to bring our questions to Him rather than countering them with our own intellect. When we open our hearts to Him in faith, He strengthens our faith to the point of admitting that we don't have to know; we don't have to understand, but we will still love and trust Him in faith because we know that He is good. And therein is the good for us. **The strengthening of our faith is always a good that comes from suffering.** "Consider it pure joy, my brothers and sisters, whenever you face trials of many kinds, because you know that the testing of your faith produces perseverance. Let perseverance finish its work so that you may be mature and complete, not lacking anything," (James 1:2-4). I want my faith to mature. But sometimes I fight the process that God must use to get me there.

BUT instead of fighting the process, if in the darkest hours of wrestling with your pain…if you stop trying to NOT feel the pain but instead invite God into it, there is a special intimacy with Him that comes from that. David describes this in Psalm 42. He talks of his tears day and night and how other people are even saying that God has deserted him. But his pain caused him to write, "As the deer pants for streams of water, so my soul pants for you, my God. My soul thirsts for God…put your hope in God, for I will yet praise him. My soul is downcast within me; therefore I will remember you…why, my soul are you downcast? Why so disturbed within me? Put your hope in God, for I will yet praise him, my Savior and my God," (Psalm 42 excerpts). **David's desperate need caused him to hunger for God more. And that is good.**

When we wonder why God isn't doing anything about our suffering or about the evil in the world, we can rest in the certainty that He already has. We can look to the cross and know that He has redeemed our suffering. He has put an end to all evil by sending His Son to bear the iniquity of us all. God has already put an end to all pain and suffering. We are just in the waiting room for the culmination of that work. What a glorious assurance we have in the certainty of that hope! We have a hope that triumphs over death, sin, and suffering. We long for Christ's return with the eternal perspective of seeing an end to the grief and evil of this world. "For our light and momentary troubles are achieving for us an eternal glory that far outweighs them all. So we fix our eyes not on what is seen, but on what is unseen, since what is seen is temporary, but what is unseen is eternal," (2 Corinthians 4:17,18).

Our grief is not sin, but it's also not a license to sin. We have to be willing to let grief do its work in us. "Search me, God, and know my heart; test me and know my anxious thoughts. See if there is any offensive way in me, and lead me in the way everlasting," (Psalm 139:23,24). We can ask God to help us discern if we are letting our emotions lead us toward sinful thinking. Next time we have thoughts of "This isn't the way it should be" or "This isn't fair," we can change those thoughts to "This is what God has ordained for me." We can ask God to help us trust His will and His goodness. We can rejoice and be sorrowful at the same time. And God is there in the midst of it.

Roots of Faith

Lord, like a knife this hurt has come
To slice me to the core.
I'm so overwhelmed by pain
I can't see You anymore.
I can't see the Good, Good Father.
I just see shock and disbelief.
I want to trust You, but it's hard
When I'm drowning in my grief.
I believe you really love me,
But I just don't understand
How Your sovereign will allowed this
To pass right through Your hand.
You could have stopped this if You wanted to.
You have that power and control,
But for some yet unknown reason,
You allowed this pain to pierce my soul.
That knowledge almost angers me.
I feel the rebellion well within
And fight that bitter, stubborn spirit
That will lead my heart toward sin.
Instead, I turn my heart to Jesus
And cling to what I know.
Secure in my salvation,
I should use this time to grow.
For you know when I am hurting,
And I feel that all is lost,
I shed my stubborn independence
And fall, broken, at the cross.
I will trust my Good, Good Father
To complete His work in me.
For, God, you know things I don't know
And see things I can't see.
So I'll stop asking you for knowledge, Lord,

That's too heavy for me to hold
And trust You when life makes no sense,
To take my heart to shape and mold.
In the journey through this process,
My roots of faith grow deep and strong
When cries of pain are transformed to
A symphony of song.

— © 2000 BOBBIE PERKINS

REFLECT:

Have you ever been angry at God for something He allowed to happen?

Has God ever used suffering to draw you closer to Him?

Are there any "Whys?" you need to lay at the foot of the cross right now?

—✝—

Dear God, Suffering is not something I would ever choose for my life, but I understand that it is a crucial tool to help me grow closer to You. I want to be cooperative and responsive to the things You allow into my life, even when it's hard. Thank You that in all things You are my hope. Amen.

HEINIE HAZARDS

WE ALL HAVE THOSE FUNNY FAMILY memories that are a source of laughter every time the story gets retold. An incident that happened with my daughter Regan is one of those funny memories.

Regan was 4 years old when we went to Disney. We were at the water park, leisurely enjoying floating on the lazy river. We came around a curve and spotted a cute little sign that said, "Sharks ahead" with a picture of a cartoon shark on it. Regan became terrified that there were sharks in that lazy river. It is hard to describe what she did next, but she somehow managed to travel the rest of the way around that lazy river lying on the donut float screaming while holding her heinie really high up so that it wouldn't be hanging down into the water. She was going to make sure that no sharks could bite her in the booty! We tried to convince her that no sharks were there, but she had her own understanding of the circumstances and was convinced that we just didn't know about the dangers ahead. We were obviously poor deluded adults who had no idea of the imminent peril we would be experiencing.

I wonder how a four-year-old can think she knows more than an adult....

...until I think about times I have acted like I know more than God. Oh, I would never actually say it or consciously even think it, but there have been times in my life when I have looked at a situation and thought surely I would have done things differently.

I wouldn't have allowed a seventeen-year-old athletic girl to have a diving accident that left her a quadriplegic...

But God did...and the world has been encouraged and inspired by Joni Eareckson Tada.

I wouldn't have allowed a twelve-year-old girl to contract Lyme's disease that would make her suffer excruciating pain and eventually be bedridden for the rest of her life...

But God did...and my dear friend Lisa Marie Angotti has taught friends, family, and strangers about what it means to trust God in the midst of suffering.

I wouldn't have allowed a precious two-year-old girl to lose her life in the church parking lot as a car ran over her tiny body...

But God did...and her mother, Lilly Minor, who is my dearest friend, taught me about joy in the midst of sorrow and how God's sovereignty and goodness always coexist, even when I don't understand.

I don't have to understand it all. But I have learned to trust God because He knows more than I do. I can trust that He is good even if I never see the good played out in the tragedies I see. I know that in my own life, the good has often been intangible spiritual growth. Romans 8:28 tells us that because we love God, "He works all things for the good." What is that good? It's in the next verse. "To be conformed to the image of His Son." Sometimes we must go through sorrow to become more like Christ.

I trust God a lot more now than I did when I was young. And if He tells me there are sharks in the water, I'm going to be holding my heinie up! He knows what He is doing!

REFLECT:

Can you think of situations in your own life or in the lives of others where good came from a bad situation?

If you were to experience a tragedy and never saw anything good come out of it, can you still trust that God is good?

What lessons has God taught you from your own tragedies?

✝

Dear God, You are holy, righteous, and good. I trust You because You alone are the all-knowing One who holds all wisdom. Help me to trust You even in sorrow and surrender myself to You, knowing that I don't have to understand it all because I can trust You. Amen.

15 THINGS JESUS ACCOMPLISHED ON EARTH

> *"The Son is the image of the invisible God, the firstborn over all creation."*
> — Colossians 1:15

GOD CAN USE ANYTHING TO encourage us when we are looking for Him. It was just a stray sandal. I saw it lying in the road, missing its mate, as I drove to work this week. It looked like the kind Jesus would have worn. It made me think of Jesus walking this earth and the purposes He fulfilled.

That simple sandal was kind of like God's message to me, "I was there. I walked the earth in human flesh. I changed everything."

Jesus does change everything. He was here physically. And He is still here, living inside every believer through the Holy Spirit. The redemption of mankind is His greatest gift to us, the greatest gift anyone could ever give us. But have you ever thought about the fact that He came for even more than that incredible gift?

Why did the God of all creation leave heaven, dress Himself in humanity, and humble Himself to experience our struggles, to suffer, and to die? Could He not have just come and died for us right away? To technically fit the description of a spotless sin offering, He could have died at a younger age, as a child or in adolescence. What else was significant about His thirty-three years? What else was He accomplishing? The following is definitely not an all-inclusive list, but it is a reminder that Jesus came to earth to accomplish many things. Yes, He changed everything, bringing life to all those who believe.

15 THINGS JESUS ACCOMPLISHED ON EARTH

1. TO TEACH- (Mark 6:34) "When Jesus landed and saw a large crowd, he had compassion on them, because they were like sheep without a shepherd. So he began teaching them many things."

2. TO SHOW COMPASSION AND DEMONSTRATE HIS POWER BY HEALING THE SICK- (Matthew 15:30) "And large crowds came to Him, bringing with them those who were lame, crippled, blind, mute, and many others, and they laid them down at His feet; and he healed them."

3. TO EXPERIENCE TEMPTATIONS AND STRUGGLES IN ORDER TO UNDERSTAND OURS- (Hebrews 4:15) "For we do not have a high priest who is unable to empathize with our weaknesses, but we have one who has been tempted in every way, just as we are—yet he did not sin."

4. TO BRING ABUNDANT LIFE- (John 10:10) "I have come that they may have life, and have it to the full."

5. TO BUILD THE CHURCH- (Matthew 16:18) "And on this rock I will build my church."

6. TO DESTROY THE WORK OF THE DEVIL- (1 John 3:8) "The reason the Son of God appeared was to destroy the devil's work."

7. TO REVEAL HYPOCRISY AND TEACH TRUE WORSHIP- (Mark 7:6b,7) "These people honor me with their lips, but their hearts are far from me. They worship me in vain; their teachings are merely human rules."

8. TO OPEN EYES THAT ARE BLIND- (Isaiah 42:7) "I will make you…to open eyes that are blind."
9. TO SET THE CAPTIVES FREE- (Isaiah 42:7) "I will make you…to free captives from prison."
10. TO SET AN EXAMPLE FOR US- (Mark 1:35) "Very early in the morning, while it was still dark, Jesus got up, left the house and went off to a solitary place, where he prayed."
11. TO BRING SALVATION TO THE GENTILES- (Acts 28:28) "Therefore I want you to know that God's salvation has been sent to the Gentiles, and they will listen!"
12. TO ESTABLISH HIS AUTHORITY OVER ALL CREATION- (Matthew 8:27) "The men were amazed and asked, 'What kind of man is this? Even the winds and waves obey him!' "
13. TO SHOW US WHAT GOD IS LIKE- (Colossians 1:15) "The Son is the image of the invisible God, the firstborn over all creation."
14. TO GIVE US HOPE IN ETERNAL LIFE- (Romans 6:8,9) "Now if we died with Christ, we believe we will also live with him. For we know that since Christ was raised from the dead, he cannot die again; death no longer has mastery over him."
15. TO RECONCILE A WORLD BROKEN BY SIN- (2 Corinthians 5:19) "That God was reconciling the world to himself in Christ, not counting people's sins against them. And he has committed to us the message of reconciliation."

God has commissioned believers as His ambassadors to this same ministry of reconciliation. "We are therefore Christ's ambassadors, as though God were making his appeal through us. We implore you on Christ's behalf: Be reconciled to God" (2 Corinthians 5:20).

"Implore" is a strong word. It means to beg or plead. Are we just as strongly begging people to come to Christ as if their very life depended on it? Because their eternal life does.

Are we telling people about all the things that Jesus did? We certainly are quick to update our friends on the latest accomplishments of our kids or what some celebrity or political figure did. Do we talk about Jesus just as much?

Are we imploring people to agree with our political party or to try the newest restaurant in town? What would the world be like if, in the same way, we were imploring them to be changed completely by a God who loves them?

What are we talking to people about? We talk about what we think about it. Are we thinking about our Savior throughout the day? Are we really telling people about Jesus? He did many things. John 21:25 says, "Jesus did many other things as well. If every one of them were written down, I suppose that even the whole world would not have room for the books that would be written."

The lost world doesn't need to know every little thing that Jesus did. But they do need to know that Jesus is the only way for sinful man to go from being alienated from God to becoming an heir of God. And THAT is what we should be talking about.

REFLECT:

Which accomplishments on that list of things Jesus did means the most to you?

Do you ever have spiritual conversations with your friends when you are not deliberately sharing the gospel? Try brainstorming some creative ways to turn conversations toward spiritual things.

Make an effort to look for Jesus throughout your day, as seeing that sandal in the road brought my thoughts to Him.

—✝—

Dear God, You are incredible beyond words. Help me to look for You throughout my day and to talk about You with others. Help me to be more excited about Jesus than I am in the things of this world. Let others see Jesus in me. Amen.

UNREACHED BUT NOT UNREACHABLE

I'VE HAD THE PRIVILEGE OF KNOWING some families who have provided foster care for a number of children. What a challenging ministry! It takes a lot of patience and understanding to help kids who have been hurt by hard circumstances in life. My husband and I have never been foster parents, but we did act as temporary guardians for a troubled teenager for about two years. It was a friend of a friend kind of situation, and we were saddened to hear that nobody in her family was able to take responsibility for her care. We thought that by providing her with a stable home, we might be able to help her.

It was a much harder task than we expected. We had none of the training that foster parents receive. Her grandmother retained custody but assigned us legal guardianship, and we were off on a new adventure! We tried to treat her the same way we did our own children. We made sure she had more than she needed, including a big birthday party with plenty of gifts, and all the clothing necessities she could need. I had no clue how to fix hair for black girls, so I paid my friend's daughter to braid her hair regularly. I tried to cook foods that she liked. We added her to our car insurance and began to teach her how to drive. We had some fun together, but more often than not, she stayed in trouble. I didn't understand her obsession with stealing things, and many of our friends had things come up missing after she had been around them—wallets, cash, cell phones, movies and video games, electronic devices, etc.

Aware that she had suffered much family hurt, I took her to counseling. We taught her about God's love and got her involved in our church. We tried EVERYTHING to try to connect with her, but she pushed us away and fell further and further into rebellion. We gave her ultimatums regarding her behavior, but she continued to ignore the rules. She began sneaking out at night while we were sleeping, meeting up with questionable friends, doing drugs, breaking into apartments, and making many other rebellious choices. It came to the point where I was spending so much time dealing with her, that my youngest daughter's schoolwork began to suffer (we were a home-school family).

We made the difficult decision to contact her grandmother and tell her we could no longer allow her to live in our home. She ended up going into foster care, and later, jail. I don't know where she is today, but I hope that someone has been able to help her.

I struggled when she left our home. Didn't we do everything God wanted us to do? We tried to love her, but she just pushed our love away! She chose to steal, living like a pauper, when we were willing to shower her with anything she truly needed. She preferred rebellion to obedience and refused the love we tried to offer. I questioned God, asking Him what we had done wrong. As I grieved for this young girl whom we had invested so much time and energy into but had been unable to reach, God had a message for me. He showed me that I was no different from her. God had done all of those things for me, and I had responded to Him in the exact same way that she had to me. He gave me love but I pushed Him away. He called me to obedience, but I chose rebellion. I was living like a pauper when He wanted to give me riches. I had closed my heart to the gospel.

And I began to see....

I began to see that God isn't finished with her yet. Maybe I was just called to plant those first seeds. And I pray that in time, she will open her heart to the One who can love her in a way that nobody else ever has. I pray that someone can reach her for the gospel, even if it isn't me. There is still hope for her.

Because we are more alike than I realized. And hope got through to me.

REFLECT:

Have you ever given up on someone whom you thought was unreachable? Is anyone really unreachable for God?

Are you willing to do the hard work of tilling the hard ground and planting the first seeds, even if you don't get to see the harvest?

Can you see glimmers of yourself in some of the people you may see as difficult?

⁓✝⁓

Dear God, Loving like Jesus is sometimes hard. Help me to patiently serve others out of obedience and love for You, even when I don't see a result. Help me to see with Your eyes, that nobody is unreachable. Amen.

MY REFUGE

My one-year-old granddaughter Lana has terrible "stranger-danger." It is so bad, she won't even let her aunts or grandfather hold her. It took her a while to decide I was okay, but she used to cry even if I got too close. Whenever she is afraid, she goes running straight to her Daddy. He is her strong protector who comforts her and makes her feel safe.

God gives us the body of Christ for many reasons, one being a supportive network for comfort and encouragement. But how many times do we go running to our friends with our fears and problems instead of going to our Father? I remember a specific time when I had a problem and called a friend because I was sure I had figured out a way to fix the problem, and it would involve her help. I was in mid-sentence with her when I suddenly felt a stab from the Holy Spirit. "Sheila, I'm so sorry," I confessed in embarrassment. "I don't know why I'm coming to you with this when I haven't even prayed about it yet!" I realized that I was trying to fix the problem instead of asking God what He wanted me to do about it. It ended up that the solution to the problem was not the direction I had been heading toward. I'm glad the Holy Spirit gave me a swift elbow to the side before I made a big mistake!

The same kind of situation can happen in grief as well. Believers should lift up other believers who are grieving. Scripture tells us to "mourn with those who mourn" (Romans 12:15) and to "comfort those in any trouble with the comfort we ourselves receive from God," (2 Corinthians 2:3,4). But there is a time during the grieving process when God wants us to come all alone...to HIM alone for comfort. There is a holy time during grief when our Father comforts us in a way that only He can. Friends are beautiful examples of love to us, but nobody understands our heart like God does. There is something about fear and pain that drives us to the heart of the Father, and that is where He wants us to run. He is our Healer, our Comforter, our Protector, and so much more.

It's ok to talk to your friends. But make sure you're talking to God, too. He is our "refuge and strength, an ever-present help in trouble," (Psalm 46:1).

My Refuge

I hear the taunting
Of memories haunting.
Lord, my heart cries out to You.
Can there be healing
From the pain I am feeling?
I thought that these hurts were all through!
Lord, you alone are my refuge.
I seek solace in Your Holy Word.
I can't even put words to my heart thoughts,
But in You every prayer has been heard.
Oh, Lord, how I long for a "soul-mate,"
Yet my feelings are so hard to share.

Then I'm reminded Your love is unfailing.
YOU'RE my rock who will always be there.
So I praise You, my God of salvation.
I will trust You through bittersweet tears,
And as Your grace brings a cleansing within me,
I'll rejoice as Your healing appears.

— © 1998 BOBBIE PERKINS

REFLECT:

Is it easier for you to run to friends for comfort instead of God? Or do you find it hard to confide in friends?

Have you ever tried to fix a problem without consulting God, only to have it turn out badly?

How has God been your Rock?

—✝—

Dear God, I want to come running to You before I go to anyone else for comfort or help. You are the only One who sees my heart and understands it. Help me to release my desire for control to You and ask You for guidance before going off in my own direction. Amen.

LESS THAN

I RECENTLY HAD THE PRIVILEGE OF helping with a retreat for women who have abortion in their past. It was a time of raw emotions of every spectrum—grief, anger, shame, hope, joy, peace, and so much more. Their stories were all different but amazingly similar in the struggles that each woman wrestled with.

One of the common threads women always share is the feeling of being "less than." Comparing themselves to other women in their church, they often feel less worthy to serve, less respected, less beautiful, less righteous, less whole. LESS THAN.

Oh, how I can relate to that feeling of less than! I remember when my pastor's wife first asked me to lead a women's Bible study at our church. She did not yet know about my past abortion, so I felt compelled to tell her. She obviously didn't know I wasn't as squeaky clean as some of those other women. Surely there would be a moment of uncomfortable back-pedaling, and she would politely but awkwardly tell me that she was sure she could find somebody else.

But that didn't happen. I summed up my confession to her with the words, "So I just don't think I could ever be a sedate church lady." What I was actually saying was, "I can never measure up to those other women because of my past." I will never forget her reply! She emphatically said, "I don't want you to be a sedate church lady! You are exactly what we need!"

It was a simple conversation, but it was a turning point for me. Even though I had already experienced a significant amount of growth and healing before that, it wasn't until that day that I was able to embrace my identity in Christ at a deeper level. I discovered the truth of Colossians 3:3, "For you died, and your life is now hidden with Christ in God." To me, that is one of the most incredible verses in the Bible!

The old me died, and I was raised to a new life. But it wasn't a new life that was a better version of myself. My life is hidden IN CHRIST. Because Christ lives in me, when God looks at me, HE SEES THE RIGHTEOUSNESS OF CHRIST! It doesn't get any better than that! When God looks at me, He sees the same level of righteousness as He does when He sees those other church ladies or my pastor's wife... because my life is hidden—God sees the righteousness of Christ instead of me!

I don't struggle with comparing myself to other women anymore. Well, actually today I did tell a friend that I am dorkier than she is... But I digress....

Why does the enemy work so hard to make us feel less than? One reason is that a defeated Christian isn't exactly a glowing advertisement to draw other people toward Christ. But there was another reason for me. If I thought of myself as less-than, then I would only expect myself to have a less-than walk with the Lord. It's not that I was living in any blatant sin, but living a life of holiness seemed too lofty to reach if I didn't see the holiness God had already given me through Christ. Finding my identity in Christ made me desire to live in a way that glorifies God. And I began to serve Him from my identity instead of for my identity.

Those sedate church ladies? I found out they have struggles, too.

Their sin may be different, but the pain from sin wounds all of us. Don't fool yourself into thinking there is respectable sin on one end and ostracizing sin on the other. All sin ostracizes us from God. The sedate church ladies, the choir director, even the pastor…they are all ostracized from God apart from Christ. "But God demonstrates his own love for us in this: While we were still sinners, Christ died for us," (Romans 5:8).

If you are still carrying that burden, you don't have to. Romans 8:1 says, "Therefore, there is now no condemnation for those who are in Christ Jesus." If you have questions, please read Appendix B. If you are hurting from a past abortion, please read Appendix A also!

I may be a church lady, but I'll never be sedate. Jesus wasn't exactly sedate either!

REFLECT:

Do you struggle with things in your past that make you feel like a second-class Christian?

How can mature believers help women who are struggling with these types of feelings?

Have you ever been hesitant to serve because you felt you weren't "good enough?"

─✝─

Dear God, What an amazing thought that when You look at me, You see the righteousness of Christ instead of my past! Thank You for that cleansing blood. What an affront to You that after such a great sacrifice I would still choose to live in condemnation! Thank You for setting me free from that, and please help me to walk in that freedom every day. Amen.

SEPTEMBER

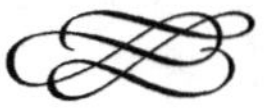

WHAT IS THE LIE?

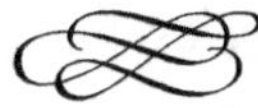

> *"The heavens declare the glory of God; the skies proclaim the work of his hands."*
>
> — Psalm 19:1

"THE HEAVENS DECLARE THE GLORY OF God; the skies proclaim the work of his hands," (Psalm 19:1). Despite the visible evidence of a Creator, the number of people who identify themselves as atheists has drastically risen in recent years. According to Gallup polls in the 1950s and 1960s, 98% of Americans expressed a belief in God. However, a recent study revealed that today 28% of U.S. adults are religiously unaffiliated (indifferent), 4% identify as atheist, and 5% identify as agnostic.[1]

We wonder how in the world could this shift have happened?

God has made it plain to all of mankind that He does indeed exist. Creation itself testifies that there is a Creator, so that people are without an excuse for their disbelief (Romans 1:20).

---

1. "Reviving Evangelism:Current Realities That Demand a New Vision for Sharing Faith," 2019. www.accessbarna.com

So why do people not believe if creation is shouting the existence of God? Scripture explains it plainly.

Romans chapter 1 repeats two key points—the word exchanged (verse 23 and 25) and God gave them over (verse 26 and 28). What is being exchanged?

People are exchanging the truth about God for a lie. But the lie isn't simply that God doesn't exist. There is plenty of proof that God exists. So what is the lie they are exchanging the truth for?

The lie is that there is something better than God.

Gratifying self. Living for this world. Continuing in sin. These are the things mankind has decided is better than God.

To a lesser degree we have all entertained that thought. Every time we willfully choose sin over God, we are deciding that sin is better than God.

To the alcoholic, that drink is better than God. To the workaholic, money is better than God. To the person who has been hurt and refuses to forgive, holding onto bitterness is better than God. We have all chosen sin over God, deciding in that moment that whatever it is that we want, it is better than God.

Verse 28 makes the sad statement that "God gave them over to a depraved mind so that they do what ought not to be done." Every time we choose sin, it's easier to choose it again the next time and the next time, until eventually our mind is corrupted. It's hard to choose truth with a corrupted mind, and eventually God gives us over to our sinful choices.

And that's why people don't believe in God. They are living for a false God instead of the true one.

How do we reach those people? I don't think the arguments of theology make an impact on them. They don't need to understand God more. They need to DESIRE Him more.

They need to stop believing that there are things that are better than God.

The question I am pondering is this: How will they begin to believe that?

I think that when the body of Christ begins to truly love others like Jesus, unbelievers will see that God is better. When they see the joy that Jesus gives and how He makes a difference in our daily lives, they will see that God is better. When we stop focusing on our differences in political and social issues and start focusing on the ways we are the same, they will see that God is better. When we stop seeing them as part of a label or a group and see them as individuals with a story that we should try to understand, they will see that God is better. When we tell them what Jesus did in our own lives, they will see that God is better.

Some will continue to believe that there are things better than God. But there might be a few who will change their minds. And I really want to find them, one by one.

The Jesus I Need

You tell me God loves me but how can I know
When each time you see me, you've a new stone to throw?
You look at me, listing all the things I should change.
The way you show love seems judgmental and strange.
I need to see how life is better for you...
That God is there in your struggles and helps you make it
*   through.*
I need to know that He cares about my sorrow and loss.
I don't need your harsh Jesus. I need the one on the cross.
So please just be patient and keep loving like Him.
If I feel I can trust you, I might let you in.
If you'll listen to me, I might listen to you,
And maybe then I will see that I need Jesus, too.

— © 2025 BOBBIE PERKINS

Reflect:

When you meet someone who is radically opposed to Christianity, do you feel reluctant to engage them in conversation?

Have ever seen Christians spouting negative narratives about unbelievers?

We can't expect unbelievers to think like we do. What kind of ideas do you have that might help to break down barriers?

Dear God, Teach me to look at others with compassion instead of judgment. Help me find small ways to share the love of Christ with those who don't believe. Help me to establish trust, so that I may gain an opportunity to have meaningful conversations with those who don't know You. Amen.

DO YOU MAKE GOD SMILE?

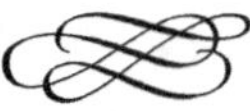

I HAVE BEEN BLESSED WITH FIVE BEAUtiful grandchildren. The crazy part is that four of them are ages 2 and under! I could film a hilarious reality tv show when they are all at my house for a visit at the same time! I have learned to embrace the pandemonium and laugh at the antics that unfold while they are playing together.

My newest grandbaby Evan is currently 8 months old. He is the happiest boy! I call him Mr. Smiley because every time I see him, he breaks out into a huge grin that melts my heart! There is no way I can look at that happy little smiling face and not smile back.

As I was thinking about how happy I feel when I see his sappy grin, I started thinking....

I believe God smiles back at us sometimes, too.

The priestly blessing in Numbers 6:24-26 contains the phrase, "The Lord make his face to shine upon you." I imagine the glory of the Lord would be so brilliant that it would shine brighter than anything we've ever seen. But when I think about a face shining, I also think about a beaming smile.

The Bible talks a lot about being joyful. When we are smiling and overflowing with joy, I think it makes God smile back, kind of in the same way that I smile back at Evan when I see his joy.

God created beauty and gives us good gifts because He loves to bring joy to us. I love the way Randy Alcorn describes it in his book Heaven. He says, "God isn't displeased when we enjoy a good meal, marital sex, a football game, a cozy fire, or a good book. He's not up in heaven frowning at us and saying, "Stop it—you should only find joy in me. This would be as foreign to God's nature as our heavenly Father as it would be to mine as an earthly father if I gave my daughters a Christmas gift and started pouting because they enjoyed it too much. No, I gave the gift to bring joy to them and to me...I am delighted that they enjoy the gift."[1]

God is delighted when we are delighted in His good gifts. It kind of makes me delighted even now to think about it! When I think of how much I enjoy watching Evan giggle over his dancing cactus, enjoying my gift to him, I love the thought that God enjoys my delight at the tree-lined trails I love so much or the mountains, beach, and other beautiful things He's created for me to enjoy.

Some research even shows that smiling can lower cortisol levels (the stress hormone), which may strengthen the immune system. It can also release neurotransmitters that contribute to a sense of peace and well-being. Maybe that leads right up to the last part of that priestly blessing.

The last part of that priestly blessing says, "The Lord turn his face toward you and give you peace."

I can't think of a better way to have peace than smiling, knowing that God is smiling at me.

---

1. Randy Alcorn, *Heaven*. (Eternal Perspective Ministries, 2004), 177.

Reflect:

Smiling and laughter tend to be contagious. Try intentionally smiling when you pass people throughout your day. Spread some joy instead of grumpiness!

Think about the last time you really had an all-out really long burst of laughter. How did you feel afterward? That great feeling is from those neurotransmitters. Laughter and smiling are like natural antidepressants! Turn on a comedy instead of the news. Tell some corny jokes. Have some fun!

Next time you are especially enjoying some of God's good gifts, thank Him for His good gifts, knowing that your delight in them brings Him delight.

—✝—

Dear God, I love the fact that you enjoy our joy! It makes me want to be a more joyful person. Help me to delight in Your good gifts and to be thankful to You, the Giver of all good things. Amen.

THE MIRACLE OF JUSTICE AND MERCY

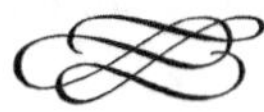

"IT ISN'T FAIR!" HOW MANY TIMES have you heard your kids say that when you were disciplining them or breaking up an argument over a toy? I know I myself have said those words even as an adult. I have heard of horrific crimes in which the criminal was never convicted for the offenses they committed. How unfair it seemed that they got away with their crimes! Sometimes people manage to escape the justice system. But there is no escaping the justice system of God.

There are no flaws in the justice system of God. He is always fair. Psalm 119:68 speaks of God's character, "You are good, and what you do is good." God's fairness means that no guilt goes unpunished. After all, a judge is not a good judge if he doesn't enforce the penalty for a crime.

But the amazing part is where God's justice and mercy meet. We are ALL guilty of crimes against God. "For all have sinned and fall short of the glory of God," (Romans 3:23). The penalty for that sin is death. "For the wages of sin is death, but the gift of God is salvation through Jesus Christ our Lord," (Romans 6:23).

God's love for us caused Him to do an amazing thing. "For God so loved the world that He gave His one and only Son, so that whoever believes in Him will not perish, but have everlasting life," (John 3:16).

God's justice demanded death for our crimes. But He sent His Son to pay the penalty for our sins. When I was young, I had heard that Jesus died for our sins. But I didn't understand what it meant. I thought it meant that He was so upset over our sins that He died, kind of like dying of a broken heart.

I later understood the substitutionary aspect of the cross— that Jesus died in my place so that I wouldn't have to. And it broke me. I knew my sinful rebellion didn't deserve mercy like that. "But God demonstrates his own love for us in this: While we were still sinners, Christ died for us," Romans 5:8.

He didn't just die for the Corrie Ten Booms and the Adrian Rogers of the world. He died for the cold blooded murderer and the twisted pedophile. Hard to imagine isn't it? Now take that one step further… imagine letting your beloved child die in order to save the lives of criminals like that. THAT's the love of God! I can't fathom it!

Let us never forget the price of the cross and His unfathomable love. Let us remember that God made a way so that His justice and mercy met both our need and the righteous requirements of the law. But at great cost to Himself.

God is good. So very, very good.

John 3:16

God loved the world so much He gave
His Son— the Bible tells us.
A deeper love man has not known.
The depth of it compels us.
I've known that verse for many years,
Put to memory for safe-keeping,
But its truth meant something more to me

As I watched my children sleeping.
"I love them so much, Lord," I whispered,
As I prayed for and gazed at each one;
Then I realized the devotion I felt for each child
Was a mere reflection of His for His Son.
How much I desired to protect them;
And I thought as I looked at each face—
How I'd do all in my power to keep them from harm,
Even if asked to die in their place.
And my God had a Son whom He cherished—
Love so perfect, I can't comprehend
How He gave His Son, not for the righteous,
But to die for those reeking with sin.
For it's one thing to die for a good man,
For someone you love or admire,
But it's another to die for a rapist,
A murderer, a cheater, or liar.
And it's one thing to give up your own life.
Many have done it for bravado or guile,
But it's another to watch pain and suffering
In the face of your own precious child.
O Great Love that surpasses my knowledge—
"God so loved the world that He gave..."
How sweet to receive grace and mercy—
How His love found us worthy to save!

— © 1997 BOBBIE PERKINS

REFLECT:

Can you imagine offering your own child to die in order to save a person who had committed vile crimes?

. . .

What amazes you the most about God's plan of salvation? Do you understand it? If not, please read Appendix B.

Think back to when you first understood the gospel. Let the wonder of that moment bring fresh appreciation for God's grace to you right now.

✝

Dear God, Thank you for being both just and merciful. Thank you for the mercy I received at the cross so that I could be washed clean. Help me to live in a way that reflects my gratefulness for my salvation and to help others know You as well. Amen.

HOW TO BE HAPPY

EVERYONE WANTS TO BE HAPPY. As believers in Christ, many of us have heard the statement, "God is more interested in your holiness than your happiness." Although I agree with that, I also know that the Bible actually does talk a lot about our happiness!

The problem is…we often don't follow the instructions found in the Bible on how to obtain happiness.

In John 13:17, Jesus is in the upper room with his disciples. It's just hours before his crucifixion. I imagine He wants to leave them with some important truths on their last night together. What does He say?

"Happy are you if you do these things I've taught you."

He doesn't say, "Happy are you if you KNOW these things." He doesn't even say, "Happy are you if you memorize these things, highlight them in your Bibles, or do a word study on them."

Happy are you if you DO these things.

James 1:25 reminds us that we shouldn't be forgetful hearers of the word but that we should follow through with what it says and obey it.

He says if we do that, we will be "BLESSED in the DOING of the Word."

Happiness and blessings come from obedience.

The opposite is also true. Life just gets hard when we don't do things God's way. Psalm 32:10 tells us, "Many are the sorrows of the wicked." That's a sad statement. I have seen deep sorrow from sin, both in my own life and in the lives of others.

Obedience comes in so many forms, and it looks different for different people. To one of my friends, it means leaving her home to live in a foreign country to share the gospel with unchurched people. To another, it means cutting the grass for her elderly neighbor.

It has looked different for me at different times. It has meant forgiving that person who wronged me. It has meant limiting my tv time to spend time in God's Word and tightening my budget so I can give to my church and other ministries. It always means seeking God to ask Him…what is my next step of obedience?

And sometimes that next step is scary. Even recently I wrestled with something God wanted me to do, and I was afraid. And I admit I have too often turned away from that step of obedience.

I remember my first roller coaster ride. I stood uncertainly in line, nervously trying to conquer my fear. I took the plunge and found it was a thrilling experience, and I got right back in line to do it again.

That is what obedience looks like. When I trust God, even when what He asks me to do is scary, there is a thrilling joy of knowing I am following His plan for me.

And I want to get back in line to do it all over again.

Because I have experienced the happiness that comes from obedience.

Reflect:

Have you ever felt that God wanted you to do something that you were afraid to do?

. . .

If you answered yes, were you feeling happy afterward?

What steps of obedience has God asked you to take that might look different from the obedience of some of your friends or family?

How have you felt after you didn't obey God?

—✝—

Dear God, Thank you for your forgiveness during my times of disobedience. There is no joy like following You! I want to obey Your plan for me. Please help me to obey even when I am afraid, and help me to hear Your voice clearly as you instruct me in the way I should go. Amen.

STARTING OVER

I'VE GOTTA GIVE IT TO MY GRANDSON. He's a determined little fellow. His perseverance first became obvious to me when he was 4 years old, attempting to draw a picture of Spiderman.

His first attempt was wadded up in a ball after only a few strokes of the marker. "That's not right. I need to start over," he informed me.

Then another wadded up paper. And another. The stack kept increasing, and I saw his frustration growing. "That's NOT what his eyes look like!" He wailed in exasperation at each wadded up paper that was added to the pile. He knew better than to ask me to draw for him. I had already been informed by him that I am "not a very good draw-er." His wadded up papers all looked better than what I would have achieved!

After eight attempts, he finally seemed satisfied with his completed picture of his favorite superhero. I praised him for his tenacious spirit in not giving up.

And I realized that those eight attempts were nothing compared to the number of times I've had to start over.

I thought about how many times I have sheepishly approached the Father's throne, asking Him to forgive me for the same sin I asked forgiveness for last month. Frustrated at myself, I've been tempted to give up on this thing called obedience. Surely I had already used up my quota of God's grace.

But that grace just kept flowing like a river. I discovered that God's grace is like a well that has no bottom. And it was that grace that made we want to try even harder to live the life of holiness He asked me to pursue. Romans 2:4 tells us, "God's kindness is intended to lead you to repentance." That makes sense. I think if I had approached that throne only to be yelled at or belittled, I wouldn't have wanted to come back.

But there was only grace at that throne.

God was happy that I kept starting over! He just didn't want me to give up.

Maybe you have a pile of wadded up attempts in front of the throne of grace. Keep repenting. Keep starting over. God's grace has no limited supply.

Starting Over

Lord, this time I've really messed up.
I don't see how You can forgive.
You must be disappointed
By the way You've seen me live.
I don't really know what happened.
I don't know how the sin crept in,
But I lay my guilt before You
And ask for strength to start again.
I turn from my rebellion, Lord.
Though I fell, I'm up again.
When my will is Yours, I just can't stand
To lie there in my sin.
It's been a painful lesson,

But I'm learning over time
To focus and abide in You—
Fruit grows when on the vine.
I know at my salvation
Your spirit made me free,
But the grip of sin is tight and strong
And my past still tugs on me.
But there's strength within Your Spirit,
A great power I can't express
As I'm learning how to use Your Word
In this battle of the flesh.
It hurts to know I've failed You, Lord.
My desire is to obey.
Please cleanse me and remind me
All disgrace is washed away.
The accuser likes to bring it back—
That guilt from sin that's past,
And though You have long since cleansed me,
I let Satan's false guilt last.
I turn from my rebellion, Lord.
Though I fell, I'm up again.
When my will is Yours, I just can't stand
To lie there in my sin.
It's been a painful lesson,
But I'm learning over time
To focus and abide in You—
Fruit grows when on the vine.

— © 1987 BOBBIE PERKINS

REFLECT:

Have you ever been frustrated with yourself and felt that you had used up your quota of God's grace?

. . .

Have you ever battled feeling guilty from sin that you had already been forgiven for? Next time can you remember where that false guilt comes from?

Have you ever asked for forgiveness without truly repenting?

—✝—

Dear God, I am sorry for the times I have hurt You by turning to sin. Help me to abide in You and the strength You give through the Holy Spirit that helps me to walk in obedience. Thank you for Your kind mercy and abundant grace that makes me want to please You. Amen.

THE FRAGRANCE OF CHRIST

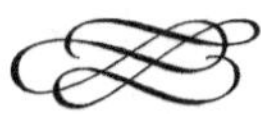

I HAVE A VERY SENSITIVE NOSE. I CAN smell cigarette smoke in the car next to me while I'm driving down the road. I have come home and immediately taken a shower because I could still smell cigarette smoke in my hair after walking past someone who had been smoking. It's hard to believe I smoked for over ten years because I absolutely hate the smell of cigarette smoke now!

I'm the same way with pleasant fragrances, too, though. One of my favorites was on our trip to Cancun. I got an amazing massage, but the scents that emanated from the spa were just as amazing! I don't know what they used, but I wanted to just hang out there all day and smell the tantalizing aromas that were wafting all around me!

Have you ever been around someone who radiated such a love for the Lord that you could almost smell the fragrance of Christ in their presence? Paul describes committed believers as "the pleasing aroma of Christ among those who are being saved and those who are perishing," (2 Corinthians 2:15).

It's interesting that he compares the presence of Christians to an aroma. Did you know that our olfactory bulb that is responsible for our sense of smell is also connected to our limbic system? The limbic system is where most of our emotional responses are regulated, including pleasure and anger.

Christians can leave people feeling angry or happy, depending on how we interact with them. We can leave behind the fragrance of Christ, or we can leave behind the stink of self-righteousness.

Pleasing aromas attract us and want us to draw closer for more. I hope people want more of Jesus after being around me. Sadly, I'm sure there have been times in my life when my own negativity, selfishness, or other ungodly traits repelled them. Like acrid cigarette smoke, sin and selfishness can leave a lingering stench. I don't want people to smell that after being with me.

As I draw closer to the sweetness of Jesus, the aroma of Christ changes me a little more each time. Oh, how I pray that the lovely aroma of our Savior will draw others to inhale more deeply of Him.

He is way better than a day at the spa!

REFLECT:

Have you ever been around a Christian who made you want more of Jesus?

On the other hand, have you ever been around a Christian who made their faith a turn-off?

What kind of things have you seen Christians do or say that turns others away from Christianity?

How can we engage a lost world but still hold fast to what is right?

—✝—

Dear God, I want to draw others to You, not turn them away. Help me to live in a way that shows that I have something different that they are missing out on. Help me to stand for righteousness without coming across as self-righteous and to respond with love to others. Amen.

ACTING LIKE A TWO-YEAR-OLD

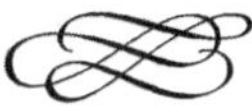

My granddaughter Nora is tall for her age. (I know that's hard to believe...that ANY of my descendants would be tall!) Nora also talks very well for a two-year-old—probably because my daughter is a speech therapist. Sometimes when I take Nora out somewhere, people mistakenly think she is older than she actually is. I may have to explain to people that she is only two years old because some of her childish behaviors that aren't appropriate for a 5-year-old are perfectly normal for a two-year-old. She is a smart, sweet, loving kid, but two-year-olds will be two-year-olds!

I've been thinking about that and realized something. We also need to remember that principle in relation to believers. Two-year-old Christians will often exhibit behaviors that aren't appropriate for twenty-year-old Christians. Just as we can't expect a two-year-old child to have the maturity of a five-year-old child, Christians shouldn't expect new believers to have the maturity of those who have been Christians for many years. We need to be careful that we aren't passing judgment on people who just need more time to grow.

Growth is a slow process. I can attest to that in my own life. I have often claimed that I hold the world-championship title as the slowest growing Christian ever. But I'm ok with that because I trust God's timetable. And honestly, I probably would have grown a lot faster if I had cooperated with God a little more in those earlier years! Spiritual growth happens at different rates for different people, depending on their life experiences and how they respond to those experiences and to God's work in their lives. Physical growth varies from person to person as well. Some kids have a growth spurt at 13, while others might not have one until 17. (And some, like me, never do have a growth spurt, but let's NOT apply that to spiritual matters! Lol!)

When Moses first began his walk with God, he spent a lot of time questioning God and trying to convince God that he wasn't the right person for the job. But Moses eventually grew into one of the greatest leaders in Biblical history. Instead of faltering to follow God as he had in the beginning, he eventually had such a desire to know God that he begged God, "Show me your glory," (Exodus 33:18). Moses had a passion to know God more intimately. That is what Jesus talks about in John 15.

In John 15 Jesus describes how He abides in us and how we must also abide in Him. "As the Father has loved me, so I have loved you. Now remain in my love," (John 15:9). Remaining in His love is like falling in love with someone. We aren't content to just know facts about that person. We want to know that person intimately. Our thoughts remain in that love. We think about that person over and over. I want my thoughts to remain in the love of Christ.

Like Moses, I want to see the glory of God. Do you? It means remaining in His love. It means when the world distracts us from our Savior, we make a concentrated effort to refocus our gaze. We keep that abiding relationship by prayer, reading the Bible, connecting with other believers, and all of those other spiritual disciplines that help us to grow. The important thing is that we want to grow and take steps to grow, remaining in His love.

And God's plan is that we eventually mature from the baby

believer to someone who is mature in the faith and able to help others to grow, "mature and complete, not lacking anything."

I still have a ways to go. But in the meantime, I'm abiding in Him. I don't want to act like a two-year-old Christian!

Reflect:

How has spiritual growth happened in your life? Fast or slow? What events or people in your life have affected that growth?

Think about times of spiritual dryness in your life. At that time would you say you weren't abiding in Him very well?

What specifically has helped you to grow the most as a Christian?

✝

Dear God, Thank you for showing me glimpses of Your glory! I want to see more of it as I grow more mature in my faith. Help me to abide in You always and to teach new believers to do the same. Amen.

WILDERNESS

"Whoever wants to be my disciple must deny themselves and take up their cross and follow me."

— Matthew 16:24

My pastor recently started a new sermon series called "Life Hurts, Jesus Heals." It has been an impactful series for many of our church members, including me. In one of those sermons, he talked about "coming out of the wilderness." He explained that we all have wilderness times in our lives. He talked about the experiences of Moses and even Jesus himself, as they had experienced their own struggles in the wilderness.

When my pastor was talking about coming out of the wilderness, I facetiously told him that recently I have felt that God led me out of the wilderness only to lead me to the raging sea instead. Unpredictable. Scary. More than I planned for.

And then, I thought later about what I had said to my pastor. I realized it wasn't actually a raging sea that God was beckoning me to after leaving my wilderness. No...it was actually the same place He had led Jesus.

To the cross.

To surrender my will to Him.

Our wilderness time causes us to either resist God or cling to Him. God wants to use it to teach us how to wield the Word and call out to Him. Leaving that wilderness is a time of experiencing God's rescue and following Him to the next chapter He has planned for us.

And sometimes that next chapter stretches us more than the wilderness did. I'm sure Jesus would attest to that.

Oh, how that cross changes us! We all have to start there to meet the Savior. And we have to keep going back...to continue in that surrender over and over.

To surrender yet another layer.

I have a friend who has helped me peel my layers. I jokingly told her that she is the one who is handing Jesus the cheese grater. But God gave her to me to teach me about that surrender. She has been to the cross many times herself. Surrendering things that I'm glad God hasn't asked me to surrender, at least not at this point in time.

My own surrender is of a different kind. So I'm at the cross once again, asking Him to help me lay it down.

This book was part of that surrender. I've had to carry the manuscript with me to the cross. It has been a growing experience for me. One of peeling another new layer.

Love so amazing, so divine, demands my soul, my life, my all...

What do you need to surrender at the cross?

When I Survey the Wondrous Cross
on which the Prince of glory died,
my richest gain I count but loss,
and pour contempt on all my pride...

...Were the whole realm of nature mine,
that were a present far too small.
Love so amazing, so divine,

demands my soul, my life, my all. [1]

REFLECT:

Has God ever asked you to do something that seemed too hard? Too uncomfortable?

Have you found a friend who can walk next to you with the cheese grater?

What do you need to surrender at the cross? Are you willing to do it right now?

~✝~

Dear God, I come to you now, laying down my will at the cross. I want to surrender all to You, layer by layer, as you lead me deeper in my walk with You. Help me to be humbly obedient to Your will for me. Amen.

---

1. Isaac Watts, "When I Survey the Wondrous Cross," 1707 Public Domain.

SUCCESS

SUCCESS. WE ALL WANT TO HAVE IT, right? We want to be financially comfortable and have a fruitful career. We want to have plenty of friends and a nice home that never gets dirty or needs repairs.

We want dogs that never chew up shoes.

We want children who score the winning touchdowns, make the honor roll, and obey the first time they're told to do something.

And if we aren't careful, we can tend to turn our kids into trophies, looking to them to make us feel that we did a successful job in parenting. It's okay to be proud of our kids. But we should never look to our kids for our self-worth that should only come from God.

There will be times our kids will let us down. They will embarrass us by throwing a tantrum in public. They will refuse to share a toy in the church nursery or strike out in baseball. They may grow into adults who walk away from God. And that is something that happens even to the best of parents. Adam and Eve had the perfect parent, and we all know how that turned out.

Are we focusing more on what our kids accomplish than what the Savior accomplishes in their lives? Are we more concerned that they do well in Bible drill or instead that they apply Biblical principles to their lives?

In his book Parenting: 14 Gospel Principles That Can Radically Change Your Family, Paul David Tripp[1] says that parents "tend to be angry and disappointed with their children, not first because they've broken God's law, but because whatever they have done has brought hassle and embarrassment to them." Ouch! (By the way...if you haven't read it, get that book! It is the best parenting book I have ever read!)

Our role as parents isn't to mold our children into little robots who do whatever we want them to do. Instead we are to mold them into people who do what GOD wants them to do. Tripp says to parents, "God has designed that you would be a principal, consistent, and faithful tool in his hands for the purpose of creating God-consciousness and God-submission in your children."

As we discipline our children and grandchildren, it's important to remember that instilling a God-centered life in those little impressionable souls is more important than anything else.

Are we living a God-centered life as an example to them?

And are we praying for God to accomplish His work in their lives?

What is our measure of success?

Success

I look in wonder at your faces, and I life my heart in praise,
So glad God gave us children to mold and love and raise.
Each one of you is different, yet my love for each the same...
Love not changed by circumstances—devotion words cannot
    explain.
    I

---

1. Trip, David. *Parenting: 14 Gospel Principles That Can Radically Change Your Family.* (Wheaton, Illinois: Crossway, 2016, 20).

hold a tiny body closer and feel warm breath upon my
cheek.
Too soon the baby years are over, lost in routine week to week.
I hear the sound of playful laughter and the squeals of joy and
singing,
Dancing feet in stocking sleepers, unaware the joy they're
bringing.
You look so fragile and unblemished, I want to shield you from
life's blows,
To preserve somehow your innocence before your childhood
goes.
Yet I watch your independence as you learn so much each day.
God has special plans for each of you, and as parents we must
pray.
We pray that as you're growing, you will seek God with a
thirst,
Persevering through life's problems to still love and serve Him
first.
And we pray that through your lifetime your faith will deepen
and mature
To instill you with commitment to give God a life kept pure.
Sometimes it's hard to live for Jesus. You can't do it on
your own.
That is why you'll find us daily kneeling at the Father's
throne.
You see, our biggest job as parents isn't making shopping
sprees,
Or paying bills or cleaning—it's the time spent on our knees.
And when our children take our teachings, some lessons saved
and others tossed,
If they don't have a love for Jesus, "success" won't matter—all
was lost!

— © 1995 BOBBIE PERKINS

REFLECT:

Do you tend to focus more on what behaviors your children are exhibiting or what is going on in their hearts that caused the behaviors? Which is more important?

Do you pray regularly for your kids and with your kids?

Do you admit your own mistakes and model what it looks like to repent and seek God's help?

—✝—

Dear God, Thank you for the privilege of helping to mold the souls of my children and grandchildren to seek after You. Help me to be an example of how to live that out. Please give me patience and wisdom to point them to Christ. Amen.

PLAYGROUND PRISONERS

 call her the feral bobcat. My granddaughter Haven is a very opinionated, outgoing little two-year-old. Fearless. Bossy. Never met a stranger. The only time I can get her tiny little body to sit still is when I am reading her book after book in endless succession. That book thing must be in the genes!

Haven's outgoing personality can be a little intense for more introverted kids. She will approach other toddlers on the playground, saying things like, "You be my friend. Come here, friend. I be your friend, etc."

She will follow them around, almost demanding they play with her because it doesn't make any sense to her that they wouldn't want to play. Doesn't everyone want to play? Some of them see that she has a toy they don't have or that she is having fun, and they finally do play with her. But some of them just aren't ready for it. They need time to warm up to her first. It's kind of amusing to watch them try to escape to the other side of the playground.

I've seen some Christians have that same kind of style in sharing the gospel.

They chase people down on the street and demand that people listen to them. They don't understand why anyone wouldn't want to be a Christian. Doesn't everyone want to go to heaven? Some people do respond to that invitation. But there are some others who are turned off by it. They need more time to warm up to the gospel. It's kind of sad to watch them try to escape to the other side of the playground.

I don't have anything against tracts or talking to strangers, but to some people, that type of interaction can be a big turn-off. How do we reach them without being too intense? How do we engage them in conversation without turning them off?

I recently came across some interesting research[1] about methods of sharing the gospel and how it impacts different generations of people. The baby boomers and Gen X generations have a much higher percentage of people who identify as Christians. But there is another interesting slant on that....The research also showed that the Millennial and Gen Z generations are actually having more conversations about spiritual things, even though fewer of them identify as Christians.

What this means is that the younger generation values a discussion over a sermon. They are much more likely to be open to the gospel if they are first allowed to share what it is that they themselves believe. They value diversity and inclusion, so most of them enjoy talking about beliefs in a more natural setting that isn't forced upon them. Faith conversations that arise naturally from an interaction or situation are much more welcomed and accepted.

I'm a Gen X who barely missed the baby boomer generation. Because I work at a pregnancy center that is a faith-based ministry, I have faith conversations with younger people almost every day. I've

---

1. Barna Group and Alpha USA (2019), Reviving Evangelism, 12.

learned a lot from them. (Some things I really didn't want to know...
Lol!) But I do know that I don't want them running to the other side
of the playground when I mention Jesus.

I want them to be drawn to me because I have something they
don't.

I want them to see that I am having fun. And then, maybe...

Just maybe...they'll come over to play.

Reflect:

If someone from a different faith, such as the Muslim or Hindu faith,
were to approach you in order to proselytize you, would it be a turn-
off to you? Could you have a friendly faith conversation with them,
allowing them equal time to talk?

What are some creative ways to share the gospel or to spark interest
in others to cause them to want to hear more about your faith?

Make sure you are ready and able to give a testimony of your own
coming to faith, keeping it short, such as a couple minutes long.
Nobody can dispute what your personal experience has been.

⁓✝⁓

*Dear God, Thank you for saving me. There are so many people out there who
are missing out. Please give me wisdom and discernment as I interact with
them to point them to You. Let them see the difference You make in my life,
and help me to converse with them with compassion and respect, so that they
want to know You. Amen.*

OCTOBER

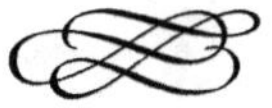

ARE YOU ASKING THE RIGHT QUESTION?

"Such knowledge is too wonderful for me, too lofty for me to attain."
— Psalm 139:6

Have you ever looked at the world around you and asked God, "Why?" I sure have. The horror of war. The murder of an elderly woman. The rape of a four year old. The suffering of a child with cancer. We hear about these atrocities and wonder, "How could God allow that to happen?"

Maybe what you're asking God "why" about is something in your own life. You look at your deep sorrow and wonder why He has allowed the hurtful things in your life. You wonder why a good God would allow such pain and suffering.

I don't pretend to know the answers to those questions. God is much too big for my finite brain. It would be like trying to explain computers to a cockroach. Or space travel to an ant. I am not capable of understanding the things of God. David felt the same way when he wrote, "Such knowledge is too wonderful for me too lofty for me to attain" (Psalm 139:6).

God Himself even makes it clear that we can't begin to understand

His ways when He basically spent four full chapters (Job 38-41) taunting Job about how "wise" Job really wasn't! There are things about God and the things of God that we are just not meant to know. "The secret things belong to the Lord our God..." (Deuteronomy 29:29).

Maybe we are just asking the wrong questions. Instead of asking "why," perhaps we should be asking "who?"

Who is God? Who is He in relation to mankind? Who is He in relation to me?

The problem is that we look at the world around us and try to define God by what we see in the world. It doesn't work that way. 1 John 5:19 tells us, "The whole world is under the control of the evil one." That is not to say God isn't sovereign, but God has allowed Satan a certain degree of power initiated by the first sin of mankind. Satan's agenda is to alienate us from God. He wants to make us believe that God is not good. The truth is, we can't define God by looking at this world.

How do we know who God is? By looking at Jesus. Jesus was all-God and all-man. God loves us so much that He came to earth in the form of a man in order to rescue us from our sin. So if you ask the question, "Who is God?" The answer is to look at Jesus.

Read the gospels (especially the book of John) to see how Jesus interacted with people. He was compassionate, gracious, patient, and loving. He served others to the point of exhaustion. He sought out the outcasts. He gave dignity to women. He relieved the suffering of many.

Jesus suffered more trauma than any of us can ever imagine. Being both God and man, He knew He had come to die upon the cross, but in His humanity, he was sickened with dread at the thought of the physical suffering. He was overwhelmed at the thought of the emotional suffering of being separated from His Father and covered in the vileness of our sin. Yet Jesus willingly did that for us. OUR GOD willingly did that for us. That is who God is.

He died to save us. We deserved God's righteous wrath. God couldn't just let us go free. He is righteous. Would it be right for a judge in our court system to let a murderer go free? Of course not. Justice must be served. Jesus took our punishment upon Himself, thus satisfying the penalty for our crimes. Our God purchased our salvation with His own blood. How incredible!

But there is an additional reason that He went to the cross that you might not have thought about. If you look at your own suffering, you can see that He mirrors yours. The pain you feel of being hurt by someone you loved- the sting of His betrayal. The physical pain of illness- His physical suffering. The grief, anxiety, depression, and other things you might struggle with- His emotional and spiritual turmoil.

"For this reason he had to be made like them, fully human in every way, in order that he might become a MERCIFUL and FAITHFUL high priest in service to God, and that he might make atonement for the sins of the people" (Hebrews 2:17, emphasis mine).

Merciful and faithful. That's who God is. And that is always the right question.

REFLECT:

Do you think remembering that the "secret things belong to God" could comfort you next time you are struggling to understand suffering?

Jesus came to save us. But that salvation is a gift that must be opened. When did you open that gift? If you're not sure, please read Appendix B.

What things do you need to release to God, accepting the fact that you don't have to understand them?

—✝—

Dear God, Thank you for the love poured out on the cross so that I can know You. I release to You the things I don't understand and trust You with them, knowing that you are righteous and good. Help me to stop asking "why" and to start remembering "who." Amen.

STRENGTH TRAINING

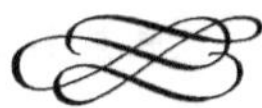

I'M NOT A GYM PERSON. I REALLY WISH I was. My idea of fun exercise is to go for a run where I can see trees and enjoy nature. A gym just doesn't appeal to me.

Another reason I'm not a gym person is because I don't know much about weight training. I don't know how to use the machines or how to use proper body mechanics with free weights. My daughter Hannah does. I went to the gym with her, and I asked her to help me work my arms. The next day I exclaimed, "Well, now I know how I will lose weight!" "How?" she asked, curious about what new information I may have discovered. I told her, "Well, you worked my arms so hard yesterday, that today my arms are so sore, I can't even lift a fork to my mouth!"

Muscle growth takes effort. And so does spiritual growth. How can we "work out" our spiritual muscles? Just as physical growth takes discipline and a workout plan, spiritual growth does, too. The problem is that most people don't have a plan. Their Bible may be on a shelf collecting dust. They may claim, "I don't have to go to church to be a Christian." That's true. But just as athletes with the strongest muscles usually go to the gym, Christians who are the strongest usually connect with other believers.

So what steps can we take to grow and stay strong as a Christian? This is not an all-inclusive list, but here are some good places to start to flex those spiritual muscles. When I was doing a lot of Biblical Counseling, I would often talk about these things with my counselees before I "graduated" them so they would have a plan for continued growth after I was no longer seeing them.

WAYS TO STAY STRONG AND GROW AS A CHRISTIAN

Attending church:

> "The eye cannot say to the hand, "I don't need you!" And the head cannot say to the feet, "I don't need you!"

> — 1 CORINTHIANS 12:12-26

Reading the Bible:

> "I gain understanding from your precepts; therefore I hate every wrong path. Your word is a lamp for my feet, a light on my path."

> — PSALM 119:104,105

Memorizing Scripture:

"I have hidden your word in my heart that I might not sin against you."

— PSALM 119:11

Praying:

Do not be anxious about anything, but in every situation, by prayer and petition, with thanksgiving, present your requests to God."

— PHILIPPIANS 4:6

Worship:

"Ascribe to the Lord the glory due his name; bring an offering and come before him. Worship the Lord in the splendor of his holiness."

— 1 CHRONICLES 16:29

Meditation:

"You will keep in perfect peace those whose minds are steadfast, because they trust in you."

— ISAIAH 26:3

Stewardship:

"Now it is required that those who have been given a trust must prove faithful."

— 1 CORINTHIANS 4:2

Surrounding yourself with good influences:

"As iron sharpens iron, so one person sharpens another."

— PROVERBS 27:17

Being accountable to someone:

"Therefore confess your sins to each other and pray for each other so that you may be healed. The prayer of a righteous person is powerful and effective."

— JAMES 5:16

Fasting:

"Even now," declares the Lord, "return to me with all your heart, with fasting and weeping and mourning."

— JOEL 2:12

Renewing your mind:

"...We take captive every thought to make it obedient to Christ."

— 2 CORINTHIANS 10:5

Sharing the gospel:

> "Therefore go and make disciples of all nations, baptizing them in the name of the Father and of the Son and of the Holy Spirit, and teaching them to obey everything I have commanded you..."

> — MATTHEW 28:19,20

Serving the body of Christ:

> So Christ himself gave the apostles, the prophets, the evangelists, the pastors, and teachers, to equip his people for works of service, so that the body of Christ may be built up..."

> — EPHESIANS 4:11-12

REFLECT:

Which area of spiritual discipline comes the easiest for you?

In which areas of spiritual discipline do you need to flex your muscles more?

Pick one discipline to focus on each day this week to see if you can establish some new habits.

—✝—

Dear God, I want to flex my spiritual muscles to grow stronger as a disciple of You. Help me to establish spiritually healthy habits to make me a stronger

Christian and glorify You. Thank you that your Holy Spirit empowers me to walk in obedience. Amen.

MARRIAGE GOALS: LEARNING TO LOVE

Even though the next few devotions are about marriage, some of the principles can be applied to any relationship. There are certain things we have to learn in marriage that just don't come naturally to us. Although the list could be much longer, a lot of our relationship struggles can be helped with the following principles:

Learn how to love

Learn how to forgive

Learn how to communicate

Learn how to live

I honestly didn't mean to make a rhyme there, but knowing my poetry-loving self, I thought that worked out perfectly! Let's take a shallow dive into each of those things. Today we will talk about learning how to love.

What is the purpose of marriage? It's about something way bigger than two people! The purpose is found in Ephesians 5:21-33. "Submit to one another (lay down your rights) out of reverence for Christ

(Christ is in that equation). Wives, submit yourselves to your own husbands as you do to the Lord (The Lord is in that equation). For the husband is the head of the wife as Christ is the head of the church (Christ is in that equation)...husbands, love your wives, just as Christ loved the church and gave himself up for her (Christ is in that equation)...Do you see the repetition? Marriage is a reflection of Christ's relationship to the church. We can't lose sight of the main character: Christ! If we lose sight of Jesus, we lose the motive behind sacrificially loving, submitting, and respecting.

When we have marital strife, we may think to ourselves, "The way he is acting, he doesn't deserve my respect," or "The way she is acting, she doesn't deserve for me to love her that way," but we can't look to our spouse for the reason why. We have to look to our sacrificial, serving Savior. HE is our reference point. We didn't deserve what He did for us on the cross, but He did it anyway. Love isn't based on merit or what the other person deserves. That's the love of Christ—loving sacrificially even when the other person is not deserving of that love. "But God demonstrates his own love for us in this: While we were still sinners, Christ died for us," (Romans 5:8).

I Corinthians 13 describes the kind of love we should have. "Love is patient, love is kind. It does not envy, it does not boast, it is not proud. It does not dishonor others, it is not self-seeking, it is not easily angered, it keeps no record of wrongs. Love does not delight in evil but rejoices with the truth. It always protects, always trusts, always hopes, always perseveres."

Living that out in our marriage will teach us how to love.

Reflect:

Can you respond in love to your spouse even when the feelings of love aren't there at the moment?

Are you willing to sacrifice your own wants and desires for those of your spouse?

. . .

Do some random small acts of love for your spouse this week. See what it does for your marriage!

⁓✝⁓

Dear God, I thank you for my spouse and the way marriage reflects the relationship of Christ to the church. Help us to love each other sacrificially and respond with patience and grace, especially when the other is hard to love at that moment. Amen.

MARRIAGE GOALS: LEARNING TO FORGIVE

"Be kind and compassionate to one another, forgiving each other, just as in Christ God forgave you."

– Ephesians 4:32

MARRIAGE PROBABLY REQUIRES MORE forgiveness than any other relationship. The only relationship I can think of that needs a greater amount of forgiveness is the one between ourselves and God! But I have noticed something about forgiveness in my own marriage. The longer I've been married, the less forgiveness we seem to need. We just don't seem to argue or annoy each other as much as we did in our early marriage. I hope that is because we have grown spiritually, but it may also be that as we have gotten older, we have learned the virtue of thinking before speaking!

Forgiving our spouse should be patterned after God's forgiveness toward us. Scripture has a lot to say about forgiveness.

"Bear with each other and forgive one another if any of you has a grievance against someone. Forgive as the Lord forgave you." (Colossians 3:13)

How did the Lord forgive us?

"I, even I, am he who blots out your transgressions, for my own sake, and remembers your sins no more." (Isaiah 43:25).

He remembers our sins no more.

I don't know about you, but sometimes it's hard to erase the sin of others out of our memory. We might complain about it to other people. We bring it back up to our spouse in a future argument. We might hash it around in our mind for a while and stew over it, bringing more internal discord.

But God says we are to remember their sin no more. That means no talking about it to other people. No bringing it back up to that person who offended us. No rehashing it in our mind or dwelling on it.

That takes grace. But that's what God gives to us. Undeserving, healing grace. "Be kind and compassionate to one another, forgiving each other, just as in Christ God forgave you," (Ephesians 4:32).

I hope you're not needing to do a lot of forgiving. But I hope that next time you do, you'll do it the way God does.

REFLECT:

In a new argument do you tend to bring up past offenses that should have been forgotten?

Do you rehash old hurts in your mind or talk about them to other people when they should have been given to the Lord and forgotten?

How can you show the grace of God to your spouse? By not answering a sharp word with a sharp word in return? By doing something nice for them when they are grumpy? Plan in advance how you will respond so that you can act in love.

. . .

Read Matthew 6:14,15, "For if you forgive other people when they sin against you, your heavenly Father will also forgive you. But if you do not forgive others their sins, your Father will not forgive your sins." According to those verses, how does our forgiveness of others affect our relationship with God?

—✝—

Dear God, I thank You for the forgiveness You have given me that I don't deserve. Help me to forgive my spouse and others in the same way. Help me to hand those offenses over to You so that I don't rehash them in my mind. Please give me the grace to live in that forgiveness with actions of love. Amen.

MARRIAGE GOALS: LEARNING TO COMMUNICATE

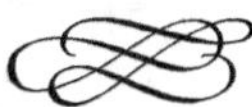

> *"Let your conversation be always full of grace."*
>
> — *Colossians 4:6*

Have you ever said something and instantly regretted it? I think we all have. The words we utter are an overflow of what is in our hearts. So in learning to communicate better, the goal is not so much to guard our words but to guard our hearts. "Above all else, guard your heart, for everything you do flows from it," (Proverbs 4:23).

What is in our hearts that causes arguments? James tells us it is our sinful desires. "What causes fights and quarrels among you? Don't they come from your desires that battle within you?" (James 4:1). We want what we want because we are sinful humans. When that other person interferes with our getting what we want, that's when the arguments start. James goes on to tell how we can avoid those arguments. "God opposes the proud but shows favor to the humble. Submit yourselves, then to God. Resist the devil, and he will flee from you," (James 4:7).

We have to submit our desires and rights to God. Admit to Him that you wanted A but got B instead. Acknowledge your disappointment, but choose in that moment to resist the enemy's assault to act in the flesh. The enemy is not your spouse. The enemy is the one urging you to be angry at your spouse.

How do we communicate well in these types of conflicts? If we can remember 6 principles of communication, many arguments could be avoided.

1. ATTACK THE PROBLEM, NOT THE PERSON. "Do not let any unwholesome talk come out of your mouths, but only what is helpful for building others up according to their needs, that it may benefit those who listen," (Ephesians 4:29).

2. LISTEN WELL. Truly try to understand the other person's perspective. If we are thinking about what we are going to say while the other person is talking, we are not listening well. "Everyone should be quick to listen, slow to speak and slow to become angry," (James 1:19).

3. CONTROL VOICE TONE. Why do we yell in an argument? Because we tend to talk louder when we are excited, whether it is from happy excitement or from anger. Being aware of this and concentrating on controlling voice volume and tone will help keep the conversation calm, aiding communication.

4. KEEP CURRENT. This goes back to the principles of forgiveness. Don't rehash old offenses or bring them into the current conflict.

5. DON'T USE ABSOLUTES- Don't use words like "always and never." For example, you don't want to accuse with "You always…" or "You never…" That is just going to put the other person in a defensive mode.

6. RESTATE WHAT THE OTHER PERSON IS SAYING. Let them know you are trying to understand what they are saying and how they feel.

REFLECT:

Which principle of communication is hardest for you? Why don't you ask God to help you with that?

If you need a moment to gather your thoughts, ask your spouse to give you a moment to pray or even pray together before you discuss a problem. It will help you both be in a better frame of mind.

Next time you are angry, try to determine what is in your own heart. As the passage in James explained, what desire in your heart is not being met? A clean house? Peace and quiet? Some free time to yourself? Appreciation? Are you able to surrender that desire to the Lord and glorify Him with that surrender instead of arguing with your spouse?

—✝—

Dear God, Thank you for giving us principles of communication as believers. Your Word says our tongue is powerful, and I want to use it to build up my spouse and others. Help me to filter my words through the Holy Spirit. Amen.

MARRIAGE GOALS:
LEARNING HOW TO LIVE

THE SECRET TO HAVING A GOOD marriage isn't to have the goal of having a good marriage.

It's true. Our goal isn't to focus on the marriage. Our goal is to focus on Christ. In fact, that is our goal for life itself!

Why did God even create us? For amusement? For company? To exercise His creative talents?

The answer to why God created us is found in Isaiah 43:7. "...everyone who is called by my name, whom I created for my glory..."

God created us for the purpose of bringing glory to Himself! Marriage is a beautiful platform from which to bring Him glory as we reflect the relationship of Christ to the church. We do that as we live out self-sacrifice and unconditional love and as we forgive and serve one another.

The success of our marriage is linked to the strength of our relationship with God and applying His principles found in Scripture to the way we interact with one another. It's fine to work on our marriage. But our goal isn't to solely focus on the marriage, but to focus on our true goal for life...

It's the same goal that Paul had in 2 Corinthians 5:9. "So we make it our goal to please him..." Bringing glory to God and pleasing God in all we do is our goal. And THAT will lead to building a strong marriage as we follow Biblical principles.

And that's how we live...Marriage goals=God goals.

Oneness

God knew what He was doing
When He made us man and wife,
For God has a special purpose
And a plan for every life.
And His plan for every marriage
Is for two to become one
With the goal of growing closer
To the likeness of His Son.
And sometimes we need to look inside
Our hearts to really search
To see if we're a mirror to
Reflect Christ and the church.
Jesus loved the church with willingness
To suffer as He died,
As a husband's love should model Christ's
With honor for his bride.
And wives should love their husbands
With respect—for God has said
He holds the man accountable
For how his home was led.
The two-as-one in marriage
Isn't such a mystery
Knowing God the Father, Son, and Spirit
In their Holy Trinity.
We fall so short of righteousness,

Forget the prayers that we have prayed,
And often don't live up to all
The wedding vows we made.
It's not that we don't want to,
But we fall flat on our face
When we let our selfish thoughts preside
Instead of love and grace.
But we're learning as we blunder
Just what love was meant to be.
It's not a feeling—it's commitment
To last throughout eternity.
And that is how a unity
In spirit can begin—
Our love will deepen only
As we go through thick and thin.
My prayer is God will teach us
To live out self-sacrifice.
As we serve each other, Lord, we pray
Please make us more like Christ.

— © 1988 BOBBIE PERKINS

REFLECT:

How can you grow together spiritually as a couple? Do you pray together? Have you studied the Bible together? Are you meeting with other believers to encourage one another?

Start your day with the goal of pleasing God in everything that you do. Do you think you will have many arguments with your spouse if you have that as your goal?

. . .

Make some marriage goals together. Just make sure God is at the center of it all.

—✝—

Dear God, Thank you for my spouse who is Your perfect match for me. Help me to glorify You in my marriage and have love like that described in 1 Corinthians 13, knowing that can only happen as I abide in You. Amen.

TASTE AND SEE

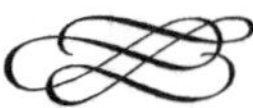

It was my husband's birthday. We were celebrating in the usual fashion with a family get-together. The grandbabies ran around the den, playing and scattering toys everywhere, giggling and creating the normal chaos of a room full of toddlers.

I keep a small folding children's table in my playroom for the kids to eat at when they visit. I typically bring it into the den when we are ready to eat.

I knew it was getting close to naptime for the littles. We needed to go ahead and eat and let my husband open his gifts. But the casserole wasn't ready yet.

I decided to reverse our usual order of events and have him blow out the candles on his cake and open his gifts first, and by then the casserole would be ready. We could eat cake after we ate lunch.

Two-year-old Haven studied the mound of chocolate as I lit the candles on the cake. She looked up at me with an impish grin. She knew what cake was. Chocolate had earned her approval on previous birthday gatherings.

I carried the cake over to Denny while everyone sang "Happy Birthday." But Haven was nowhere to be seen. She had disappeared into the playroom. We called for her to come back to the den, and as she rounded the corner, the room erupted into laughter.

Her tiny little body was struggling, but she was making it happen! She staggered into the den, lugging that children's table into the room all by herself. She was ready to sit down at the table because she was eager for a piece of that cake!

She had tasted cake, knew how good it was, and was eager to have some more! She was willing to put forth some effort for that cake!

"Taste and see that the Lord is good; blessed in the one who takes refuge in him," (Psalm 34:8).

When we taste of the goodness of God, it should put a desire in us for more of Him. When the Holy Spirit directs a specific Scriptural truth to our heart, it should make us want to make an effort to pull up to the table of God's Word for some more. Even if it's a bit of a struggle, we will make it happen.

"How sweet are your words to my taste, sweeter than honey to my mouth!" (Psalm 119:103)

Sweeter than chocolate cake. Pull up a table and see.

In the Dust

> *Your Word is like a precious jewel,*
> *Giving me my daily fuel*
> *To face the battles of my day,*
> *To light my path and guide my way.*
> *You are my heart's desire, my thirst.*
> *Above all else, I'll love you first,*
> *For, Lord, You've never failed to be*
> *A Help and Hope and Rock to me.*
> *So often I have hit the dirt,*

Lost and lonely, broken, hurt...
With friends on earth who can't quite be
The comfort that You've been to me.
But in those lonely times You've come...
Brushed off the dust, scrubbed off the scum,
And bound my wounds with tender hands.
You are the One who understands.
How precious are my thoughts of You...
That You, God, care what I go through
And have it all in Your control
To mold my life toward You, my goal.
So teach me, Jesus, more of Thee
In any trial my life may see,
And when I taste the bitter dust...
You've been there, too.
In You I'll trust.

— © 2019 BOBBIE PERKINS

REFLECT:

Are you willing to put forth an effort to read your Bible and spend time with God? Maybe get up a little earlier or block off part of your day as an "appointment" with Him?

Do you look forward to reading God's Word with excitement and anticipation of something good?

Think of a particular Scripture that has especially ministered to your heart. There is more of that to be found. What is keeping you from pulling up a table to taste some more?

—✝—

Dear God, Your Word feeds my soul and ministers to my needs. It is living and active to reach places in my heart that I didn't know needed changing. Help me to discipline myself to spend time in Your Word every day, even when it takes effort on my part. Amen.

HE ISN'T SAFE, BUT HE'S GOOD

SHE HANDED ME A LITTLE GIFT BAG (actually, she stuffed it into the pocket of my lab coat) while we were at work. "What's this?" I asked, as she caught me by surprise.

"It's nothing. Just a little something for you," she responded with a roguish grin. I was in the middle of drawing blood from a baby, so I had to wait for a peek. By the time I looked into the bag, my dear coworker had disappeared off to another task.

When I peeked inside, I had the strangest feeling— like God had told her my secrets! She had written me a sweet note, thanking me for being an encourager and enclosed a beautiful pair of hand knitted socks with the logo of a lion on the package. It may have seemed like a simple, sweet gesture, but it was oh….so much more than that! Socks are really a random gift…but there was nothing random about this.

You see, I have Raynaud's syndrome. It causes vasoconstriction of blood vessels, especially in the hands and feet. My hands will sometimes turn white or blue and feel numb or tingly. It is worse with cold weather or emotional stress. With all of the cold weather we've had lately, my feet have been very cold and uncomfortable. I had even thought about trying to find some kind of heated slippers.

This friend who loves to knit had no idea that I have Raynaud's. That just floored me that she would randomly give me a beautiful pair of warm, knitted socks just when I had been bothered with my feet being cold. But that's not all. The Lion logo on it was especially significant for that day...THAT day in particular.

That exact morning in my devotional time, I had been reading in Acts chapter 2 about the Holy Spirit coming down at Pentecost. Verse 2 described it as a sound like a violent wind. That morning I had been pondering about the mighty power of God, how He is fearful and awesome like a violent tornado, like a ferocious lion— yet good, compassionate, and loving.

As I was musing over the complex nature of God, it reminded me of a quote from a book I love—*The Lion, the Witch, and the Wardrobe* from the Chronicles of Narnia series by C.S. Lewis. It is an allegorical story in which the character Aslan, who is a Lion, represents Jesus. In the book there is a conversation between Lucy and Mr. Beaver about the nature of Aslan. Lucy asks, "Is he safe?"[1]

"Safe?" said Mr. Beaver. "Who said anything about safe? 'Course he isn't safe. But he's good. He's the King, I tell you." I had been thinking about that quote describing Aslan in regard to the nature of God, and my friend not only gave me socks with a lion on them, but she even mentioned Aslan in her note to me! It was a totally weird God-wink moment...or as another dear friend would say— "A kiss from the King!"

Something so simple. Yet such a WOW moment. That a friend cared enough about me to do something kind. That my God cared enough about me to make it obvious that He was behind the whole thing.

"And my God will meet all your needs according to the riches of

---

1. C. S. Lewis, *The Lion, The Witch, and the Wardrobe* (New York: Macmillan Publishing Company, 1950), 75-76

his glory in Christ Jesus" (Philippians 4:19). Oh, yes, He does. Sometimes He just stuffs it into your pocket and smiles.

REFLECT:

Consider the complex nature of God and worship Him today.

What kind of "God-wink" or "Kiss from the King" moments have you had? What did it do for your faith?

Think about that statement, "Course He isn't safe. But he's good. He's the King, I tell you." How would you explain that statement in relation to God's character?

—✝—

Dear God, You are always good, holy, and righteous, even in Your judgement against sin, when You aren't safe! I thank You that I am safe from Your wrath through the blood of Jesus on the cross. Help me to lead others to safety as well so that they can experience the goodness of You. Amen.

DADA

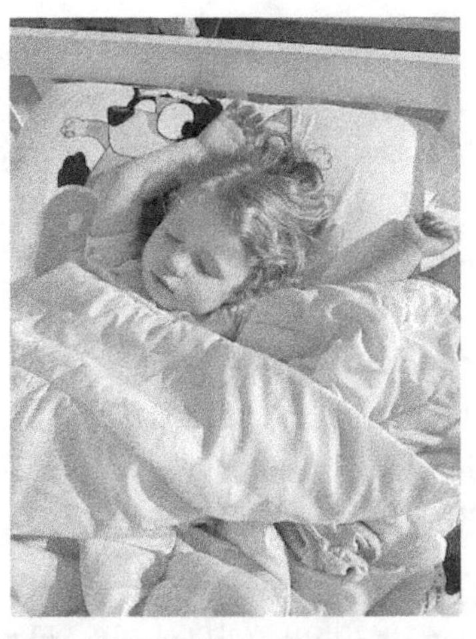

SHE LOVES HER DADDY. THERE'S NO doubt about it that my two-year-old granddaughter Nora is a Daddy's girl. She always wants to know where he is. She wants to be in his lap or playing right next to him. She loves spending time with her Daddy.

My daughter Regan said that lately Nora has been so preoccupied about where her Daddy is that when Regan wakes her up in the morning, Nora's first word when she opens her eyes is always, "Dada." (As a point of reference, my granddaughter Haven's first word of the day is almost always "snack.") No kidding! Lol!

Nora's daddy is the first thing she thinks about when she opens her eyes in the morning.

Needless to say, that made my son-in-law very happy. He knows he is loved by his daughter and that she wants to spend time with him.

I have to admit I was a little convicted when I considered the spiritual parallel. Is my heavenly Father the first thought on my mind when I wake up in the morning? Honestly, coffee usually hits my thoughts first! Yes, I spend time with Him in the morning, but I can't say He is always the very first thought I have when I open my eyes.

Just as it made my son-in-law happy that Nora's thoughts are focused on him when she wakes up, it must make God happy when my thoughts for the new day begin with Him, seeking Him out before I begin my day.

It's a new goal for me, inspired by a two-year-old. When I awaken each morning, I want to talk to God before I head for my coffee. It might be a short conversation, but I want Him to have that first waking moment of my day. Like my son-in-law Weston, I want God to be happy knowing that He is loved by His daughter and that she wants to spend time with Him.

David had that kind of relationship with God. He wrote in Psalm 63, "You, God, are my God, earnestly I seek you...on my bed I remember you; I think of you through the watches of the night." The watches of the night represented blocks of time in which guards began their duty in Roman culture. The spiritual parallel for both the Jews and Christians indicated a ceaseless contemplation of God throughout the night, being vigilant in prayer during a time of greater risk for danger. That fourth watch would be the time period of 3 am to 6 am. It's interesting to note that some very momentous spiritual things happened during that fourth watch of the night—Jacob wrestled with God, Moses led the Israelites across the Red Sea, the angels appeared to the shepherds, Peter and Jesus walked on water, Jesus was resurrected from the dead, and I'm sure there are several others.

I have to admit I was a little convicted when I considered the spiritual parallel. Is my heavenly Father the first thought on my mind when I wake up in the morning? Honestly, coffee usually hits my thoughts first! Yes, I spend time with Him in the morning, but I can't say He is always the very first thought I have when I open my eyes.

Just as it made my son-in-law happy that Nora's thoughts are focused on him when she wakes up, it must make God happy when my thoughts for the new day begin with Him, seeking Him out before I begin my day.

It's a new goal for me, inspired by a two-year-old. When I awaken each morning, I want to talk to God before I head for my coffee. It might be a short conversation, but I want Him to have that first waking moment of my day. I can have more conversation with Him after my coffee, too!

Like my son-in-law Weston, I want God to be happy knowing that He is loved by His daughter and that she wants to spend time with Him.

I always wake up early anyway. Instead of fighting to go back to sleep, I often feel that God just wants me to spend that special time, that fourth watch of the night, in prayer. There is something special about that early morning hour. No distractions. A clear mind for the day. Solitude with my Savior. In fact, today I signed up for a time slot for a twenty-four hour prayer vigil for a special family in deep need of prayer. I was happy to see an available time slot during that fourth watch of the night. My special time with Jesus.

I look forward to that time with Him. How about you?

REFLECT:

What are your first thoughts of the day? Are you thinking about your to-do list? Maybe wishing you didn't have to get up to go to work?

When do you usually have your first thoughts of God in the day? Is He in your everyday thoughts? Would you say that it is evident that you love spending time with Him?

How can you make God the first priority in all areas of your life?

—✝—

Dear God, You are a good, good Father. Thank you for caring for me better than any earthly father can. Help me to make You my biggest priority and to start my day with You. I want to spend time with you and live in a way that shows I love You. Amen.

SOJOURNERS

I HAVE A FRIEND WHO RECENTLY retired from teaching school for many years. Lilly didn't teach Science or Math. She taught an interesting subject—English as an Alternative Language. Her students were kids who were studying in the United States on visas, and they were learning how to integrate into their new surroundings and learn the English language. They often needed help understanding their homework or studying for tests due to the language barrier.

Lilly also taught them about the culture and customs of the United States. She was always careful to respect their own cultural customs as she assisted them with learning to adjust here.

I thought about this as I completed the wonderful Bible study, *Heaven*, by Jennifer Rothschild. (One of my favorite Bible studies yet!) In the Bible study we looked at Hebrews 11:13, a passage in which the great heroes of the faith called themselves "foreigners" and "strangers" on earth.

They remembered that their true citizenship wasn't on this earth — it was in heaven. The same is true for us. We need to remember where our true citizenship is! We are citizens of a better country. We are just sojourners while we are on this earth.

My question is...how much time do we spend thinking about our homeland? I was excited to study Heaven because I had never studied it before. And I began to realize that I had not been spending a great deal of time even thinking about Heaven.

I had to admit that I have spent more time planning get-aways and exploring fun vacation destinations than I have spent learning about my final destination!

But isn't that what the enemy wants? His goal is to have us so consumed with this world that we don't think about the next. We would do a lot less sharing the gospel. A lot less living for the glory of God. A lot less pursuing the mission that God has set before us. And a lot MORE pouring our hearts into things that don't last.

But Heaven is a greater reality than my vacation! That condo might just burn to the ground before I get to leave for my trip. There could be an earthquake that destroys the interstate route for me to get there. But Heaven is a sure thing for me.

Is it for you? If you're not sure, please read Appendix B in the back of this book.

That Bible study left me with a lot of good quotes to consider. Think about these:

"What if you live how you want to leave?" [1]

"Living with focus reduces dying with fear."

And one that has been attributed to several people, including Leonard Ravenhill and Adrian Rogers— "Is what I'm living for worth what Christ died for?"

I'm a sojourner here. But I don't want to acclimate. I want to stand out as different. (That's not too hard for someone as goofy as me!) I want others to know about my real home. While I'm living here on

---

1.   Jennifer Rothschild, *Heaven* (Brentwood, TN: Lifeway Press, 2025), 201-203

this earth, I want to live as an ambassador for my true place of citizenship.

"We are therefore Christ's ambassadors, as though God were making his appeal through us," (2 Corinthians 5:20).

REFLECT:

Do you ever think about Heaven? How are you living now in preparation for it?

What do you most look forward to about heaven?

Can you say that right now you are living how you want to leave?

—✝—

Dear God, Thank you for the certainty we have of heaven. Help me to live in anticipation of it and build my life around that eternal destination instead of this temporary one. I want to help others find the way through You. Amen.

NOVEMBER

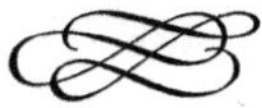

WHAT BRINGS US GRATITUDE?

WHAT ARE YOU LIKE WHEN YOU GO ON vacation? Do you pack lightly, bringing just the necessities? Not me. I unashamedly bring everything I can think of that will make our condo feel like home. I pretty much move in! I put boxes of food in the kitchen, my fuzzy robe and books in the den, my fan in the bedroom—I am not staying there; I am DWELLING there during our vacation.

I thought about that as I considered what it means to let the Word of Christ dwell in me richly, as Paul instructs in Colossians 3:16. I think it's kind of like my vacation style. God's Word isn't like a suitcase to be put in the corner, for me to be living out of it for one little area of my life. Letting His Word dwell in me richly is letting His Word MOVE IN to every room of my heart, so that people can see the evidence that He lives there.

If you were to walk into my vacation condo, you would see my fuzzy robe, my books, my comfortable belongings and know that someone was at home there. I want Christ and His Word to make their home in my heart in the same way, so that people see the evidence of Him in my life.

This verse tells us exactly what the evidence will be in our lives when we allow His Word to dwell in us richly- "teaching and admonishing one another in all wisdom, singing psalms and hymns, and spiritual songs with thankfulness in your hearts to God."

As His Word is living in us, it bubbles over to others. We are learning from one another, keeping each other accountable, encouraging one another, and praising God with one another. We are reflecting on God's character and His truth. The end results? Gratitude. Thanksgiving. His Word ultimately brings "thankfulness in your hearts to God."

This Thanksgiving as I lift my heart in gratitude to the Giver of all good gifts, I thank God for other believers like you. I am thankful for all those little things you do that give evidence that Christ has made His home in your heart.

I thank God for the times you have been kind to the harried server at the restaurant. When you have let the other driver over into your lane. The time you have sent a card or a text to a hurting friend and been faithful in prayer for the one burdened with grief. When God's Word dwells in us richly, it makes us love each other a little more like Jesus does.

Thank you for allowing Jesus to unpack in your heart. Thank you for allowing Him to make His dwelling place in you more beautiful each day as He continues to conform you into the image of Christ. It brings gratitude to my heart to know that He is there, leaving the evidence in how we live. I pray that today gratitude is dwelling in you richly as well as you look toward Thanksgiving!

Colossians 3:16

"Let the word of Christ dwell in you richly, teaching and admonishing one another in all wisdom, singing psalms and hymns and spiritual songs with thankfulness in your hearts to God." – Colossians 3:16

REFLECT:

Are others able to see the evidence of Christ in your life?

In what ways do you live differently because of Him?

Do you have friendships in which you keep each other accountable and encourage one another in the faith?

—✝—

Dear God, I want Your Word to dwell in me so richly that it overflows to others. I want to live differently because of You. Help me to encourage others and unpack Jesus everywhere I go. Amen.

TURNING THANKSGIVING INTO THANKSLIVING PART 1

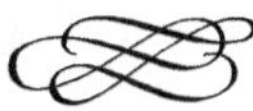

As Thanksgiving approaches, I've been reflecting on what scripture has to say about living a life of thankfulness, not just for a holiday, but as a lifestyle. It has made me want to be more thankful! How about you? Would you consider yourself a thankful person? Or are you a habitual grumbler? What kind of person do you want to be? In the next three devotions, we will look at how to change Thanksgiving into THANKSLIVING! Today we will look at why it matters that we as believers live with gratitude.

* * *

Why It Matters That Believers Live in Gratitude:

OUR THANKFULNESS MATTERS TO OTHERS. Thankful people are refreshing souls who bring encouragement to our day. Unthankful people are negative, miserable people who poison our outlook. What kind of impact do you want to have on those around you? Do you enjoy being around someone who is always complaining?

OUR THANKFULNESS CHANGES US. When we begin to practice gratefulness, it trains our hearts. There is something transformational about praising God when we don't feel like it. Psalm 34:1 says, "I will extol the Lord at all times; his praise will always be on my lips." The result of that praise is in verse 4. "I sought the Lord, and he answered me; he delivered me from all my fears." When we seek Him with a grateful heart, we find Him.

OUR THANKFULNESS MATTERS TO GOD. I Chronicles 23:30 describes one of the duties given to the Levites. "They were also to stand every morning to thank and praise the Lord. They were to do the same in the evening." Do you think God just instructed them to perform this ritual just to keep them busy? God knows what is best for us. He knew that their praise would make them love God more.

OUR THANKFULNESS GLORIFIES GOD. Psalm 69:30 states, "I will praise God's name in song and glorify him with thanksgiving."

This fulfills our purpose, for Isaiah 43:7 states that we were made for God's glory.

REFLECT:

Would those around you say you are a thankful person or a complainer?

Have you ever found God in a deeper way by thanking and praising Him?

Try starting your day every day this week with worship music and see how it impacts your outlook on the day.

―✝―

Dear God, I want to glorify You by being thankful. Help me to make gratefulness a natural outpouring of my love for You. Help me to encourage others with a grateful spirit and praise You in all I do. Amen.

TURNING THANKSGIVING INTO THANKSLIVING PART 2

Why It Matters That Believers Live in Gratitude:

OUR THANKFULNESS IS GOD'S COMMAND AND WILL FOR US. I Thessalonians 5:18 states "Give thanks in all circumstances; for this is God's will for you in Christ Jesus." I don't want to be outside of God's will for my life!

OUR LACK OF THANKFULNESS IS SIN. When we aren't thankful, God sees it as sin. It was the complaining of the Israelites that elicited God's wrath to them in Numbers 21:4-8. Their grumbling was considered rebellion because they weren't trusting God. Romans 1:21 states "That although they knew God, they neither glorified him as God nor gave thanks to him." That passage goes on to list some serious sins, and ungratefulness is right there in the ranks with those other sins. In Luke 17:11-19, Jesus denounced the lepers who did not thank God for their healing, but he praised the faith of the one who did thank him.

OUR THANKFULNESS IS A TRADEMARK OF OUR FAITH. Joy is one of the fruits of the spirit mentioned in Galatians 5:22,23. It is our joy through difficult circumstances that intrigues unbelievers and draws them to the faith. A despondent, cranky Christian is not an inviting advertisement for Jesus! That doesn't mean we can never be sad. We will talk about that in the next devotion!

OUR THANKFULNESS DEFEATS THE ENEMY. II Chronicles 20:22 tells the story of how Jehoshaphat, the fourth king of the Kingdom of Judah, managed to defeat his enemies. He appointed men to go out ahead of the army to sing and praise the Lord. "As they began to sing and praise, the Lord set ambushes against the men... who were invading Judah, and they were defeated." As we go forth with praise and thanksgiving, Satan's power is defeated in our lives.

REFLECT:

Have you ever thought about a lack of thankfulness being a sin?

What are some ways you can be more intentionally thankful?

What attacks of the enemy in your life have you been able to defeat with thankfulness?

⁃✝⁃

Dear God, I confess that I haven't always been giving thanks for the blessings You have given me. Lord, I want to be thankful in all things and be thankful for YOU, even when other things in my life are difficult. Help me to make it a habit to praise and worship You every day. Amen.

TURNING THANKSGIVING INTO THANKSLIVING PART 3

> "Let us continually offer to God a sacrifice of praise."
>
> — *Hebrews 13:15*

Today we will talk about how to be thankful when it is hard.

We want to be thankful, but sometimes it is really hard! How do we take the truths of Scripture and integrate them into our lives? We live in a broken world as broken people. We have daily disappointments, difficulties, and frustrations. Car repairs. A leaky roof. Traffic jams. Rude people. Work stress. I must admit that my reactions aren't always thankful. I think it's even harder for me to think about God in those small, seemingly insignificant things than it is in the big ones. The thing is... God isn't surprised by those little annoyances any more than He is by the big tragedies. He is there in the midst of all of them. I want to look for Him in all of those things.

But how do we do that? How can we transform our responses to become more thankful? We have to recognize that being grateful isn't about feeling good about something. It is about giving God the gift of our praise from an obedient heart. Hebrews 13:15 says "Let us continually offer to God a sacrifice of praise." It is a sacrifice to praise God when it hurts. How do we actually do that? I think Scripture teaches us to do it in these two ways– Remember and Relinquish.

Remember

- Remember that God understands our pain. Being thankful doesn't mean we can't ever be sad. Hebrews 4:15 tells us "We do not have a high priest who is unable to empathize with our weaknesses." Jesus suffered and understands our suffering. He was filled with agonizing dread in the Garden of Gethsemane as He wept and mourned His fate. And His Father gave Him strength to do what He was destined to do.
- Remember that God is trustworthy. Can we trust God to bring something good even out of the worst tragedies of our lives? Romans 8:28 says, "For we know that all things work for the good of those who love God, who have been called according to his purpose." We may never know the good, but we can trust that it is there.
- Remember what God has done for us in the past. When we focus our thoughts on what God has done for us, instead of what He hasn't done for us, it brings rest to our souls. Psalm 116:7 states, "Return to your rest, my soul, for the Lord has been good to you." Remember all those times in the past when He has seen you through other times of difficulty. He is faithful.
- Remember that God sees the big picture. Can we trust that God has our good in mind, even if He never tells us why? I always want to understand. Somehow if I can know the good that is coming out of something, then I somehow feel better. But sometimes we can't see the good. And sometimes we just aren't supposed to understand. We look through a limited scope of vision, but God sees the whole picture. He is eternal and sees the future that I don't

see. Some suffering seems so senseless and unfair. Then I think back to the cross. If I had been standing there, I would have thought how senseless and unfair that the compassionate, gentle Jesus was wrongly accused, tortured, and murdered. I would have questioned God for allowing that suffering. But God saw the big picture. He was up to something bigger than human eyes could see. He was conquering sin and death! He isn't limited by constraints of time. I have to ask God to help me see past the here and now and trust that He sees the future that I don't see.

- Remember how great a salvation we have. Psalm 105:5 says, "Remember the wonders He has done." Remember the wonder of salvation. How can we receive such undeserved mercy and that not be enough? When was the last time we pondered our own sin and the incredible gift of grace we have received? If someone gave you an incredible gift- say a brand-new Ferrari, you would be very grateful. Would you be complaining the next day if they didn't give you their old 1973 rusted clunker? The first incredible gift is enough. Salvation is the greatest gift we will ever receive.
- Remember to talk to God in your heartbreak. Be honest with God. Admit to Him that you don't understand. Tell

Him you are afraid. Then choose by faith to thankfully acknowledge that He is trustworthy. It was during his moments of deepest pain and desperation that David had his greatest encounters with God and wrote some of the beautiful Psalms of praise. Psalm 22:3 says that God inhabits our praises. Praise invites us to a deeper intimacy with God. What beautiful story of praise does God want to write with your life?

- Remember to form thankful habits. When we act in obedience even when we don't feel like it, it eventually becomes a habit. A lifestyle. An automatic response that becomes second nature. When we feel the grumbling coming, we need to "demolish arguments and every pretension that sets itself up against the knowledge of God, and we take captive every thought [even the desire to grumble] to make it obedient to Christ" (2 Corinthians 10:5).

That's a lot of things to remember! In the next devotion we will talk about what we need to relinquish. Hang in there!

REFLECT:

How have you seen the faithfulness of God in your life and how can remembering that help you when you are discouraged?

Are you remembering to talk to God in your times of struggle? Are you praising Him?

What thankful habits do you need to establish?

—✝—

Dear God, I thank you right now for Your goodness and mercy to me. My salvation is the greatest gift I could ask for, and it makes everything else pale in comparison. I praise You for Who You are and what You have done in my life and ask You to continue Your work in me to make me a grateful follower of You. Amen.

CONVERT YOUR GRATEFUL
THOUGHTS TO ACTIONS

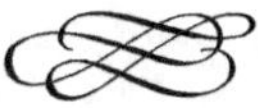

"I will praise God's name in song and glorify him with thanksgiving."

— Psalm 69:30

God has continued to reveal to me where I fall short in the area of thankfulness. I think my journey of deliberately trying to be more thankful actually began in May of this year. We were taking a vacation to the beach, and things didn't exactly go as planned. The funny part was that I was in the midst of a Bible study that focused on giving God honor through our gratefulness. I just didn't plan to actually have to apply what I was learning!

After traveling safely over seven hundred miles, we had a wreck twenty-six miles before arriving at our condo. A big wreck. The other car was totaled, and our car had massive damage. Instead of it ruining our vacation, the strangest peace and gratefulness flooded me. I was grateful for the miracle of no injuries other than mild bruises. Grateful we were twenty-six miles from the condo and not two hundred, since we had to pay a cab to take us the rest of the way. Grateful for Walmart grocery delivery since we would have no car until our rental would arrive two days later. Thankful for the beautiful ocean reminding us that God is in control. Then, on top of it all, our condo had this picture hanging in it! How cool is that?

I think being thankful is mostly about making a shift in our perspective. We think beyond ourselves and try to look at life from God's perspective. One of the people who is so practiced at doing that is Joni Eareckson Tada. Many of you may be familiar with Joni, who has spent most of her life in a wheelchair after becoming paralyzed from the shoulders down in a diving accident at the age of seventeen. Joni's story of faith has changed countless lives, both through her ministry to the disabled community and her ministry to anyone who is experiencing struggles. In 2010, Joni was diagnosed with breast cancer. When I heard about her diagnosis, my immediate thought was, "Lord, hasn't she suffered enough?" Joni's reaction to the diagnosis, however, shows her God-centered focus. After the initial shock, Joni expressed that God was giving her a new group of people to relate to — people with cancer." How humbling to think of this woman of faith having those unselfish thoughts despite all the suffering she has already endured. And I have to wonder...would Joni's teachings be as beautiful if she had not suffered greatly? Her life struggles enhance her message. Oh, Lord! May our lives and our messages intertwine in such a beautiful way!

REFLECT:

I hope that these devotions have helped to bring Thanksliving into your life! So how about it? Are you ready to turn your thoughts into action? Here are some ideas on how to convert those thankful thoughts into thankful actions:

1. Tell your family or others some specific ways you appreciate them.
2. Write a note to your pastor or a person who has spiritually encouraged you. Don't assume they know how you feel. Thank them for their faithfulness. Think back to people who planted spiritual seeds in your life who may not know the impact they had.
3. Thank strangers for their friendliness, helpfulness, even their smile. Be the Light.
4. Listen to praise music. Think about the words. Give the words to God.
5. Make a blessings list- Don't ignore the fact that those things come from God. James 1:17 says, "Every good and perfect gift is from above." Some of mine- family, hilarious laughter, a sunrise, mountains, the ocean, puppies, kittens, prayer with friends, music, a soft bed, air conditioning, my fuzzy robe, coffee, chocolate! Thank God for all of it!
6. Make a spiritual blessings list. We made a pumpkin this year with spiritual blessings from Scripture written on it. Make your own or use the list that we made. I have included my list of Spiritual blessings on the next devotion. There are a lot, and I'm sure you can find many more! This is a great activity to do with kids and grandkids!

May your Thanksgiving be filled with grateful enjoyment of your blessings!

—✝—

Dear God, Your blessings are so abundant, and I thank You for them and for Your perfect love. Help me to look for the blessings even in my struggles. Help me to have a more positive outlook on life. Amen.

SPIRITUAL BLESSINGS

WE TEND TO THINK OF BLESSINGS AS tangible things, but consider some of the intangible spiritual blessings listed below.

That His ears are attentive to my cry- Psalm 34:15

That while I was a sinner Christ died for me- Romans 5:8

That Jesus intercedes for me- Romans 8:26

For God's grace given through Jesus- 2 Timothy 1:9

For The beauty of His Creation-Psalm 19:1

For The church as the body of believers and my own church- Romans 12:4,5

For friends who encourage in the faith- Hebrews 10:24,25

For Our Pastor and other spiritual leaders- Hebrews 13:7

For the passages in the Bible that thrill my soul- Psalm 119:97

For how the Bible convicts us and changes us- Hebrews 4:12

For the blessed assurance of salvation- 1 John 5:13

That I have redemption and forgiveness of sin through Jesus-
Ephesians 1:7

For the Holy Spirit who advocates for me against the enemy- John
15:26

For the Holy Spirit who guides me into truth- John 16:13

For the Holy Spirit who testifies to me that I am a child of God-
Romans 8:16

For planning a way of salvation before the world began- Ephesians
1:4

That He delights to show mercy- Micah 7:18

That His compassions never fail and are new every morning- Lamen-
tations 3:23

That He cares about everything in my life- I Peter 5:6,7

That He is a personal God- Psalm 23

That He directs my steps- Proverbs 16:9

That He set eternity in our hearts so we would seek Him- Ecclesiastes
3:11

That He disciplines us for our own good and to make us holy-
Hebrews 12:10

That He restores my soul- Psalm 23:3

That He redeemed me- Isaiah 43:1

That God conforms me to make me more like Jesus- Romans 8:29

That Jesus has prepared a place in heaven for us- John 14:2

For God's relentless pursuit of my soul- Matthew 18:12

For giving me an inheritance with the saints- Colossians 1:12

For equipping us by inspiring the writing of His Word- 2 Timothy
3:16

For calling saints who made mistakes so I could have hope- 1
Timothy 1:13-16

That He keeps me from sin- Psalm 19:13

For beautiful hymns and music that draw me in worship- Ephesians
5:19,20

For God's faithfulness when I am unfaithful- 2 Timothy 2:13

For God's trustworthy, true, and unchanging nature- Malachi 3:6

For God's holy nature- Psalm 96:9

That I am precious and honored and loved by Him- Isaiah 43:4

For The peace that only He can give even in the midst of trials- John 14:27

That I am chosen- Ephesians 1:4

God's unfathomable power to accomplish whatever He wills to do- Jeremiah 32:17

That He knows me fully and still loves me- Psalm 139:16

That He heals the brokenhearted- Psalm 147:3

That He can comfort me like no one else can- 2 Corinthians 1:3,4

That He rescues out of the deepest pit- Psalm 40:1,2

That He is slow to anger and abounding in love- Exodus 34:6

That He clothes me with righteousness- Isaiah 61:10

For His power that keeps me from stumbling- Jude 24

For bringing good out of what the enemy intends for evil- Romans 8:28

For God's calling to deem me worthy of serving Him- 1 Timothy 1:12

That His divine power gives us everything we need to live a godly life- 2 Peter 1:3

That He gives a song to my soul- Psalm 40:3

That His power is working in me- Ephesians 3:20

That He is with me through every trial and hardship- Isaiah 43:2

That He counsels me and instructs me- Psalm 16:7

That my testimony is used along with Jesus' blood to defeat the enemy- Revelation 12:11

That He gives spiritual gifts to the body of Christ- 1 Corinthians 12:7

He gives us strength to fight our battles- Psalm 18:32

That He delights in me- Psalm 18:19

That He walks with me in the dark valleys- Psalm 23:4

He turns my wailing into dancing- Psalm 30:11

He delivers me from my fears- Psalm 34:4

That He makes known to me the mystery of His will- Romans 12:2

That God loved me so much He sent His beloved son to die for me- John 3:16

Reflect:

What Spiritual blessings are the sweetest to you?

Did you find any verses that were new to you or that especially stood out?

Which one do you most need to cling to in this season of your life?

—✝—

Dear God, You are more than sufficient to meet my every need. Thank you for the abundant blessings and promises you have given in your word. Help me to walk in victory as I remember them. Amen.

GOD'S GIFTS

WHEN MY KIDS WERE LITTLE I DID ONE of my rare attempts at doing something crafty. For Thanksgiving I cut a large tree out of felt and glued it to another large piece of felt to make a banner. I bought fall leaves from a hobby store and had the kids write things they were thankful for on the leaves. Every day starting a couple weeks before Thanksgiving, they would attach one of their leaves to the tree.

I have to admit there weren't a lot of deep spiritual thoughts going on...lol. They were usually thankful for things like pizza and toys. But it did get them thinking about the everyday things around them that they are thankful for. And the closer we got to Thanksgiving, the more we talked as a family about some of those intangible blessings in addition to the goofy things they loved.

I'm a nature lover, so aside from salvation and spiritual blessings, most of my gratitude was usually pointed toward the beautiful things in God's creation and the relationships I have with those I love. Doing this made us realize there are so many little things we take for granted in our everyday lives! Heat! Air conditioning! Hot water! A soft bed to sleep on! We don't think of being thankful for those everyday things, but a homeless person would be so grateful to have those. It's all a matter of perspective.

As Thanksgiving approaches, you don't have to make a tree, but you could make a list by writing down one thing every day. It's also fun to see what other people appreciate that you might not have thought about.

Don't let God's gifts go by unnoticed!

God's Gifts

Looking back at all my life, I decided that today
I'd sit down and think about the gifts God sends my way.
There's the beauty of a sunrise in a morning's dawning hour,
The melody of singing birds, the fragrance of a flower;
A rose's sun-kissed dewdrops, a baby's trusting cry,
The cleansing wetness of the rain, the stars up in the sky;
Trees swaying in the breeze to form a work of art,
A love that slowly reached out and gently touched my heart;
A stranger's smile, a winter's snow, a cool refreshing stream;
Songs sung with gladness, an accomplished hope or dream;
Many hours spent with family and close friends-
Oh, Lord, I've never noticed the beauty each day sends!

— © 1990 BOBBIE PERKINS

REFLECT:

What are some everyday blessings that you take for granted?

What things are at the top of your blessings list?

. . .

As a family, try talking about what others are thankful for. It may make you think of things you haven't thought of?

—✝—

Dear God, I walk by beauty every day without seeming to notice or to thank you for it. I want to notice Your good gifts. Help me to think about the goodness You bring to my life as I go about my daily activities. Help me to celebrate Thanksgiving every day. Amen.

LOOKING BACK

"He has made everything beautiful in its time."

— Ecclesiastes 3:11

We do it every year. Setting those clocks back... as if we can really gain another hour of time. I once heard someone describe it as like cutting an inch off the bottom of a blanket, sewing it to the top of the blanket, then claiming to have a longer blanket!

This year when we turned the clocks back, a friend mentioned how she wished she could turn the clock back even further in time and do some things differently. I felt sad for her because I have definitely felt that way before. But I don't really struggle with those thoughts much anymore. As much as I remember the messes and mistakes I've made, I realize they have impacted me in ways that have made me who I am today. If I had never needed God's comfort, I might not know Him the way I do as my Comforter. If I had never needed God's deep well of grace, I might not have ever known Him as the God of Amazing Grace. God's sovereignty reigns even in my mistakes. Even in my sin. He has a good plan for my life and can use even those bad things to teach me more of Him and to bring good.

I don't have to live in regret. And neither do you. If you start to feel preoccupied with thoughts of the past, think about it like this—it's okay to look back. But look back in a different way….

Look back to remember the people God placed in your life, the ones who brought you closer to Him…and thank them. Write them a letter, a text, or go tell them in person. It will make their day!

Look back to remember the lessons you learned through times of sorrow or sin….now go share that with someone else who is struggling.

Look back to remember what it was like to be on the other side of the chasm, to not know Jesus….and go find someone else who is still there. Tell them your faith story and share the gospel with them.

Look back and remember the goodness of God. And tell your children and your grandchildren all about that goodness.

…And suddenly you are looking back on the past with a smile instead of regret.

Reflect:

How can you make regrets into opportunities?

Have any of your regrets helped you to know God in a deeper way?

How has God brought victory out of your defeats?

⁓✝⁓

Dear God, I am thankful that You reign over all, even my own poor choices. Thank you that You are still fulfilling your plan for my life, even despite my mistakes. You are good, powerful, and trustworthy. Help me to walk in the victory that You have already provided after my defeats. Amen.

THE THINGS WE
AREN'T THANKFUL FOR

"*He comforts us in all our troubles so that we can comfort others.*"
— 2 Corinthians 1:4

I AM CONTINUING THIS MONTH TO reflect on the many things for which I am thankful. A loving husband and family. Beautiful grandchildren. Dear friends who make me laugh and point me to Jesus. Not having to worry about practical needs such as shelter, food, and clothing...the list goes on and on. I am wondering if you, like me, tend to think of tangible things or people when you think of what you are thankful for.

Those tangible things and people are definitely gifts from God. But about the intangibles? What about those THINGS in our lives that have brought turmoil? Can we thank God for those events in our lives that we look back upon with sorrow or regret? Can we thank God for adversity that taught us how to trust Him in a deeper way? What about thanking Him for the mistakes we've made that weaved a new thread of wisdom into our lives?

Hmm. That's a new one. Thanking God for our mistakes? But God wasn't caught off guard by those things. He lovingly uses them to teach us more of Him. "For we are God's workmanship, created in Christ Jesus to do good works, which God PREPARED IN ADVANCE" (Ephesians 2:10, emphasis mine). I see how God prepared me to minister to others by allowing some things in my life that I would not have chosen. But He knew in advance the good that would come of it.

God's purpose for all believers is to conform us to the likeness of Jesus. The amazing thing is that nothing that happens in our lives is outside of God's sovereign will, and He brings about His purpose for good in our lives through the mysterious dance of our free will and His sovereign will. God's sovereign plan even includes our failures, and He lovingly uses them in our lives for good. "And we know that in all things God works for the good of those who love him, who have been called according to His purpose" (Romans 8:28).

That verse doesn't say all things work for good except our bad choices. It says ALL things work together for good. He has a purpose even in our grief and mistakes. And that purpose is always for our good and His glory.

What things in your life do you wish had never happened? Can you thank God for them? In one of my favorite books, *31 Days toward Trusting God,* Jerry Bridges writes, "Over all the actions and events of our lives, God is in control, doing as He pleases– not apart from those events or in spite of them but *through* them."[1]

What is God accomplishing through the difficult things in your life? This Thanksgiving, thank Him for the intangibles. Choose thankfulness by an act of your will, and see the truth of Jeremiah 29:11, "For I know the plans I have for you," declares the Lord, "plans to prosper you and not to harm you, plans to give you hope and a future." God's plan is always good. Even in those things we aren't thankful for.

---

1. Jerry Bridges, 31 Days toward Trusting God (Navpress in alliance with Tyndale House Publishers, 2013), 23.

Reaching Out

The past has left scars, and though my life has been made new,
I still have some regrets from the things I've been through.
I remember the shame as sin stole my self-worth,
But your love had a plan for my life before birth.
So, Lord, I give you the past- all the pain through the years.
I know you can use it to dry others' tears.
And, Lord, I give you the future and lift praise to Your name
That I can tell those around me how my life's not the same.
Take everything You can use in my life.
Lord, I offer myself. Make me a pure sacrifice.
And the hurts fade away as I look in the face
Of one finding Your mercy and experiencing Your grace.
And the aches are now blessings- a welcome stab to my heart
As you work changes in lives and allow me to take part.
Oh, Lord, now I see just how sovereign You are.
It's as I reach out to others that You heal my own scar.

— © 2000 BOBBIE PERKINS

REFLECT:

What is God accomplishing through the difficult things in your life?

How has God allowed you to use your scars to help others?

Are there things in your life that once brought tears that now bring thanksgiving?

━✝━

*Dear God, Thank you that You have always had a good plan for my life,
even when it included tears. Help my aches turn to blessings as I learn to
reach out to minister to others. Thank you that You are our Healer and
Deliverer. Amen.*

THANKSGIVING AND
LYME DISEASE LESSONS

I MADE A NEW FRIEND A FEW YEARS ago. Lisa Marie is the adult daughter of a dear couple from my church. She is beautiful, intelligent, unique, talented, joyful, and so many other wonderful things. I didn't meet her at a party or an event. I actually met her in a dark room where we had to speak in hushed whispers.

The quiet darkness was not a temporary situation. Astonishingly, Lisa Marie has been confined to a dark bedroom for almost 30 years. Her captor is not a person but an illness called Lyme Disease. When Lisa Marie was 12 years old, contracting this illness changed the trajectory of her life forever. Lyme disease is caused by a bacteria often found in ticks and can be transmitted when an infected tick bites a person.

Lisa Marie went from being an active girl involved in sports, music, church youth gatherings, and other fun activities to suffering from debilitating joint pain, light sensitivity, dizziness, crushing migraines, and a host of other physical ailments that cause her to require a caregiver to attend to all of her needs. Her parents have faithfully cared for her all of these years. She can't tolerate the noise of the television or the sound of her favorite music unless it is played very, very softly. She can't walk. She can't bear any noise above a whisper.

I can't imagine the boredom. The loneliness. The longing for the life she once knew. Yet Lisa Marie has a joy that surpasses understanding. She trusts God with her life. She can truly say with the Psalmist, "In him our hearts rejoice, for we trust in his holy name," (Psalm 33:21). It is her trust in God that sustains her, and she has spent many hours in the quietness of that bedroom communing with her Maker. She reads her Bible in the dark with a small flashlight and has memorized large passages of Scripture. Her favorite verse is Psalm 73:26, which reads, "My flesh and my heart may fail, but God is the strength of my heart and my portion forever."

The thing that amazes me the most about this precious woman is that the maturity of her faith started at a very young age. She began writing poetry about her struggles when she was barely a teenager. Her writing is a beautiful testimony of how God has worked in her life to teach her contentment, hope, and joy in her extraordinary circumstances. I feel a strange connection to her because I, too, have found writing poetry to be the way God teaches me, encourages me, and helps me sort through difficult emotions.

It seems fitting that I met Lisa Marie during the season of Thanksgiving. When I reflect on what I am thankful for, I realize that I have so much more than I ever imagined. I never thought to thank God for the ability to turn on a light without piercing agony in my head. I never thought to be thankful that I can laugh loudly with friends, enjoy music, walk, care for myself, and go outside whenever I want.

I am convicted when I look at Lisa's Marie's life in comparison to mine and the amount of complaining I do in comparison to her. I realize I have nothing at all in my life to complain about. I am convicted about the many things I take for granted.

I am including some of Lisa Marie's poems that show her sweet, humble spirit and love for the Lord. Her mother, Karen Angotti, also wrote a magnificent and heart-wrenching book about their experience that is available on Amazon. It is called *Lyme Disease: A Mother's Perspective*.

What are you complaining about? What are you taking for granted? What are you thankful for this Thanksgiving? I am thankful for my friend Lisa Marie, who has taught me much about being thankful.

I want to glorify God with my life, and His Word says we glorify Him when we are thankful. "I will praise God's name in song and glorify him with thanksgiving," (Psalm 69:30).

The following poems were written by my friend, Lisa Marie Angotti.

Hold My Hand

Lord, life sometimes is oh, so hard.
With mountains high and valleys low.
Please hold my hand with gentle strength.
Oh, never let me go.
Lord, at times I feel like giving up;
The road is rough and long.
But if you'll hold my hand real tight,
My heart will always sing Your song.
Lord, some days I seem to want my way,
To do what I think's best.
Instead, please lead me by the hand
Into the perfect will You've blessed.
Lord, I know You said You'd never leave me,
Yet now and then I feel alone.
Clasp my powerless hand in Yours
For I am never on my own.
Lord, what do You think when I'm afraid
When I've no cause for doubt or fear?
It must cause You unfathomed pain
When you are standing there so near.

So, Lord, when I start to cry for You
Begin to wonder if You understand,
May I always know with a perfect peace
You are there – waiting – to hold my hand.

— © 1995 LISA MARIE ANGOTTI THIS POEM WAS WRITTEN WHEN LISA MARIE WAS A YOUNG TEEN. I AM AMAZED AT HER SPIRITUAL MATURITY AT SUCH A YOUNG AGE. BOTH POEMS USED WITH PERMISSION.

Cup Of Anguish

Sometimes it all seems too much,
This overflowing anguished cup.
I say, "I can't; I'm not this tough."
But then I see upon that tree
The Man of Sorrows slain for me —
Unshakable even to death.
And though my strength has nothing left,
I feel a deep, steadying Breath.
For a sacrifice so infinite,
May my gratitude be evident.
In Your strength, I know I can,
So, precious Lord, with all I am, I surrender to Your perfect
plan.

— © 2018 LISA MARIE ANGOTTI

Reflect:

When you think about the suffering of someone like Lisa Marie, does it change your perspective of your own problems?

. . .

Do you think Lisa Marie has a special relationship with God BECAUSE of her pain? Do you think God has used that in her life to draw her even closer to Him than she might have been otherwise?

James 4:8 says, "Draw near to God, and he will draw near to you." How do you think that describes Lisa Marie's life?

—✝—

Dear God, Suffering can be such a double-edged sword that I wouldn't choose, but that brings things that I desire in my life. Help me to seek after You with a passion and desire holiness, even when I don't have to walk such a difficult path. Amen.

DECEMBER

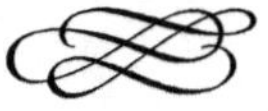

CAN WE SEE GOD?

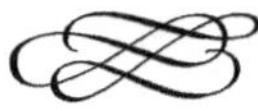

I John 4:12 tells us that no one has seen God. The indescribable glory of seeing the essence of His being would devastatingly overwhelm us in our sinful state. Though it is true that I may never have visualized Him as a material substance, this week I did see God. It was an amazing experience.

In December every year my running group, the 901 sole sisters, participates in the run for St Jude Children's Research Hospital to raise money to help kids with cancer. It's an emotional race because many of us know someone who has lost a child to cancer. During 2020 the race was made virtual due to Covid, so we held our own event, complete with a makeshift finish line and an after-party! Emotions were also fragile because it was a momentous accomplishment for six of our runners who ran their first full marathon—Heather Volner, Patricia Prather, Michelle Bledsoe, Catherine Smith, Cat Tankersley, and Ashley Snow. Three in the group ran the half-marathon—Judy Reynolds, Jayn Lando, and Steven Henry (we have a few random dudes in our sole sister group). It was an emotional day for Ashley for an additional reason: Saturday was the anniversary of her sister's death. I shared about Ashley's story in the January devotions. I was recovering from knee surgery, so I didn't get to run, but I organized food and the after-party.

What I saw that day was the reflection of God as He was perfecting His own image in us. I John 4:12 tells us "No one has ever seen God," but if you continue reading, the second half of that passage says, "But if we love one another, God lives in us and his love is made complete in us."

(pictured, Heather Volner, Catherine Smith, Michelle Bledsoe, Patricia Prather, Ashley Snow, Ann Marie McCalla, Steven Henry, Cat Tankersley, and Jayn Lando)

It is God's nature to love. The provision He made for our sin through Jesus stems from his lovingkindness, perfectly combining the fact that his nature is to be both loving and just. We need only to look to the cross to see the depths of that love. An astonishing thing about that love is that if we were to search the universe for a visible representation of that astonishing love, John tells us that this love is gloriously displayed in the relationships between believers as we love one another. When God dwells in us, His Spirit causes love to reign in our hearts. As the work of God's spirit in our hearts grows closer to completion, His love becomes more and more evident in our lives.

That love was so evident on Saturday. It was in running for a cause to help kids and families. It was in sharing supplies like Gu chews, water, sunblock, and pickle juice. It was in sharing experiences during brutal training– like running in the dark, heat, cold, fog, rain, wind, and hills. It was sharing the experiences of muscle cramps, blisters, chafing, and getting up at ridiculous hours of the morning to run before work. It was in sharing encouragement when a member of the group was struggling and fighting insecurities. It was in sharing tears at the finish line, celebrating the victorious realization of a shared goal that had been so very difficult to achieve. It was in sharing preparations by those who couldn't participate due to injuries or conflicts with training schedules and being there before the sun came up to cheer and organize an after-party.

Love that will suffer the unthinkable at the cross. Love that will get up at 2:50 a.m. for a friend. They are mysteriously and splendidly intertwined through the roots of grace.

No one has ever seen God, but Jesus has made Him known (John 1:18). We love because He first loved us (I John 4:19).

Reflect:

How can you show an extra measure of love to someone this week?

John 13:35 says, "By this everyone will know that you are my disciples, if you love one another." Would people know you are a disciple by how you treat others? Not just your family and friends, but what about the cashier at the grocery store or the server at the restaurant?

Dear God, Thank You for the fellowship of other believers to encourage me and help me see an extra glimpse of Your love for me. Help me to love others in a way that gives them a visible representation of Your love for them. Thank You for Your great love that surpasses all others! Amen.

ALL ABOUT JESUS

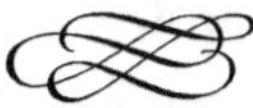

WORKING AS A NURSE FOR ALMOST 40 years, I have seen just about everything. Weird stuff. Sad stuff. Joy. Blood. Death. Teamwork. Miracles. I vividly remember certain patients and their families, even though our paths may have only crossed for a matter of hours. Gracie is one of those memories.

I was bummed to be working on Christmas Day, but that's all part of being in the healthcare profession. I entered my postpartum patient's room to find a little girl with beautifully wild, curly hair sitting on the sofa, holding her new baby brother. Her big brown eyes looked at the baby, then her mother. She was sobbing. "No, Mommy! No! That's not right!"

"Not too happy with her baby brother?" I questioned her mom.

"Oh, she loves the baby, mom responded. It's his name she isn't happy with. She is insistent upon naming him something else."

Curious, I asked, "What does she want to name him?"

"Baby Jesus," the mom replied with an exasperated laugh. She explained, "This Christmas we have been showing Gracie the baby Jesus in the nativity scene, and she is all about that baby Jesus! All she will talk about is the baby Jesus. She plays with the manger scene at home and tells everyone that baby Jesus is coming at Christmas. Now Gracie expects our baby to be named Baby Jesus because he came at Christmas. "Help!" she laughed. "I think we have confused her!"

I sat next to Gracie and asked her if she would like to use my stethoscope to hear her baby brother's heartbeat. I managed to get a smile out of her as she listened with wonder to his heartbeat and then her own. When I left the room, nothing more was said about the baby's name. To be honest, I don't even remember what the baby's name really was. But I remember Gracie.

Gracie was all about that baby Jesus. I felt God speaking to me through that strong-willed, intelligent child. I need to be more like Gracie! Oh, how I want it to be all about Jesus as I celebrate His birth! I began to think about the holiday hustle and bustle and my own rushing around to get everything done. Did everything really need to be just right? Our Savior definitely didn't come into a world that was just right. His birth in a stable reminds me that Christmas is not about elaborate preparations. The only preparation He asks for is the one in my heart. The redemption of my soul is so much like the miracle of birth! What a miracle to look at new life with eyes of wonder! Lord, may I always look at the new life you created in my soul with eyes of wonder! Like Gracie, this Christmas I want it to be all about Jesus.

REFLECT:

What preparations have you made, not in your home, but in your heart for Christmas this year?

Are your children and grandchildren learning that Christmas is about Jesus more than holiday celebrations, gifts, and food?

· · ·

If you have a job that requires you to work on Christmas, how can you share the beauty of Christmas at your job that day?

—✝—

Dear God, I want to focus on the true meaning of Christmas. Help me to communicate that to the children around me who are learning about Jesus. Help us to be able to look back after the holidays and be able to say, "It really was all about Jesus!" Amen.

WHAT I LEARNED FROM THE YEAR OF COVID CHRISTMAS

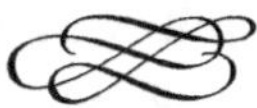

"My soul glorifies the Lord and my spirit rejoices in God my Savior."

— Luke 1:46

THE FAMILIAR SONG JOYFULLY proclaims the arrival of the Christmas season as "The Most Wonderful Time of the Year!" What is it about Christmas that makes it so special? Is it really the giving and receiving of gifts that we look forward to? Or is it something more?

As a Christian, my desire at Christmas is to commemorate the birth of my Savior and not get caught up in the "Whoville" busyness of the season. But there are still preparations that are necessary in order to host a family gathering, even a small gathering. How do I strike a balance between worship and work, praise and provision? Surprisingly, it was Covid that changed my perspective on what is necessary and what is superfluous. I learned it is okay to spend less time cooking and more time enjoying my family. That's a big jump for someone like me who thrives on feeding people!

When I think back to that dreadful Covid year, I see the spiritual parallels between sin and Covid. I don't know a single person who didn't get impacted in some way by Covid. In the same way, nobody is able to escape the impact of sin. Like that virus, sin also brings so much of the same type of calamity. Fear. Sickness. Death. Struggles. Separation. But there is an important difference between Sin and Covid! Our sin virus doesn't just have a vaccine; it has a cure!

Born out of mercy and birthed in a stable, God's rescue from the wretched consequences of sin is what we celebrate at Christmas.

There is no greater gift than this deliverance. But there is something else. Another precious gift was wrapped in those swaddling clothes. It was the gift of family. Mary and Joseph started their family in that humble stable. They looked in wonder at their firstborn child just as we have looked with wonder at our own children. And their hearts were filled with joy. May our hearts be filled with joy this Christmas as we reflect on the gift of family. If anything, I think that the year of Covid with social distancing brought me a new appreciation for connecting with family and friends.

No matter what the year has brought, my prayer is that the precious gifts of redemption, family, and friendship bring celebration to you this Christmas. "And Mary said: My soul glorifies the Lord and my spirit rejoices in God my Savior" (Luke 1:46). This truly is our something more...that makes it the reason why it is the "most wonderful time of the year."

REFLECT:

Would downscaling your preparations of cooking and decorating help you to enjoy more time with your family?

What are some of your favorite Christmas memories?

If we found out about a cure for Covid, cancer, or some other disease, we would be telling people! Are you telling people about the cure for sin?

―✝―

Dear God, I want my heart to be filled with joy, not filled with stress of things I need to do when I look at the blessing of my family. Like Mary, help me to remember the important thing about Christmas is that "my spirit rejoices in God my Savior." Thank you for giving us a cure for sin. Amen.

HAPPY BIRTHDAY JESUS!

> *"Blessed is she who has believed that the Lord would fulfill his promises to her!"*
>
> — Luke 1:45

WHAT KIND OF CHRISTMAS TRADI-tions do you have in your family to keep Jesus in the forefront of your celebration? One thing our family does is our "Happy Birthday Jesus Box." It is just a decorative cardboard box that says "Happy Birthday Jesus" on the front. What we do with it is similar to making a New Year's Reso-lution. We do it as a family, but it is a private matter that nobody else sees. We think about what God is speaking to us about in our walk with Him and what we might like to do better for the upcoming year. It is basically our gift to Him, our desire to be obedient in what He is leading us to.

An example may be to spend more time in prayer or Bible study. It may be to devote more time to ministry or improve in an area of struggle. We write it on an index card, place it in an envelope, write our name on the outside, seal it up, and place it in the box. The following year, we each take out our previous year's envelope without showing it to anyone else, reflect on it and decide if we kept our promise to Jesus for that year. Then we write our new one for that year.

Some years I have been happy about my progress. Some years I could have done better.

When the kids were little, we had to help them with this. The entries were amusing, such as not annoying the cat or fighting with a sister. With maturity has come deeper goals. But the tradition has always been a part of our family Christmas celebration. One year I promised to reconnect with an estranged family member. I was obedient, and God miraculously made it happen. One year I promised to step out in faith with my writing. This book is the slow fulfillment of that promise to the Lord.

There have been some promises I made to God that I have broken. I am grateful for His grace to give me new mercies every morning. The sweetest thing about it is that no matter how many promises to Him I fail to keep, God always keeps His promises to me. What a sweet reminder in reading the Christmas story that God blesses us when we believe His promises! Luke 1:45 says of Mary, "Blessed is she who believed that the Lord would fulfill his promises to her!"

Believe with me for this upcoming year in the promises that God is fulfilling in your life. And while you're at it, think about what promises you can make to Him. This is your gift of obedience. Your heart of love and obedience is the gift He most desires.

REFLECT:

What promises has God fulfilled in your life?

What promises does He want you to fulfill to Him?

What act of obedience has He prodded you toward that you still haven't done?

—✝—

Dear God, I want my heart to be sensitive to take steps of obedience You are pointing me toward. Help me to be sensitive to the Holy Spirit to take those first steps, even if the first step is to make You that promise. Thank you that You are always growing me toward godliness. Amen.

HOW TO GET READY FOR CHRISTMAS

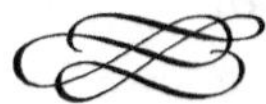

IN YEARS PAST, IT DIDN'T START UNTIL after Thanksgiving. The Christmas aisles in stores. The Christmas carols on the radio. Back then, the festivities and the decorations all would obligingly wait until the end of November. Now Hobby Lobby has their Christmas décor out in October. Everywhere we look, months before Christmas, every store is clamoring for us to get ready for Christmas.

How do we really get ready for Christmas? As Christians, we know that this holiday is so much more than shiny paper and wreaths. And as much as we love our families, Christmas is even more than spending time bonding with family and gathering over a delicious meal. It is more than being generous to those in need and giving to the poor. We ask each other, "Are you ready for Christmas?" But how do we really get ready for Christmas?

Isaiah 40:3-5 gives us a glimpse of how to prepare for the coming of a king. "A voice of one calling: 'In the wilderness prepare the way for the Lord; make straight in the desert a highway for our God. Every valley shall be raised up, every mountain and hill made low; the rough ground shall become level, the rugged places a plain. And the glory of the Lord will be revealed, and all people will see it together. For the mouth of the Lord has spoken.'"

John the Baptist preached the same message. He urged people to "prepare the way for the Lord, make straight paths for him" (Matthew 3:3, Mark 1:3, Luke 3:4, John 1:23). He urged everyone to get their hearts ready.

In ancient days, the people didn't have our modern system of highways for travel. When a king wanted to travel through an area that wasn't heavily traversed, he would send crews of men to clear a path through the debris of rocks, trees, and other obstacles blocking the way. These men would clear a path specifically for the king, removing all that was in the way of his arrival.

What debris needs to be cleared from my heart today so that the One True King can make His arrival evident in my heart? In the wilderness of my heart, what is blocking Jesus from being visible on every path and corner? Are prickly branches of worry and doubt inhibiting His advent? What about roots of bitterness blocking His thoroughfare? Are there boulders of strongholds that need to be removed? What rubbish and rubble needs to be cleared in order for Jesus to pave a highway in my heart? How can I prepare my heart for Him this Christmas?

Isaiah says, "Every valley shall be raised up." Are you in a valley of despair? The King's arrival will raise you up. "Every mountain and hill made low." Our pride is made humble before His great majesty. "The rough ground shall become level." God shows up in the rough places of our lives and gives us stability. "And the glory of the Lord will be revealed, and all people will see it together."

May all of your loved ones together see the glory of the Lord's arrival this Christmas. His arrival to the manger. His arrival in the flesh. His arrival to the cross. His arrival to life from death. His arrival to your hearts and lives, not just at Christmas, but every day. Christmas is Emmanuel! God with us! Pave a highway in your heart so His glory can be revealed. Merry Christmas!

Reflect:

Is there any accumulation of debris or prickly branches currently blocking the advent of Jesus in your life?

What rough places has Jesus made level and stable in your life?

How is God revealing His glory in and through Your life?

—✝—

Dear God, Thank you that You raise us up out of the valley of despair and put us on stable ground. I want to pave a highway in my heart to receive You every day. Help me to live so that Your glory can be revealed in and through my life. Amen.

GETTING PAST THE CHRISTMAS CHAOS

> *"My soul glorifies the Lord and my spirit rejoices in God my Savior."*
>
> — Luke 1:46

IT HAPPENS TO SOME DEGREE EVERY Christmas. You may have the same struggle. Every year before Christmas I contemplate the glory of the season and vow that THIS year will be less hustle and bustle and more spiritually focused. THIS year I won't be so busy with the preparations of cooking and cleaning and wrapping gifts. Although I have come a long way, I must admit that there is always some hustle and bustle to our Christmas every year.

Is that displeasing to God? Have we taken the focus of Christmas off the Christ child and put it on shopping and preparing for gatherings? Let me ask you this: When you read Luke 10:38-42, do you relate more to Martha or Mary? I must admit I understand Martha's frustration that she was doing all the work while her sister sat and enjoyed the company of their special guest.

But Jesus said, "Mary has chosen what is better." I have to remember that Jesus chastised Martha instead of Mary. Martha wasn't wrong in making preparations, but she had her priorities out of order.

Jesus is always the better. I pray amid the hustle and bustle that we always make Jesus the focus of our Christmas celebrations.

How do we do that? Jesus gave a hint in his reprimand to Martha. I must confess, I used to feel that Jesus was kind of hard on Martha. I mean, after all, shouldn't Mary have been helping? But maybe… just maybe…Martha was trying to overdo it. Maybe…Bobbie…I mean Martha…was trying to fix eight casseroles when three would have been sufficient. Jesus' reprimand wasn't that she was preparing things. It was that it captured all of her attention instead of just some of it. What exactly did Jesus say?

"Martha, Martha, you are worried and upset about many things, but few things are needed—or indeed only one. Mary has chosen what is better, and it will not be taken away from her."

Maybe Jesus' reminder that few things are needed means to trim some of those preparations. Maybe he was saying she could have prepared a few simple things to eat instead of an elaborate meal so she could have time to enjoy His company. How does this relate to our Christmas preparations?

Instead of putting up five Christmas trees, maybe one is enough. Instead of decking out the yard in Christmas Vacation style lights, what about a few simple lights? Instead of slaving in the kitchen and missing that time with family, what about a simpler meal or having everyone sign up to bring something or even having a meal catered? "Few things are needed" so we can enjoy the One who is the focus and enjoy the gift of family and friends that He has given us.

Christmas is still chaos at my house. But it's a bit more relaxed chaos now. I'm enjoying the gift of family and the sweet blessings of grand babies. And I'm remembering the One who is our greatest gift. I have chosen what is better. And when I look at my Christmas chaos, I remember that on that long ago night of His special birth, Mary and Joseph had some chaos, too. My chaos looks pretty minimal compared to being in labor while riding on a donkey!

Reflect:

On a scale of 0-10, how would you grade the level of holiday chaos at your house?

What few things could you trim off your preparations in order to have more time to focus on the meaning of Christmas?

Make an effort this Christmas to spend MORE time in Scripture, prayer, and meditation instead of less.

—✝—

Dear God, I am glad that You understand the chaos of life. It is comforting to know that even The Prince of Peace entered this world in a chaotic way. Thank you that You are the One who brings calm to all our chaos. Help me to remember that few things are needed, and You are the one thing that is always needed. Amen.

GOD'S MERCY MANGER

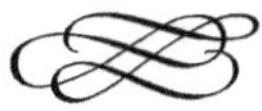

"For God so loved the world that he gave his one and only Son, that whoever believes in him shall not perish but have eternal life."

— John 3:16

CAN YOU IMAGINE WHAT THE ANGELS were thinking? As they watched the birth of Jesus, the hope of all mankind, bringing redemption to all who would believe, can you imagine the rejoicing of that heavenly host? My church has the best music ever, but I am confident that the praises lifted by heaven's choir easily surpasses even the music at my church!

Can you imagine what the shepherds were thinking? As that angel brought them the news in that quiet field, overwhelming them with fear at the glory of the Lord, it must have been the most exciting moment of their lives! Luke 2 says they HURRIED to go see the newborn king. I'm sure they had some adrenaline on board after seeing that angel!

And what are you thinking? Are you thinking about decorating, cooking, and gifts to wrap? Have you ever unwrapped the greatest gift? After all, He is the reason we are celebrating! "For God so loved the world that he gave his one and only Son, that whoever believes in him shall not perish but have eternal life," (John 3:16). I pray you don't leave that gift unwrapped this Christmas! If you have any questions about God's gift of salvation, please read Appendix B in the back of this book.

The heavenly host is still watching with excitement as the salvation of mankind continues to unfold. Luke 15:10 tells us, "...there is rejoicing in the presence of the angels of God over one sinner who repents." That repentance was made possible because God sent mercy in a manger.

God's Mercy Manger

The light breaks through the darkness
Redemption draweth nigh.
Man's freedom has been purchased.
Chains broken by a baby's cry.
Joy and sorrow intermixed...
Heaven's glory only known
By angels singing praises
As they gather 'round the throne.
O fathom deepest riches
That this earth would shame to boast
As they lift up praises to the King,
Songs from a heavenly host!
Glory, Honor to our God!
Sing praises to His name!
There is no other God like Him!
Eternally the same!
Proclaim to all the earth aloud:
Great things that he has done!
His righteousness shines brighter
Than the blazing noonday sun!
Celebrate His mighty power!
Rejoice within His grace—
That He should make a way
For man to look into His face!

Amazing love that ushers us
To come sit at His feet,
Brought to earth incarnate
As a helpless babe so sweet.
Born to die so we could live,
Saved from death's wrathful danger...
The babe, the only path to life...
Cooing in God's mercy manger.

— © 2023 BOBBIE PERKINS

REFLECT:

How do you think you would have felt if you had been one of those shepherds? Skeptical? Excited? Afraid? Did you have any of those feelings when you first heard the gospel?

How did the birth of Jesus bring a mixture of both joy and sorrow?

Mary's song in Luke 1:46 contains the words, "My spirit rejoices in God my Savior." How do you imagine Mary felt as she held her helpless baby? Do you think it struck her that He needed her, but that she also needed Him?

—✝—

Dear God, Thank you for Your incredible, perfect plan of salvation. There was no other way. Help me to join in the anticipation of the heavenly host to be excited about others coming to Christ and to be obedient to help lead them to the mercy manger. Amen.

GOD WITH US

WHAT IS YOUR VERY FAVORITE Christmas decoration? Is it your tree with a combination of beautiful ornaments mixed in with toilet paper rolls made by your kids? Or maybe it's the manger scene handed down to you by your grandmother. As much as I love those, I must say I absolutely love looking at the lights!

We have lights on our tree, on the mantle, on the television console, and even some light-up pictures hanging on the walls. Watching them twinkle relaxes and mesmerizes me, reminding me that Jesus came as the Light of the World. "In him was life, and that life was the light of all mankind. The light shines in the darkness, and the darkness has not overcome it," (John 1:4,5).

There is a lot of darkness in the world. But there is One who overcomes ALL darkness. He laid His glory aside to put on flesh, to suffer and die to pay the penalty for the sin of His creation who had rebelled against Him. "But God demonstrates his own love for us in this: While we were still sinners, Christ died for us," (Romans 5:8). It's an amazing thought to think of the powerful, glorious Creator God laying His glory aside to be born as a helpless infant! Why? To suffer an agonizing death to save us from the penalty of our sin! What kind of love is this?

It is a love that pierces EVERY darkness. I don't know what darkness you have wrestled with, but God does. He is there, present in your own darkness, reminding you that the darkness you have experienced cannot overcome His light. He is there with you this Christmas, as you wrestle the dark places of grief, isolation, sickness, poverty, addiction, brokenness, pain...HE IS THERE WITH YOU. His very name, Immanuel, means, "God with us." Matthew 1:23 says, "The virgin will conceive and give birth to a son, and they will call him Immanuel, which means, God with us."

So if Christmas is especially hard for you this year, I am so very sorry! And I encourage you to look at those lights and remember that He is there with you in those dark places, promising that He overcomes your darkness. "The Lord is close to the brokenhearted and saves those who are crushed in spirit," (Psalm 34:18). He is with you: Immanuel.

The Light has come!

REFLECT:

When we walk into a dark room, we turn on the light in order to see better. How can you turn on the light of Jesus into the dark places in your life?

What things in your life do you see better in His light?

If you are feeling brokenhearted, I encourage you to read through the book of Psalms and ask God to help you feel his presence as Immanuel, God with us.

—✝—

Dear God, This world will always bring darkness at different times in my life, but I thank You that no darkness can extinguish the light of Christ that is living in me. Help me to turn on that light instead of sitting in darkness. Help me to share it with others who are also struggling. Amen.

A LEGACY OF FAITH

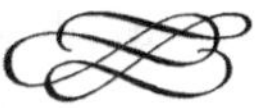

THE LAST DEVOTION IN THIS BOOK WAS written by my grandson Bryce, who at the time of this writing is in the first grade. I noticed when Bryce was very young that he had deep spiritual thoughts. I remember once when he was four years old, he was riding in the car with me and being unusually quiet, deep in thought. Then he looked at me and out of the blue asked, "Nana, what is Jesus doing right now?"

Wow! When I was four years old, I was thinking about cookies and playing with dolls! Bryce and I talked about how Jesus is preparing a place for us in heaven, how He is interceding for us, how He lives in us through the Holy Spirit, and all kinds of things. And I marveled at the little four-year-old who was pondering thoughts about Jesus.

Where does he get this from? The Holy Spirit has blessed him with a keen understanding of Scripture. I love that he came to know Christ at the tender age of five. My daughter and son-in-law have taught him well, as they are much wiser than I was when I was raising little ones.

The legacy of faith that we leave tends to grow roots that are deeper with each generation. My mother didn't come to know Christ until she was in her fifties. I met Christ at sixteen, and it was a messy love story in the beginning. My daughter Hannah, who is Bryce's mom, was six. Bryce was five. Not that age makes a difference, but looking at that progression of generations, I see the continuation of faith that has gotten stronger and deeper and wiser.

Planted....to grow Deeper Roots. I initially chose the title of my book to refer to our individual faith growing deeper roots, being firmly established and growing in our walk with God. But it wasn't until I read Bryce's devotion that I realized the title also means those roots grow deeper for future generations in order to leave a legacy of faith.

The idea of Bryce writing a devotion for this book was last minute. Hannah mentioned to me how he loves to write stories. She said he comes home from school every day and writes stories and makes his own books. Hannah told him that his Nana was writing a real book, and he was amazed by that. So I thought it would be a great idea to let my little Jesus-loving, book-loving grandson have the privilege of writing the last devotion. He was very excited to write in a real published book!

My prayer is to eventually see all my precious grandchildren come to know Christ. They are just babies now, but my prayer is that the legacy of faith will continue, and that "they will be called oaks of righteousness, a planting of the Lord for the display of his splendor," (Isaiah 61:3b).

And I want to be faithful to water those seeds. How about you?

We all sin even though
we try to be good. The
problem with sin is, we
can get hurt, hurt other peoples
and the biggest problem with
sin is it separtes us from
God. God hates sin. God
had a awsom plan. He saved
our worlds because he sent

God's son, Jesus. He lived with no sin, he lived a perfect life, and he helped people who were sick. He died on the cross and rose from ti dead. He took the punishment of our sins, he was dead for 3 days, then he rose from the grave. He is alive waiting for us in heaven. I love God because he lets me when I

have a bad dream? he talks
to me. and he died for me. I
love God and I hope you do too.
For God so loved the world that
he gave his one and only Son that
whoever believe in him shall not
perish but have eternal life. John
3:16

Bryce
Bailey

perfect
love

If you enjoyed this book, I would greatly appreciate your honest review on Amazon. It would help further the success of my book and help further the gospel! Thank you for your support!

— BOBBIE

APPENDIX A

Sanctity of Human Life Sunday was first instituted by President Ronald Reagan and is celebrated close to the anniversary of Roe v. Wade, in which the Supreme Court in 1973 issued a ruling that guaranteed women access to abortion. Roe v. Wade was overturned in June of 2022, through Dobbs v. Jackson, giving individual states the power to regulate certain aspects of abortion. But as of today, abortion is still happening, even in states where abortion is illegal. With the advent of the abortion pill, which is currently being shipped to mailboxes even in "abortion-free" states, abortion is happening in women's bathrooms at home, without medical oversight.

BUT! God loves to redeem life! There is a way to save that little life even after the woman has taken the first abortion pill if she is able to get help quickly by receiving progesterone before she takes that second pill. The National Abortion Pill Reversal hotline number is 1-877-558-0333 and the website is www.abortionpillreversal.com. This national resource can connect women needing help with a provider in their local area.

If you live in an area with a pregnancy center, I encourage you to become involved. They need your financial support. There are also many other ways to help. You could volunteer as a mentor or to help with office tasks, donate baby items or Uber gift cards, hold a baby shower at your church to gather items to donate, participate in their fundraising events, pray for them, stay educated on the issues surrounding abortion, tell others what you are learning, and research before you vote. You could help with events, moving furniture, painting, or maintenance of their center...whatever talent you have, it can probably be put to use! Use your talents for the glory of God!

To find a pregnancy center in your area, go to www.care-net.org. Under the Pregnancy Center Tab there is a choice for "Find a center." There are also a lot of other resources available on their website.

Additional Resources to learn more:

The Alternative to Abortion: Why We must Be Pro **Abundant** Life by Roland C. Warren

Contenders: A Church-Wide Strategy to Unmask Abortion, Defeat Its Advocates, Empower Christians, and Change the World by Marc Newman

Why Pro-Life? Caring for the unborn and their mothers by Randy Alcorn

See Baby Grow App ©2023 Education Resource Fund www.ehd.org

HOPE FOR YOU IF YOU HAVE HAD AN ABORTION OR HAVE EXPERIENCED SEXUAL ABUSE

If you or someone you know has experienced the pain of an abortion or sexual abuse, I am so sorry! I want you to know that you are not alone and that there is hope and healing for you. God wants to comfort you in your grief and bring you to a place of freedom. Please see the list of resources below for help:

FOR ABORTION:

Websites:

www.abortionhealing.org

You can also call 703-554-8746 or email info@abortionhealing.org

www.reassemblelife.com

www.herchoicetoheal.com
www.anevenplace.com (virtual)
biblicalcounseling.com
ChristianCounselorsNetwork.com
ChristianCareConnect.com

If you are in the Memphis, TN area, you can contact Life Choices of Memphis by texting "HOPE" to 901-277-5808 or emailing hope@life choicesmemphis.org. Life Choices of Memphis offers counseling, a Bible study, a retreat, and a community group.

Books:

Forgiven and Set Free by Linda Cochrane

Surrendering the Secret, Pat Layton

For men:

Reclaiming Fatherhood by Jill Marquis, Guy Condon, and David Hazard

FOR SEXUAL ABUSE:

Websites:

the allendercenter.org

fearlessresources.org

hopefortheheart.org

biblicalcounseling.com

ChristianCounselorsNetwork.com

ChristianCareConnect.com

Books:

Shame Interrupted: How God Lifts The Pain of Worthlessness and Rejection by Edward T. Welch

The Path to Sexual Healing by Linda Cochrane

The Wounded Heart by Dr. Dan B. Allender

APPENDIX B

God has a story for every life. It is a love story like no other. When God created mankind, He fashioned us in His very own image (Genesis 1:26). That doesn't mean that we are gods or that we look like God, but that there are things in us that reflect His image– things that no other living creature has. Think about the exquisite creative genius of mankind to figure out space travel and computers, to create art, music, architecture, and other beautiful works. Animals can't do that, but we have creativity that stems from our Creator's imprint on us.

Another part of His image in us is that He created our souls with a longing to find Him and a spirit that is uniquely designed to know that He exists. Romans 1:20 states, "For since the creation of the world, God's invisible qualities– His eternal power and divine nature– have been clearly seen, being understood from what has been made, so that people are without excuse." We can spend our lives denying His existence, but He has given us proof of His existence through His creation. Our souls, too, give us proof by a longing within us that can't be satisfied apart from communion with Him. We can try to fill that longing with money, food, drugs, sex, power, or any other deceptive method of contentment that life offers, but none of those things will satisfy. Because we were made for God! His imprint is on your soul, and your soul was made to connect with Him.

God's perfect fellowship with mankind changed when Adam and Eve chose to rebel against their Creator. They embraced the lie of the enemy that they should disobey God and choose their own way of doing things. They passed that sin nature down to all future generations, including you and me. We live in a broken world as broken people. God's image is still imprinted on our souls, but it has become blurred and disfigured by sin. We are guilty of crimes against God, and because God is a righteous judge, our crimes have a penalty. If a judge today were to let a serial killer go free, we would say he is not a righteous judge. Well, we may not be serial killers, but we are serial sinners!

"Wait," you say. "I'm not that bad. I go to church and treat others with kindness. I try to do the right thing." Romans 3:10,12 tells us, "There is no one righteous, not even one…there is no one who does good, not even one." Because God is perfect, His standard is perfect, and nobody can achieve it. That's pretty bad news for us because the penalty of our sin is death and eternal separation from God. Romans 6:23 states, "For the wages of sin is death." BUT KEEP READING! "THE GIFT OF GOD IS ETERNAL LIFE IN CHRIST JESUS OUR LORD." John 3:16 tells us "For God so loved the world that he gave his one and only Son, that whoever believes in him shall not perish but have eternal life."

God loves us so much that He came to earth as both God and man in the person of Jesus Christ. He lived a perfect life and willingly took our punishment upon Himself. He was the only person who ever lived who had no crimes of His own to pay for, so He was the only one who could do this for us. He basically took the rap for us all. The suffering his human body endured was unimaginable, but the glory of his divine nature conquered death with his resurrection after three days. He was seen by over 500 people after His resurrection. The Bible tells His story, God's captivating story of redemption and grace. It is this story that beckons us to be restored to God. But how?

First, we have to abandon our efforts to save ourselves. Going to church and doing good works are useless because salvation is "not of works" (Ephesians 2:9), "not by works of righteousness which we have done, but according to his mercy" (Titus 3:5).

Next, we need to acknowledge Christ's payment for our sin and repent from our sin. Repentance means to turn away from it. It means to be sorry for it to the point of not wanting to go that path again. Instead, we desire to take the path of God's way. Yes, we will sometimes still sin. But we won't WANT to sin. We will desire to please God, even when we sometimes wander back to that old ugly path. But when we come to God and tell him we are sorry, He forgives us and helps us find the way back to His path again! No matter how bad the sin, "God demonstrates His own love for us in this: While we were still sinners, Christ died for us" (Romans 5:8). His blood is the only, all-sufficient cleansing agent to make us pure before God. Isaiah 1:18 promises "Though your sins are like scarlet, they shall be white as snow."

Finally, we have to accept Jesus Christ as Savior and Lord. Romans 10:9 asserts that, "If you declare with your mouth, 'Jesus is Lord,' and believe in your heart that God has raised him from the dead, you will be saved." If someone were to send you a million-dollar check, even though it is an incredible gift, it would do you no good if you didn't cash the check. God's gift of salvation is a gift, but it is our choice to accept it. God doesn't force us to love Him because love that is forced isn't really love. He invites us into a relationship with Him through the way of Jesus Christ. "I am the way and the truth and the life. No one comes to the Father except through me" (John 14:6). All roads do not lead to heaven. Jesus is the only way. If you have never received this incredible gift, you can do it this very moment. Just talk to God sincerely from your heart. There is nothing magical in saying a prayer with certain words. What matters is the attitude of your heart. You could say something like this:

Dear God, I know that I have rebelled against your standards by going my own way. I confess that I have tried to live my life apart from your authority. I thank you that you love me so much that you made a way through Jesus to rescue me from my sin. Jesus, I believe you are the

Son of God who died on the cross to pay the penalty for my sins. I believe you rose from the dead. I open my heart now, by faith, to receive you, Jesus, as my personal Savior and Lord. Come into my heart, forgive my sins, and save me, Lord Jesus. Right now I give all that I know of myself to all that I know of you. Help me to live for you and put you first in my life. Thank you for your precious gift of salvation. In your name I pray, Amen.

If you received this greatest treasure of salvation today, Welcome to the family of God! I hope that you will connect with other believers through a church that teaches from the Bible. Tell the pastor about your decision and tell him you need help to learn how to grow. Read God's instruction manual, the Bible, starting in the book of John. Start talking to God every day through prayer. Surround yourself with other believers who can help you, and get involved in a Bible study if you can.

Lastly, as you learn to make Jesus the Lord (boss) of your life, you will still sometimes mess up and go your own way. That doesn't mean you lost your salvation. Salvation is a one-time permanent change in our standing with God. When we sin, we don't "feel" like a Christian, and our fellowship with God is broken. But the assurance of our salvation is not based on our feelings or anything we do, but on the promises of God's Word. "I write these things to you who believe in the name of the Son of God so that you may KNOW that you have eternal life" (I John 5:13, emphasis mine). Sin doesn't affect our standing with God as His child, but it does affect our relationship with Him. When my kids were little, if they did something wrong, it affected our relationship, but they were still my kids. When you sin, confess those mistakes to God, turn away from your sin, and He will forgive you. "If we confess our sins, he is faithful and just and will forgive us our sins and purify us from all unrighteousness" (I John 1:9). This journey of following Jesus is a growth process. After we have received salvation, the process in which God makes us holy is a life-long growth process that won't be complete until heaven! May you grow and flourish and establish deeper roots in Him!

–Bobbie

ACKNOWLEDGMENTS

I would like to express a heartfelt thank you to the following people:

To Rose Goldfarb, the teacher who nurtured my love for writing. I wish you were still alive to read this book, but your daughter will be receiving a copy.

To my sister Karen Gaugh, who knows too much yet loves me still.

To my friend Rita Ricks, who first told me about Jesus.

To my friend Cindy Cooley, who invited me to Young Life and kept my teenage secrets.

To my friends Jan Berry, Barry Jenkins, Clay Harrington, and Linda Gilbert, who walked me to the cross. I'm so grateful for your years of involvement in Young Life Ministry.

To my friend Linda Dale Burch, who taught me how to pray, modeled what it means to walk faithfully with Jesus, and in a way, saved my life.

To Carrie Whitten, who instilled in me a love for God's Word.

To Life Choices of Memphis and other pro-life ministries, for leading women to the One True Healer.

To my friend Shirley Picou for being the impetus behind my blog and giving me the courage to share my writing with the world (for pushing me off the cliff).

To my dearest friend Lilly Minor for teaching me that God's sovereignty and goodness coexist. I have no words to express how you've impacted my life. You are the most joyful person I know.

To Ted Minor for being a faithful friend and faithful teacher of God's Word

To my Tuesday Bible Study Ladies for being vulnerable and sharing feasts of God's Word with me.

To my former pastor the late Dr. Adrian Rogers, for teaching me how to renew my mind with Scripture memory.

To my Pastor Rob Mullins for being an approachable, faithful shepherd who loves people well.

To Vicki Mullins for teaching me that my identity is in Christ and for involving this "NOT sedate church lady" in the joys of ministry

To Angela and Rebecca from 3Trees Publishing for becoming kindred spirits in my writing journey.

To Jim Neace from BrandStudio1 (www.brandstudio1.com) for website assistance and encouraging words.

To Maranatha Maurer for helping with edits and technology and for shining for Jesus in everything you do.

To Melanie Redd for being an encouragement in my writing journey (go get her books!).

To Nat Martin Photography for my professional author photo.

To many others who weaved threads of faith into my life....thank you! If you're not listed here, God has his own list in heaven!

ABOUT THE AUTHOR

Humbled by grace, I write with one simple hope: that Jesus—who is enough for every need—will meet you through these words. As a sinner saved by His mercy, I pray these pages inspire your faith, encourage your heart, and help you take deeper root in Him.

Most people who know me describe me as outgoing and energetic. I love meeting new people and hearing their own "Jesus stories." I'm not a fancy girl...I prefer a bonfire over a fancy dinner, and a cabin in the woods over an upscale hotel. If I am around trees, I am in my happy place! I have been married since 1988 to my husband Denny, who is semi-introverted but quite the comedian when you get him going! He patiently tolerates my obsession with books...don't ask how many bookshelves are in our home! We reside in Tennessee near our three daughters, sons-in-law, and at the latest count...five beautiful grandchildren. I have been a nurse for over 40 years, spending many of those years caring for moms and babies. I currently serve as the Director of Nursing at Life Choices of Memphis, a faith-based pregnancy center. I am still amazed that I have the privilege of serving at the same center that ministered to me so many years ago.

I feel a sobering responsibility to handle God's Word carefully and live my life in a way that is representative of the truths that I share. I must admit that I often struggle to appropriate those truths into my own life, and I pray that the gap between what I teach and how I live will close more with each passing day. I am an unfinished work! I am a certified Biblical Counselor through ACBC, which has reinforced what I had already found to be true— that God's Word is sufficient to give us answers for any problem in life we may encounter.

You can connect with me at bobbieperkins.com or deeperroots-blog1@gmail.com to schedule a speaking engagement at your church or pro-life event.

So then, just as you received Christ Jesus as Lord, continue to live your lives in him, rooted and built up in him. — Colossians 2:6,7

www.ingramcontent.com/pod-product-compliance
Lightning Source LLC
Chambersburg PA
CBHW051456150726
47997CB00001B/3